STUDENT
LEARNING GUIDE

MARKETING

William G. Zikmund
Michael D'Amico

Prepared by Jim L. Grimm

John Wiley & Sons, Inc.
New York Chichester Brisbane Toronto Singapore

To TREVA AND LLOYD GRIMM
DOROTHY AND CHARLES SOMAN

CONTENTS

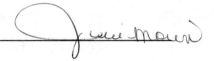

Student Feedback Form for the Student Learning Guide and Marketing.

EXPERIENTIAL ACTIVITIES

TO THE STUDENT

This student learning guide has been designed to be used with Marketing by William Zikmund and Michael d'Amico. This learning guide will assist you in learning, evaluating, and applying the concepts and strategies of marketing. For each chapter in Marketing, this learning guide contains:

1. Chapter objective,

2. Chapter outline,

3. Chapter summary by learning objectives,

4. Vocabulary building matching exercise,

5. Vocabulary building programmed learning exercise,

6. True or false statements,

7. Multiple choice questions,

8. Quick quiz,

9. Experiential activities, and

10. Answers to objective questions.

The chapter objective highlights key concepts and strategies of the chapter. The sentence outline introduces definitions, concepts, strategies, and related factual material. The chapter summary is structured around the learning objectives for the chapter. You should find a review of these three sections useful prior to studying the corresponding chapter in Marketing. These three sections will make you aware of key concepts and strategies. Consequently, your study should be more effective and more efficient. After studying the chapter, you can review these sections again prior to testing your understanding of the chapter through the matching exercise, the programmed learning exercise, true or false statements, and the multiple choice questions. You should refer to the answers to the objective questions only after completing each section of questions. The quick quiz section presents interesting commentary on selected concepts introduced in the chapter.

The experiential activities enable you to apply key concepts and strategies. Their level of difficulty and complexity varies. These activities will assist you in understanding the function of effective marketing.

Finally, the authors of Marketing and I encourage you to return the Student Feedback Form for the Student Learning Guide and Marketing. Your feedback concerning the strengths and weaknesses of these learning materials will be greatly appreciated. Your feedback will enable us to improve the learning process by building on the strengths of the total learning package. Please return your feedback form to:

Dr. Jim L. Grimm
Department of Management and Marketing
Illinois State University
Normal, Illinois 61761

ACKNOWLEDGMENTS

The author acknowledges and appreciates the assistance of J.B. Wilkinson, Sunil Patel, Scott McElroy, Scott Fraser, and Jeff Bednarz for their contributions in the development of this learning guide. For contributing experiential activities I am indebted to J.B. Wilkinson, The University of Akron, and Sunil Patel, Illinois State University.

I especially thank Frank Burrows, William Zikmund, Michael d'Amico, and Richard Esposito for their suggestions on how to structure the Student Learning Guide. In addition, George Prough and Michael d'Amico, both of The University of Akron, assisted in developing review questions. I especially appreciate the many helpful suggestions made by William Zikmund, Oklahoma State University, regarding the content of the learning guide.

I am also indebted to three very special friends--Leonard J. Konopa, Kent State University; O:.C. Ferrell, Texas A & M; and James B. Spalding, Jr., Bellarmine College--for their many insightful comments and discussions concerning effective marketing over the years.

A special appreciation is due Dr. Steven C. and Hope R. Barrowes, who own Electronic Secretary, and Merrily Corwin for typing this learning guide.

My family has been patient and consistent supporters through all phases of this project. My wife Barbara proofread each draft, and my children Michael, Andrew, and Sarah made special contributions.

CHAPTER 1

THE NATURE OF MARKETING

OBJECTIVE

This chapter explains that marketing deals with exchanges. Successful, satisfying, and profitable exchanges will result if the marketing concept is properly applied.

OUTLINE

I. Marketing: What is it?

   A. Marketing consists of activities designed to bring buyers and sellers together.

   B. Production is not a major marketing activity.

   C. The marketing process begins with an understanding of customers' needs.

II. Not-for-profit organizations are marketers too

   A. The broader perspective of marketing acknowledges that not-for-profit organizations perform marketing activities.

   B. Primary emphasis of marketing for both business and not-for-profit organizations involves the exchange process.

III. A definition of effective marketing

   A. Effective marketing consists of a consumer-oriented mix of business activities.

   B. These activities are planned and implemented to facilitate the exchange of products, services, or ideas.

C. Both parties to the exchange must receive something of value.

IV. Marketing's purpose in society

    A. The delivery of a standard of living is marketing's fundamental purpose in society.

    B. Products provide economic utility by satisfying consumers' needs.

    C. The five types of economic utility are form utility, place utility, time utility, possession utility, and information utility.

V. The marketing mix

    A. The marketing mix describes the specific combination of product, price, place (distribution), and promotion variables.

    B. Marketing mix variables are controllable variables since these variables may be influenced by managers.

    C. The product variable refers to the physical good, service, or idea that an organization (business or not-for-profit) offers to its customers.

        1. The offering (total product) of an organization includes the product and associated extras, such as credit availability and friendly service.

        2. The task of product planning and product development activities is to insure that an organization's total product provides attributes which customers desire.

        3. Other product strategy decisions are brand name selection, packaging considerations, and developing warranties and service plans.

    D. Place or distribution strategy determines how products are made available to customers.

        1. Physical distribution includes transportation, storage, and materials handling activities.

        2. A channel of distribution describes the path of a product or title from a producer to a consumer.

3. Who is involved in a basic channel of distribution?

EXHIBIT 1-1
Who Is Involved in a Basic Channel of Distribution?

Flow of Product or Title	Definition
Manufacturer	Producer of a finished product from raw materials or component parts.
Wholesaler	A middleman that neither produces nor consumes the finished product, but sells to retailers or manufacturers or institutions that use the product for ultimate resale (perhaps in another product form).
Retailer	A middleman that neither produces nor consumes the finished product, but sells to the ultimate consumer.
Consumer	A person who buys or uses the finished product.

4. Facilitating agents are specialists, such as financial institutions or transportation firms, which assist manufacturers, wholesalers, and retailers in the flow of the product or title in a channel of distribution.

E. Price is something of value (money, good, or service) given in exchange for a product.

F. Promotion is how a firm communicates with its customers.

1. Promotion is used to inform and to persuade.

2. Advertising, personal selling, publicity, and sales promotion are forms of promotion.

3. The particular combination of these communication tools is the firm's promotion mix.

G. The blending of the elements of the marketing mix is a creative activity.

VI. The marketing concept--the foundation of effective marketing

   A. The marketing concept is a philosophy of management.

   B. This philosophy stresses a consumer orientation, a long-run profitability orientation, and an integrated marketing effort.

   C. A consumer-oriented firm satisfies consumer needs.

      1. This orientation implies that a business should identify what the consumer wants first and then offer that product.

      2. A company should define its purpose for existence from a broad consumer-oriented perspective.

      3. Marketing myopia exists when a firm uses a product orientation to define its nature of business.

   D. An organization needs to stress long-run profitability to enhance its continuity.

      1. This orientation implies that the satisfaction of all consumer wants is not a feasible objective for an organization.

      2. Sales volume for its sake alone should be avoided.

   E. An integrated and coordinated marketing effort will minimize conflicts between the marketing function and other functional areas.

SUMMARY

Learning Objective One: To discuss the importance of marketing in your daily life.

   Daily you are exposed to marketing activities such as advertisements, retail store displays, transporting of products by trucks, dissemination of price information, and information provided by sales people.   These kinds of marketing activities enable you to select products which are essential in performing tasks related to such roles as student, employee, citizen, parent, or consumer.   In fact, various aspects of marketing are fundamental in the delivery of a standard of living to society.

Learning Objective Two: To define marketing in the business sense and the newer "broadened" sense.

4

Marketing activities are designed to bring buyers and sellers together by directing the flow of goods and services from the producer to the consumer. These activities should begin with an understanding of customers' needs. The "broadened" sense of marketing indicates that not-for-profit organizations are marketers too. Thus, marketing involves an exchange process requiring that two or more parties exchange things (products--goods, services, or ideas) of value. Effective marketing consists of a consumer-oriented mix of business activities planned and implemented by a marketer to facilitate the exchange or transfer of products, services, or ideas so that both parties profit in some way.

Learning Objective Three: To show how marketing creates economic utility.

Economic utility is the ability of a product to satisfy some aspect of a consumer's needs. The process of marketing provides economic utility through the creation of place, time, possession, and information utilities. Place utility is created primarily by transportation and distribution. Time utility is created by the storage activity. Possession utility is created by the conclusion of a sale while information utility is created primarily by promotion. Thus, transportation, storage, distribution, sale consummation, and promotion are marketing activities which create economic utility.

Learning Objective Four: To describe the marketing mix.

The marketing mix describes the specific combination of interrelated and interdependent marketing activities of the product, price, place (distribution), and promotion variables. These basic variables, referred to as the 4 P's of marketing, are the framework for the development of a marketing plan. Marketing mix variables are called controllable variables since they may be influenced by a manager.

The product variable refers to the physical good, service, or idea an organization offers to its customers. The product variable encompasses such activities as product planning, product development, branding, packaging, warranties, and service plans. The product variable does not include production, the creation of form utility.

The place or distribution variable is concerned with making the product available to customers. This variable encompasses physical distribution (transportation, storage, and materials handling activities), channels of distribution (selection of wholesalers and retailers to assist in the flow of product or title), and facilitating agents (specialists who assist manufacturers, wholesalers, and retailers in the flow of product or title). The place variable creates time, place, and possession utilities.

The price variable determines the amount of money, goods, or services (something of value) given in exchange for a product. The promotion variable describes how a firm communicates with its customers. The major types of promotion are personal selling, advertising, sales promotion, and publicity.

Learning Objective Five: To explain the marketing concept.

The marketing concept is a philosophy of management. This philosophy stresses a customer orientation based on an integrated marketing effort to achieve long-run profitability. An organization's purpose should be founded on satisfying the consumer--a consumer-oriented perspective. This perspective implies the firm should identify what the consumer wants first and then offer a product to satisfy this want. These customer-satisfying activities should be directed at long-run profitability rather than sales volume and short-term profits. Marketing efforts must be integrated and coordinated within the marketing function as well as with the production, finance, personnel, information, and research and development areas. Such coordination and integration minimizes marketing conflicts within these areas.

VOCABULARY BUILDING

Matching Exercise

Match the following by placing the letter of the concept or term on the blank preceding the phrase which best describes the concept or term. You should use a term or concept only once.

A.	Effective marketing	M.	Place (Distribution)
B.	Macro-marketing (Marketing)	N.	Promotion
		O.	Price
C.	Economic utility	P.	Channel of distribution
D.	Form utility	Q.	Manufacturer
E.	Place utility	R.	Wholesaler
F.	Time utility	S.	Retailer
G.	Possession utility	T.	Ultimate consumer
H.	Information utility	U.	Marketing concept
I.	Marketing mix	V.	Facilitating agents
J.	4 P's of marketing	W.	Production era
K.	Controllable variables	X.	Sales era
L.	Product	Y.	Marketing myopia

___I___ 1. Specific combination of interrelated and interdependent marketing activities.

___P___ 2. Complete sequence of marketing organizations involved in bringing a product from producer to ultimate consumer.

6

_L_ 3. The goods, service, or benefit which an organization offer to its customers.

_4_ 4. Failure of a firm to define its purpose from a broad consumer orientation.

A _G_ 5. Consumer-oriented mix of business activities planned and implemented to facilitate the exchange of products to the mutual benefit of both parties.

C _A_ 6. Ability of a product to satisfy some aspect of a consumer need.

m _F_ 7. Determination of how fast and in what condition a product gets to a customer.

_V_ 8. Specialists assisting manufacturers, wholesalers, and retailers in the flow of the product or title.

_U_ 9. A philosophy of management that stresses a consumer orientation with an emphasis on long-run profitability and an integration of marketing and other corporate functions.

_N_ 10. The marketing communication process utilized to remind, inform, and persuade.

_B_ 11. An aggregate of marketing activities within an economy or the marketing system within a society.

_S_ 12. An organization that sells a product to the ultimate consumer.

D _W_ 13. Created primarily by production.

_K_ 14. Marketing mix variables which may be influenced by managers.

_X_ 15. This era is characterized by aggressive sales and persuasive advertising efforts.

F _E_ 16. A utility created primarily by storage.

_I_ 17. The individual who buys or uses the product.

_I_ 18. The four basic marketing mix categories of product, place, price, and promotion.

_O_ 19. The amount of money, or sometimes goods or services, given in exchange for something.

R 20. An intermediary that serves between a manufacturer and another middleman (wholesaler or retailer) to facilitate the transfer of a product or title.

VOCABULARY BUILDING

Programmed Learning Exercise

1. The function of marketing is to bring _____ and _____ together.
   [buyers, sellers]

2. The primary emphasis of marketing involves a/an _____ process between at least two parties.
   [exchange]

3. Effective marketing consists of a/an _____-oriented mix of business activities planned and implemented to facilitate the exchange of products.
   [consumer]

4. _____ utility is the ability of a product or service to satisfy some aspect of a consumer's need.
   [Economic]

5. _____ utility is created primarily by the conclusion of a sale.
   [Possession]

6. _____ _____ describes the result of management's efforts to creatively combine interrelated and interdependent marketing activities.
   [Marketing mix]

7. The basic categories of the marketing mix elements are _____, _____, _____, and _____.
   [product, place or distribution, price, promotion]

8. Marketing mix variables are frequently referred to as _____ variables since a manager can influence these variables.
   [controllable]

9. A product may be a _____ good or an _____ benefit.
   [tangible, intangible]

10. Transportation, storage, and materials handling are _____ _____ activities.
    [physical distribution]

8

11. A channel of distribution is the complete sequence of marketing organizations involved in bringing a product from the _____ to the _____.

[producer, ultimate consumer]

12. _____ _____ are specialists who perform marketing activities for the channel organization but are excluded from the channel of distribution.

[Facilitating agents]

13. _____ is what is exchanged for the product.

[Price]

14. The essence of promotion is _____.

[communication]

15. A firm's _____ _____ is its particular combination of advertising, personal selling, sales promotion, and publicity.

[promotion mix]

16. The _____ _____ is a philosophy of management.

[marketing concept]

17. This philosophy has a _____ orientation, stresses _____ profitability, and an _____ marketing effort.

[consumer, long-run, integrated]

18. The satisfaction of customer needs is the _____ for an organization's existence.

[justification]

19. A firm should stress long-run profitability rather than _____ or _____.

[short-term profits, sales volume]

20. An integrated marketing effort reduces _____ with other functional areas of an organization.

[conflicts]

TRUE OR FALSE STATEMENTS

T F 1. Most people fully understand marketing's place in society and how marketing activities should be managed.

T F 2. Production is not a major marketing concern.

T F   3. The marketing process begins with customer analysis before the product is manufactured.

T F   4. Marketing activities are performed only by business organizations.

T F   5. Marketing activities are designed to facilitate the exchange of products.

T F   6. Storage is a marketing activity.

T F   7. Time utility is created primarily by transportation and distribution.

T F   8. The 4 P's of marketing are product, place, possession, and price.

T F   9. Marketing mix variables are uncontrollable variables by managers.

T F 10. A product can be tangible or intangible.

T F 11. Wholesalers and retailers are channels of distribution members for consumer products.

T F 12. Facilitating agents are middlemen in a channel of distribution.

T F 13. Price may be expressed in something other than money or goods.

T F 14. Advertising and publicity are forms of promotion.

T F 15. A standard formula exists for a successful combination of marketing elements.

T F 16. An organization with a production orientation produces the products that customers want.

T F 17. The customer orientation of the marketing concept means that an organization should find out what the customer wants before offering a product.

T F 18. The marketing concept implies that an organization must meet all needs of their customers.

T F 19. The marketing concept adheres to a short-run profit orientation.

T F 20. Integrated marketing effort will minimize organizational conflicts between marketing and other corporate functions.

MULTIPLE CHOICE QUESTIONS

1. Which statement does not help define marketing?
   a. Marketing focuses on the marketplace.
   b. Marketing activities bring buyers and sellers together.
   c. Production is a major marketing activity.
   d. Product planning is part of marketing.

2. Which statement is not encompassed by a definition of effective marketing?
   a. Both parties in the exchange of products must profit in some way.
   b. Marketing facilitates the exchange of products.
   c. Marketing consists of a consumer-oriented mix of business activities.
   d. Business activities are planned and implemented only by profit-seeking organizations.

3. Which utility is created primarily by transportation and delivery?
   a. Possession.   c. Time.
   b. Place.   d. Economic.

4. The basic categories of the marketing mix elements are
   a. product variables, price variables, consumer variables, place variables.
   b. distribution variables, price variables, production variables, promotion variables.
   c. place variables, production variables, price variables, promotion variables.
   d. distribution variables, price variables, promotion variables, product variables.

5. Marketing mix variables are classified as controllable variables because these variables
   a. may be influenced by marketing managers.
   b. are controlled by government.
   c. are controlled by marketing managers.
   d. are controlled by customers.

6. Which one is not a product strategy decision?
   a. Selecting brand names.   c. Storing the product.
   b. Designing packages.   d. Determining product attributes.

7. A complete offering refers to
   a. the basic product an organization offers.
   b. the marketing mix.
   c. the basic product and its associated extras.
   d. the services that an organization offers.

8. Which one does not involve place strategy?
   a. Materials handling.
   c. Selection of retailers.
   b. Form utility.
   d. Transportation.

9. All are channel organizations except
   a. common carriers.
   c. retailers.
   b. manufacturers.
   d. wholesalers.

10. Facilitating agents can be
    a. financial institutions.
    b. organizations in a channel of distribution.
    c. unimportant for effective marketing.
    d. wholesalers.

11. For not-for-profit organizations, price
    a. is always money.
    b. can be time or votes.
    c. is always a physical good.
    d. is nonexistent.

12. Which one of these statements is correct?
    a. There is a standard marketing mix for companies in the same indus-
       try.
    b. There is a best marketing mix inasmuch as pat solutions exist in
       marketing.
    c. The design, implementation, and revision of a marketing mix is an
       uncreative activity.
    d. Marketing is dynamic, consequently, the marketing mix must be
       altered to reflect the ever-changing environment in the marketplace.

13. The marketing concept suggests that management and employees should
    be all but
    a. long-run profit-oriented.
    c. market information-oriented.
    b. consumer-oriented.
    d. sales-oriented.

14. The marketing concept suggests that marketing activities should start
    and end with the
    a. marketing objectives.
    c. customer.
    b. organizational goals.
    d. exchange process.

15. A consumer orientation means that an organization
    a. should create a product and then find a market for this product.
    b. has marketing myopia.
    c. has developed an effective marketing mix.
    d. should define the nature of its business in terms of consumer needs.

16. Which one does <u>not</u> reflect a consumer orientation for a financial institution?
   a. Aggressive advertising pushing for conventional savings account.
   b. Branch banks close to home.
   c. Extended banking hours daily.
   d. Use of ATM's (automatic teller machines).

17. Which statement reflects the marketing era?
   a. Make the best product you can.
   b. Sell what we have.
   c. Maybe people don't want the best product.
   d. People want my product.

18. The profit-oriented aspect of the marketing concept suggests that
   a. consumer wants be evaluated in terms of cost and profit goals.
   b. sales volume is more important than costs.
   c. all customers are equally profitable.
   d. a firm may price its product to the preference of its customers without consideration of costs.

19. Which one is <u>not</u> an example of a potential conflict between the functional areas of marketing and manufacturing?
   a. New product introduction.   c. Number of items produced.
   b. Credit availability.   d. Physical distribution.

20. Integrated marketing effort refers to the integration of the marketing function with
   a. other organizational departments.
   b. customers.
   c. government.
   d. society.

QUICK QUIZ

1Q.
Why is "production" not one of the marketer's concerns while "product planning" is?

1A.
Because product planning involves analyzing buyer demand so that a product which suits buyer needs is developed. How that product is actually made (production) is of little concern as long as the product satisfies buyers.

13

2Q.
What is a simple way to explain marketing's basic function?

2A.
Find a need and satisfy it.

3Q.
How can a bank provide utilities through its marketing activities?

3A.
The customer may use an "electronic teller" which is located at a convenient <u>place</u>, during any <u>time</u> of the day, once having <u>information</u> on where it is and <u>how to use</u> it, to add to savings the <u>possession</u> of which gives a psycho<u>logical</u> satisfaction.

4Q.
Does the marketing concept require that the president of an organization be a marketer?

4A.
No, though about 25% of Fortune 500 presidents do have marketing backgrounds. The concept <u>does</u> suggest that <u>all</u> <u>organization</u> members be marke<u>ting</u>-oriented.

5Q.
How can you tell if a firm has adopted the marketing concept?

5A.
You can't, because the concept is a philosophy of business, and no claims or demonstrated success can <u>prove</u> the philosophy has been <u>adopted</u>. But an indication can be provided by the organization chart. The presence of a Marketing V.P., with the marketing functions "under" the V.P., indicates that marketing is equal to the other areas of the business and that the V.P. can integrate marketing's functions.

ANSWERS TO OBJECTIVE QUESTIONS

MATCHING

1.	I	5.	A	9.	U	13.	D	17.	T
2.	P	6.	C	10.	N	14.	K	18.	J
3.	L	7.	M	11.	B	15.	X	19.	O
4.	Y	8.	V	12.	S	16.	F	20.	R

TRUE OR FALSE

1.	F	5.	T	9.	F	13.	T	17.	T
2.	T	6.	T	10.	T	14.	T	18.	F
3.	T	7.	F	11.	T	15.	F	19.	F
4.	F	8.	F	12.	F	16.	F	20.	T

MULTIPLE CHOICE

1.	c	5.	a	9.	a	13.	d	17.	c
2.	d	6.	c	10.	a	14.	c	18.	a
3.	b	7.	c	11.	b	15.	-d	19.	b
4.	d	8.	b	12.	d	16.	a	20.	a

CHAPTER 2

ENVIRONMENTAL OPPORTUNITIES AND CONSTRAINTS

OBJECTIVE

This chapter describes the dynamic nature of marketing's environment. Effective marketing involves anticipating, reacting, and adapting to changes in these external forces.

OUTLINE

I. The environment of marketing

    A. All profit- and not-for-profit organizations are affected by environmental factors.

    B. These environmental factors are uncontrollable influences for marketing managers.

II. The environment and the marketing mix

    A. Managers must recognize the influence of environmental forces on marketing by anticipating, reacting, and adapting to external forces.

    B. Environmental dynamics refers to the external dynamic forces influencing an organization.

    C. Marketing dynamics refers to the adjustments of the marketing mix to reflect the effects of environmental changes.

    D. The success of a marketing decision is often a function of proper timing.

III. Identifying major environmental influences

    A. Physical and cultural environments are the two major environmental components.

B. Both environments have an impact on the marketing mix.

IV. The physical environment

    A. Natural resources, climate, and the earth's human population comprise the physical environment.

    B. The physical environment has an influence, sometimes devastating, on marketing.

V. The cultural environment

    A. Culture refers to social institutions, values, beliefs, and behaviors.

    B. The cultural environment includes demographic, economics, science and technology, social values, and the political and legal environments.

    C. Demography is the study of the size, composition, and distribution of the human population in relation to social factors.

        1. The world population is about 5 billion people.

        2. According to the 1980 Census of Population, there are more than 225 million persons living in the United States.

        3. Migration is an important demographic factor in the United States.

        4. Urbanization continues with growth in suburban areas rather than central cities.

        5. Growth is more rapid in the Sunbelt, particularly California, Texas, and Florida.

        6. Selected characteristics of the United States population are that women outnumber men, the median age is 30.3 years, the average household size is 2.76 persons, the median family income is slightly more than $22,000, and families have fewer children today.

    D. Economic factors determine how a society allocates its scarce resources.

1. Monopoly, oligopoly, monopolistic competition, and pure competition are types of competitive market structure.

2. Demarketing refers to a marketing strategy to discourage buying on a temporary or permanent basis.

E. Organizations must adjust their marketing strategy to changing technology.

F. Social values and beliefs impact on marketing strategy and other environmental variables in all cultures.

G. The political and legal environment can require, prohibit, or limit marketing activities.

1. Legislation affecting marketing activities can be found at federal, state, and local levels.

2. Federal antitrust legislation prohibits activities that lessen competition such as price fixing.

3. The Federal Trade Commission has broad powers of investigation into and jurisdiction over unfair methods of competition.

VI. Environmental interactions

A. Marketers must consider the interactions among the various external environments.

B. Marketing success depends on the effectiveness of the environmental analysis in identifying external constraints and opportunities.

SUMMARY

Learning Objective One: To portray the environment in which marketing managers work and to describe how that environment affects the organization.

The marketing environment consists of a physical environment and a cultural environment. These can be influenced, but not controlled, by the marketing manager. The major physical environmental factors are natural resources, climate, and people. The cultural environment includes factors related to demography, economics, science and technology, social values and beliefs, and political and legal factors. These factors provide environmental opportunities and constraints for marketing decision-making. Marketing managers must recognize the influence of these factors, singly or jointly, on their marketing activities.

<u>Learning Objective Two</u>: To discuss the impact of the environment on an organization's marketing mix.

A major responsibility of a marketing manager is adjusting the organization's marketing mix to changes in the external environment. Before altering the marketing mix, a manager must anticipate the environmental changes which will impact on the organization as constraints and opportunities. Thus, correct environmental assessment will enhance the timing and success of a marketing decision. Marketing dynamics refers to this process of adjusting the marketing mix to changes in environmental forces.

<u>Learning Objective Three</u>: To describe the interactions between the several aspects of marketing's environment.

Exhibit 2-3 in the Zikmund and d'Amico textbook shows how the physical environment impacts on the cultural environment. For example, a climatic change can affect economic conditions, social values, and legislation. Social values, such as safety and a clean environment, are reflected in legislation and products. The political and legal environments, in turn, influence economic conditions and permissible business practices. Interactions exist between changes in the economic, technological, and social environments. More dollars are invested in research and development when a country has a prosperous economy.

<u>Learning Objective Four</u>: To know a number of important demographic facts and figures that impact the marketing manager's performance.

Slightly more than 4 percent (over 225 million) of the world's 5 billion people live in the United States. Of these 225 million people, 75 percent live in 318 major metropolitan areas, and 33 percent live in the South. Over 70 percent of the U.S. population is at least 18 years old. The median age is 30.3 years. Women outnumber men. There are over 82 million households in the United States with an average size of 2.76 persons, with 23 percent being one-person households. The median family income for the 60 million U.S. families (average size, 3.27 persons) is over $22,000, even though 11 percent of the families are below the poverty level.

<u>Learning Objective Five</u>: To be familiar with a number of major demographic trends and their importance to modern marketers.

Major demographic trends include:

    ° the aging (greying) of the U.S. population,
    ° the migration to the Sunbelt states,

- the growth of suburban areas,
- the increase in single-person households,
- the increase in divorces,
- the increase in females employed, and
- the increase in household income.

Managers must understand the influence of these trends on their marketing activities for effective marketing. These trends reflect the changing composition of a market and the impact on shopping behavior. For example, employed females may require adjustments in the marketing mix regarding kinds of products offered, hours open, or location of the store. An organization is more apt to succeed when its managers recognize how demographic trends affect the organization.

Learning Objective Six: To describe the implications of migration, urbanization, and changing age structures of the population for marketing.

In general, migration, urbanization, and shifting age structures necessitate that marketing managers adjust their marketing mixes. Each of these factors create environmental opportunities and constraints. For instance, migration and urbanization impact on channels of distribution. Organizations must make their product available to people at different locations. Conversely, these same organizations close outlets in geographic market areas which become unprofitable because of fewer potential customers. The changing age structure of the population has implications for an organization's offering. For example, older people consume different kinds of products than younger people; or, a retailer can adjust product lines to retain existing customers.

Learning Objective Seven: To comment on the marketing activity known as "demarketing."

Demarketing involves a marketing strategy to discourage buying an organization's product either on a temporary or permanent basis. These activities can be directed to all customers or selected segments of customers. Product shortages usually initiate a demarketing strategy. An effective demarketing strategy stresses consumer satisfaction.

Learning Objective Eight: To relate social values, and changes in those values, to marketing.

Social values reflect a culture's idea of what is preferred behavior. Marketing practices must conform to this preferred behavior. If not, legislation is likely to be enacted to ensure marketing's conformity to social values. The requirement of safety packages for products that may be harmful to children is an example. A manager must adapt marketing activities to changes in social values.

Learning Objective Nine: To give examples of how the three levels of law in the United States affect marketing activities.

Federal antitrust legislation prohibits acts such as price discrimination, price fixing, and other deceptive practices that tend to lessen competition. Federal agencies have been established to enforce these and other laws. In addition to similar laws and agencies at the state level, specific consumer protection laws exist. Each state has unique laws regarding taxable products, unfair trade practices, and selected industry practices. Many local ordinances pertain to inspections and licensing in order to control the type and number of businesses. All three levels of law restrict marketing activities.

VOCABULARY BUILDING

Matching Exercise

Match the following by placing the letter of the concept or term on the blank preceding the phrase which best describes this concept or term. You should use a term or concept only once.

A.	Environmental dynamics	K.	Oligopoly
B.	Marketing dynamics	L.	Monopoly
C.	Physical environment	M.	Demarketing
D.	Cultural environment	N.	Science
E.	Culture	O.	Technology
F.	Demography	P.	Social value
G.	Economics	Q.	Belief
H.	Market structure	R.	Federal antitrust legislation
I.	Pure competition	S.	Federal Trade Commission
J.	Monopolistic competition		

__C__ 1. That part of the environment which consists of natural resources and the human population.

__S__ 2. Given broad powers of investigation into "unfair methods of competition" in 1919.

__M__ 3. Marketing strategy designed to intentionally discourage customers on either a temporary or permanent basis.

__F__ 4. The study of the size, composition, and distribution of human populations.

24

_D_ 5. That part of the environment which includes demographic factors, scientific knowledge, social values and beliefs, economic conditions, and political and legal factors.

_O_ 6. The application of knowledge to practical purposes.

_Q_ 7. A statement concerning the existence and characteristics of physical and social phenomena.

_B_ 8. The various activities and changes in an organization's marketing mix.

_N_ 9. The accumulation of knowledge about man and his environment.

_E_ 10. Refers to social institutions, values, and behaviors.

_P_ 11. A statement about a culture's idea of what is preferred behavior.

_A_ 12. External forces influencing an organization's marketing.

_H_ 13. Refers to number of competing firms and size of market held by each competitor.

_J_ 14. Principal characteristic is product differentiation.

_K_ 15. Distinguishing characteristic is a measure of control over the market-place--and in particular, some control over the prices at which it sells its products.

VOCABULARY BUILDING

Programmed Learning Exercise

1. _Environ_____ dynamics refers to various dynamic external forces influencing an organization.

[Environmental]

2. Marketing managers must _____, _____, and _____ to environmental opportunities and constraints.

[anticipate, react, adjust]

3. The two major parts of marketing's external environment are the _____ environment and the _____ environment.

[physical, cultural]

25

4. The physical environment consists of _____, _____, and _____.

[natural resources, climate, human population]

5. Demography is the study of the _____, _____, and _____ of the human population.

[size, composition, distribution]

6. The world population is nearing _____ people.

[5 billion]

7. Since 1940 the average size of a U.S. household has steadily _____.

[declined]

8. Total percent of all women who work exceeds _____ percent.

[50]

9. Rivalry in all areas of marketing is intensified by competition from _____ goods and services.

[substitutable]

10. _____ _____ exists when there are no barriers to competition.

[Pure competition]

11. A demarketing strategy is appropriate when _____ exceeds _____.

[demand, supply]

12. _____ and _____ are particularly volatile parts of marketing's environment.

[Science, technology]

13. A social value is a statement about a culture's idea of what is _____.

[preferred behavior]

14. Marketing legislation can be found at the _____, _____, and _____ levels.

[federal, state, local]

15. Federal _____ legislation prohibits acts such as restraint of trade, monopoly, and price fixing.

[antitrust]

16. The _____ _____ _____ Act requires banks, finance companies, and retailers to fully disclose true interest rates and all other charges to credit customers for loans, revolving charge accounts, and installment loans.

[Consumer Protection Credit]

17. The _____ Act prohibits price fixing and conspiracies to restrain trade or to monopolize.

[Sherman]

18. The _____ _____ Act requires that sellers must offer equal deals to all customers.

[Robinson-Patman]

19. Effective marketers must consider the _____ of marketing's environment, not just its _____.

[whole, parts]

20. Marketing's environment changes _____.

[constantly]

TRUE OR FALSE STATEMENTS

T F 1. Not-for-profit organizations do not have to contend with external forces.

T F 2. Both marketing and environmental dynamics are controllable by an individual organization.

T F 3. The marketing mix should be adjusted for changes in the external environment.

T F 4. When making a marketing decision, a marketing manager must take into consideration environmental opportunities and constraints.

T F 5. Political and legal factors are part of the cultural environment.

T F 6. International marketing is only mildly influenced by social values.

T F 7. Demographic statistics and trends are of great concern to marketing managers.

T F 8. Growth in metropolitan areas has not meant growth in central cities.

T F 9. Racial minority groups constitute about 10 percent of the total U.S. population.

T F 10. The median U.S. family income exceeds $20,000 today.

T F 11. Rivalry among competitors often leads to lower prices and differentiated products.

T F 12. Competition from substitutable products refers to choosing among similar products, such as fast food restaurants, only.

T F 13. Oligopoly is the same as large size.

T F 14. An oligopoly arises from the natural logic of the marketplace in some industries.

T F 15. A demarketing strategy does not stress consumer satisfaction.

T F 16. Science and technology are a volatile part of marketing's external environment.

T F 17. Social values interact with other environmental factors as well as affect marketing strategy.

T F 18. The political and legal environment constrains actions of marketers.

T F 19. Purposes of legislation are to maintain a competitive business environment, to protect consumers, and to preserve natural resources.

T F 20. Marketers should not consider environmental interactions when developing their plans.

MULTIPLE CHOICE QUESTIONS

1. Which statement is incorrect?
    a. All organizations operate within environments.
    b. Environmental factors exert no influence on marketing activities.
    c. Environmental factors are uncontrollable influences.
    d. Environmental factors affect all organizations.

2. Which one is not an environmental factor?
    a. Social values.   c. Production.
    b. Economic conditions.   d. Technology.

3. A proper analysis of environmental dynamics
    a. helps a marketer to determine the correct time to enter and to exit the market.
    b. helps the marketer to determine the controllable environmental elements.
    c. enables the marketer to influence market forces.
    d. is seldom needed.

4. The physical environment includes
    a. social values.
    b. political forces
    c. natural resources.
    d. economic conditions.

5. The cultural environment includes all but
    a. the human population.
    b. economics.
    c. demography.
    d. legal factors.

6. Demography refers to the study of
    a. cultural influences on population.
    b. physical influences on population.
    c. the total population.
    d. the size, composition, and distribution of the human population.

7. For the United States, which demographic trend is incorrect?
    a. Hispanics are increasing faster than blacks.
    b. Median family income is increasing.
    c. Increased urbanization is due to growth in the central cities.
    d. Average household size is decreasing.

8. Regarding the United States population, one finds that
    a. the total population exceeds 250 million people.
    b. minority groups comprise over 20 percent of the population.
    c. the death rate exceeds the birth rate.
    d. the number of men exceed the number of women.

9. The competitive market structure refers to
    a. the number of products available in a market.
    b. the size of the market.
    c. the range of prices within an industry.
    d. the number of competing firms and their relative size.

10. Which one is not an economic factor which affects how a spending decision is made?
    a. Consumer savings patterns.
    b. Social values.
    c. Amount of competition in several industries.
    d. Rate of inflation.

11. Which industry does <u>not</u> have an oligopolistic competitive structure?
    a. Electric utilities.
    b. Steel industry.
    c. Tire industry.
    d. Cigarette industry.

12. A supplier who is unable to keep up with demand may initiate a _____ strategy.
    a. demand
    b. consumer
    c. demarketing
    d. supply

13. When a firm uses a demarketing strategy, this firm is trying to
    a. intentionally encourage customers to purchase its products.
    b. increase the supply of the product.
    c. reduce competition.
    d. intentionally discourage customers to purchase its product.

14. Technological advances have an important impact on an organization's marketing activities because
    a. technology can revolutionize an industry.
    b. technology increases production costs.
    c. technology involves demarketing.
    d. technology does not impact on an organization's marketing activities.

15. Which statement regarding social values is <u>incorrect</u>?
    a. Social values influence marketing strategy.
    b. Social values are a culture's idea of preferred behavior.
    c. Social values are similar in all cultures.
    d. Social values can lead to regulation.

16. Which one does <u>not</u> describe how the political and legal environment impacts on marketing?
    a. Political and legal environment limits actions of marketers.
    b. Political and legal environment requires some actions of marketers.
    c. Political and legal environment has little impact on actions of marketers.
    d. The legal and political environment prohibits certain actions of marketers.

17. All are examples of specialized federal legislation affecting business-government relationships except
    a. Poison Prevention Labeling Act.
    b. Federal Trade Commission Act.
    c. Consumer Protection Credit Act.
    d. Public Health Smoking Act.

18. Which federal agency has broad powers of investigation and jurisdiction over unfair methods of competition?
    a. Federal Communication Commission (FCC).
    b. Federal Trade Commission (FTC).
    c. Food and Drug Administration (FDA).
    d. Health, Education and Welfare Commission (HOWC).

19. Local ordinances which restrict door-to-door selling are referred to as
    a. Door-to-Door Ordinances.
    b. Unfair Trade Ordinances.
    c. Green River Ordinances.
    d. Sellers' Ordinances.

20. Which statement is <u>incorrect</u> regarding demographic statistics for the United States in 1981?
    a. Median family income for white families exceed the median family income for black families by about $10,000.
    b. Metropolitan areas contain about 60 percent of the total population.
    c. Average family size is 3.27 persons.
    d. Median age is slightly more than 30 years.

QUICK QUIZ

1Q.
If the environmental forces surrounding an organization are "uncontrollable," why should a marketer be concerned with them?

1A.
Because they affect what the marketer can and cannot do in the market place <u>and</u> because the aggressive, successful manager uses information about the environment in planning effective marketing strategies.

2Q.
What impacts on American marketing do great increases in world population have?

2A.
The prospect of a world population which doubles every twenty or thirty years presents many problems, but these problems can be solved, with marketing making a major contribution to the solutions. Products tied to birth control, health care, food production, clothing, communication, ecologically sound transportation, and energy production

31

are among the many which should "boom" as world population, and concern about that population, increases.

3Q.
Why is demarketing different from the first-come-first-served, take--it-or-leave-it attitude a marketer of goods in short supply might take?

3A.
Demarketing stresses a key aspect of marketing, consumer satisfaction, even though shortages are unpleasant. It emphasizes trying to keep customers over the long run rather than antagonizing them with a take-it-or-leave-it attitude.

4Q.
Has retailing been affected by scientific and technological changes?

4A.
Yes, since retailers, like other businesses, use computers and other modern equipment. But the development of the automobile and decline of public transportation has affected retailers drastically, forcing them to move to suburban malls and resulting in the decline of many downtown areas.

EXPERIENTIAL ACTIVITIES

2-A. Demographic Data

A local real estate developer is uncertain in which of two areas to develop an apartment complex. This developer has retained you to determine which location is better. In order to make a recommendation, you recognize that you will need some demographic information. From a Census Tract Report, you obtain these data for the metropolitan area (MSA) and two Census Tracts.

ANSWERS TO OBJECTIVE QUESTIONS

MATCHING

1.	C	4.	F	7.	Q	10.	E	13.	H
2.	S	5.	D	8.	B	11.	P	14.	J
3.	M	6.	O	9.	N	12.	A	15.	K

TRUE OR FALSE

1.	F	5.	T	9.	F	13.	F	17.	T
2.	F	6.	F	10.	T	14.	T	18.	T
3.	T	7.	T	11.	T	15.	F	19.	T
4.	T	8.	T	12.	F	16.	T	20.	F

MULTIPLE CHOICE

1.	b	5.	a	9.	d	13.	d	17.	b
2.	c	6.	d	10.	b	14.	a	18.	b
c.	a	7.	c	11.	a	15.	c	19.	c
4.	c	8.	b	12.	c	16.	c	20.	b

CHAPTER 3

DEVELOPING MARKETING STRATEGY

OBJECTIVE

Effective marketing is based on well developed strategies directed toward realistic opportunities. Marketing executives must correctly interpret the environmental analysis to develop these strategies.

OUTLINE

I. Marketing management

   A. Marketing management is the application of general management techniques to marketing situations and problems.

   B. Marketing managers plan, execute, and control marketing activities.

   C. Marketing planning involves establishing marketing goals and designing marketing programs.

      1. The two general categories of marketing planning are operational planning (planning day-to-day functional activities) and strategic planning (long-range planning).

      2. A corporate mission statement should be consumer-oriented.

      3. Marketing plans specify which actions are to be implemented when future events occur.

   D. Marketing plans need to be executed or implemented.

      1. Execution involves organizing and coordinating people, resources, and activities.

2. Plans to be executed should be appropriate for existing and expected environmental factors.

E. Control involves the basic activities of investigation and evaluation.

   1. Investigation involves the determination that the marketing plan is or is not being executed.

   2. Evaluation assesses if actual performance matches planned performance.

   3. A marketing audit is a comprehensive review and appraisal of the total marketing operation.

F. Planning, execution, and control are interrelated.

II. Strategic marketing

A. Strategic marketing planning is a long-range, comprehensive framework formulated to accomplish brand, divisional, or organizational goals.

B. A strategy involves the determination of basic long-range goals, adoption of courses of action, and allocation of resources.

C. Tactics are specific marketing actions to execute a marketing strategy.

III. Developing marketing strategies

A. The development of a marketing strategy involves identifying and evaluating opportunities, analyzing market segments, selecting target markets, and planning a marketing mix strategy.

B. Market opportunity analysis involves identifying and evaluating environmental opportunities.

   1. Strengths and weaknesses of actual and potential competitors are identified.

   2. Environmental opportunities must be matched to organizational capabilities.

   3. Organizational goals (mission) must be determined.

4. Strategic gap analysis must be performed.

C. Market segmentation involves deciding where marketing efforts are to be directed.

D. A marketing mix is developed to satisfy a target market.

IV. Various levels of planning and strategy in the organization

A. Three levels of administration are top management, middle management, and supervisory management.

B. Planning and strategy are major responsibilities of top management.

SUMMARY

Learning Objective One: To be familiar with the ideas and terminology associated with planning as these apply to marketing problems.

Marketing planning involves the determination of marketing objectives and the design of marketing programs to achieve those objectives in an efficient manner. Since planning establishes the relationship between an organization and its environment, the foundation for effective planning is an accurate assessment of marketing's environment. This environmental assessment enables managers to diagnose the present, to predict the future, and to develop goals and marketing programs to shape their organization's destiny. The planning horizon can be operational (short-range) or strategic (long-range). One aspect of strategic planning is to determine a corporate mission statement that is consumer-oriented.

Learning Objective Two: To explain the planning and managing tasks performed by marketing executives.

Marketing executives perform two types of planning: operational planning and strategic planning. Operational planning involves planning day-to-day functional activities with existing customers and facilities. Strategic planning has a long-range perspective and concerns an organization's mission, strategies, and objectives. Planning involves an analysis of the environment. Based on this analysis, plans (operational and strategic) are designed to be implemented when future events occur.

The execution of marketing plans requires organizing and coordinating people, resources, and activities. Major tasks include staffing, directing, developing, and leading subordinates to implement marketing plans. To ensure that marketing plans are properly executed, marketing managers must control their activities. Control means that acceptable performance standards, usually related to marketing goals and objectives, be established. Once these standards are determined, the manager investigates if the marketing activity has been performed, and, if so, evaluates if its actual performance matches planned performance.

Learning Objective Three: To know how the three tasks of planning, execution, and control interrelate and form the basis of marketing management.

Marketing management is a decision-making process concerned with planning, executing, and controlling a set of marketing activities to achieve organizational goals. Marketing plans are based on an assessment of environmental opportunities and constraints which then are implemented. The execution of the plan is investigated and evaluated (control function). The findings from the control function provide an input for planning and execution.

Learning Objective Four: To discuss the development of complete strategic plans and to differentiate between strategy and tactics in the marketplace.

The development of a strategic marketing plan involves an assessment of the organization's mission, environmental forces, and the organization's strengths and weaknesses. A marketing opportunity analysis accomplishes this assessment. Based on the marketing opportunity analysis, the organization's desired and actual positions are determined. Any difference between these two positions is a strategic gap. Strategic plans are then developed to close the strategic gap.

A strategy consists of the determination of basic long-range goals and objectives, the adoption of courses of actions, and the allocation of resources to achieve these goals. Tactics are specific actions to implement strategy. Tactics are less comprehensive than strategies. An example of a strategy would be to provide a pleasant, but entertaining, environment for children to enjoy a wholesome moderate-priced pizza. Appropriate tactics would be to price a medium-size pizza at $6.50 and to provide a clown to entertain the children. The actual development of a marketing strategy, however, involves identifying and evaluating opportunities, analyzing market segments, selecting target markets, and planning a marketing mix strategy that will satisfy customers' needs and meet organizational goals and objectives.

Learning Objective Five: To discuss the process of marketing opportunity analysis and its purpose in identifying trends and opportunities.

Marketing opportunity analysis involves the analysis, evaluation, and interpretation of the physical and cultural environments for future environmental impacts on target markets. This analysis identifies competitors' strengths and weakness and subsequently compares competitors' strengths and weaknesses relative to one's own. Based on these analyses, environmental trends can be interpreted as potential organizational problems or opportunities. These opportunities are evaluated in terms of the firm's capabilities in order to determine realistic opportunities. Marketing opportunity analysis then determines the strategic gap which exists between the organization's desired and actual position in the marketplace. The purpose of marketing opportunity analysis is to enable marketing executives to develop more effective marketing plans by identifying impacts, trends, and opportunities created by marketing's environment.

Learning Objective Six: To know how marketing managers distinguish between opportunities in general and realistic opportunities that their organizations can profitably pursue.

Marketing managers can develop guidelines to identify realistic organizational activities. These guidelines are based on the firms' goals, strengths, and special competencies.

Learning Objective Seven: To explain how plans relate to "the strategic gap."

The strategic gap is the difference between the desired position and the actual position. Plans are the desired courses of action to move the organization from its present position to where it wants to be.

VOCABULARY BUILDING

Matching Exercise

Match the following by placing the letter of the concept or term on the blank preceding the phrase which best describes this concept or term. You should use a term or concept only once.

A. Management
B. Marketing management
C. Marketing planning
D. Operational planning
E. Strategic planning
F. Corporate mission
G. Planning horizon
H. Plans
I. Execution
J. Control

K. Marketing audit
L. Strategy
M. Marketing strategy
N. Tactics
O. Marketing opportunity analysis
P. Strategic gap
Q. Market
R. Market segments
S. Market segmentation
T. Target markets

_L_ 1. The determination of long-run goals and objectives, the adoption of courses of action, and the allocation of resources necessary to achieve these goals.

_m_ 2. Involves identification and evaluation of opportunities, analysis of market segments, selection of target markets, and planning a marketing mix strategy.

_O_ 3. The diagnostic activity of interpreting the external environment and environmental factors.

_Q_ 4. A group of individuals who are possible customers for the product being offered for sale.

_I_ 5. The organization of people and coordination of activities in an organization.

_C_ 6. The designing of marketing programs that are expected to be implemented in the future.

_H_ 7. Specific courses of action to be taken when future events occur.

_J_ 8. Ensures that planned activities are completed and properly executed.

_A_ 9. The integration of human and material resources to achieve goals.

_R_ 10. Portions of larger markets.

_N_ 11. Specific actions concerned with the execution of plans.

_E_ 12. Concerns long-range consideration relative to an organization's mission, strategies, and objectives.

_I_ 13. Specific groups of customers likely to buy an organization's product.

_K_ 14. A comprehensive review and appraisal of the total marketing operation.

_P_ 15. The difference between an organization's desired position and actual position in the market.

42

VOCABULARY BUILDING

Programmed Learning Exercise

1. The three general functions of the management process are _____, _____, and _____.

   [planning, execution, control]

2. _____ planning concerns planning for day-to-day functional activities.

   [Operational]

3. A corporate mission statement should be _____-oriented.

   [consumer]

4. _____ helps an organization to shape its destiny by anticipating changes in the marketplace.

   [Planning]

5. The length of an organization's _____ _____ is generally determined by the uncertainty of the environmental situation.

   [planning horizon]

6. Planning must result in _____.

   [plans]

7. An important aspect of the marketing manager's job is to _____ the implementation of marketing plans.

   [supervise]

8. _____ activities provide feedback to alert managers to continue with plans or to take corrective action.

   [Control]

9. Planning, execution, and control are _____ activities.

   [interrelated]

10. Control requires _____ and _____.

    [investigation, evaluation]

11. _____ _____ planning is a long-range, comprehensive framework formulated to accomplish brand or organizational goals.

    [Strategic marketing]

12. A _____ _____ is a clear image of what you want to achieve.

    [strategic vision]

43

13. Tactics are more closely associated with the _____ of plans rather than with the planning itself.

[execution]

14. After selecting target markets, marketing managers plan a _____ _____ strategy.

[marketing mix]

15. Points of no relative advantage to competitors define the _____ _____ boundary.

[competitive segment]

16. Any organization can act profitably on only those opportunities which fit its _____.

[capabilities]

17. Firms may develop _____ to distinguish between environmental opportunities and realistic opportunities.

[guidelines]

18. Identification of opportunities involves an assessment of the environment and consideration an organization's _____ and its _____.

[goals, limitations]

19. _____ _____ is defined as the dividing of a heterogeneous mass market into a number of smaller, more specific customer groups.

[Market segmentation]

20. The three levels of administration are _____ _____, _____ _____, and _____ _____.

[top management, middle management, supervisory management]

TRUE OR FALSE STATEMENTS

T F 1. Marketing management is a decision-making process.

T F 2. The three essential activities for effective management are planning, staffing, and controlling.

T F 3. Marketing planning is made difficult by a changing marketing environment.

T F 4. The primary purpose of marketing planning is diagnostic.

T F 5. Major execution activities are staffing, directing, developing, and leading subordinates.

44

T F   6. Great marketing plans will result in failure, if improperly executed.

T F   7. Planning and control are interrelated.

T F   8. An organization does not need a mission statement.

T F   9. In determining a strategy, the first stage is to commit to a course of action.

T F 10. Tactics are more comprehensive than strategies.

T F 11. One must analyze market segments before planning a marketing mix strategy.

T F 12. A marketing audit is the diagnostic activity of interpreting environmental attributes and changes.

T F 13. Survival in the marketplace requires a unique competitive advantage.

T F 14. Strategic gap refers to a condition where a difference exists between an organization's strategy and its actual plan.

T F 15. Any firm can decide on what market it wants to serve because all environmental opportunities are, in fact, organizational opportunities.

T F 16. To identify market opportunities, a firm assesses the environment and then changes organizational goals not compatible with the environment.

T F 17. A firm selects a target market because it believes the firm will have a competitive advantage.

T F 18. A marketing mix is the means by which a marketing manager achieves goals.

T F 19. Effective marketing becomes increasingly important as we move downward from top management to supervisory management.

T F 20. Effective marketing is not possible unless carefully developed guiding strategies are planned before an organization's marketing mix is created.

MULTIPLE CHOICE QUESTIONS

1. Which one does not describe marketing management?
   a. Marketing management involves planning and executing.
   b. Marketing management adapts marketing techniques and concepts to management activities.
   c. Marketing management is a special application of general management techniques.
   d. Marketing management is a decision-making process.

2. The two general categories of marketing planning are
   a. tactical and operational.
   b. long-range and strategic.
   c. audit and strategic.
   d. strategic and operational.

3. Which one does not describe operational planning?
   a. Operational planning involves broad strategy decisions.
   b. Operational planning deals with day-to-day functional activities.
   c. Operational planning pertains to existing activities in existing markets with existing customers and facilities.
   d. Operational planning's scope is more narrow than the scope of strategic planning.

4. Planning helps an organization to
   a. exercise control over the environment.
   b. eliminate competition from the marketplace.
   c. anticipate changes in the marketplace.
   d. make substantial profits in all target markets.

5. Which one is not true about marketing planning?
   a. Marketing planning must result in specific courses of action.
   b. Certain plans may be scrapped due to changes in society.
   c. Marketing planning enables the organization to react rather than act.
   d. Planning establishes the relationship between an organization and its environment.

6. Which one is not a major execution activity?
   a. Staffing.
   b. Leading subordinates.
   c. Directing subordinates.
   d. Producing the product.

7. The execution of a marketing plan involves all but
   a. selecting a strategy.
   b. setting a price.
   c. routing salespeople.
   d. making a sales presentation.

8. Carefully formulated plans that are executed properly may fail because
    a. the conditions upon which the original plans were based may have changed.
    b. there are several ways to execute a plan.
    c. control was inappropriate.
    d. marketing opportunity analysis was not performed.

9. The first aspect of marketing control is for a manager to
    a. impose strict controls on marketing activities.
    b. conduct a marketing opportunity analysis.
    c. establish performance standards.
    d. supervise the execution of all marketing activities.

10. A comprehensive review and appraisal of the total marketing operation is
    a. an audit.   c. a marketing audit.
    b. a marketing strategy.   d. an environmental assessment.

11. Of the following, who should conduct a firm's marketing audit?
    a. Marketing vice president.   c. Controller.
    b. Marketing manager.   d. Outside consultant.

12. An important aspect of a marketing strategy is
    a. offering many brands of a product.
    b. stressing sales promotion rather than production.
    c. stating tactics.
    d. determining basic long-range goals and objectives.

13. Of the following, _____ are associated more closely with execution of plans than planning.
    a. strategies   c. strategic gaps
    b. tactics   d. marketing audits

14. The development of a marketing strategy involves all except
    a. identifying opportunities.   c. controlling target markets.
    b. selecting target markets.   d. planning a marketing mix strategy.

15. Marketing strategies are designed to
    a. satisfy the consumer.   c. maximize sales.
    b. maximize short-term profits. d. fulfill a firm's social responsibilities.

16. Marketing opportunity analysis
    a. guarantees that a firm's product will be a success.
    b. helps the manager evaluate advertising copy.
    c. interprets environmental attributes and changes.
    d. determines the corporate mission.

17. Which statement regarding competition is <u>incorrect</u>?
    a. Competitors who survive have a unique advantage.
    b. Similar competitors have less severe competition.
    c. Competitors that coexist must be in equilibrium.
    d. Competitive segment boundaries exist between competitors.

18. The evaluation of the organizational mission in terms of environmental forces determines the organization's
    a. actual position.   c. strategic gap.
    b. desired position.   d. marketing strategy.

19. The difference between an organization's desired and actual positions in the marketplace is referred to as
    a. strategic difference.
    b. marketing opportunity analysis.
    c. strategic marketing planning.
    d. strategic gap.

20. Groups of customers which are seen as having good potential for the company's product are referred to as
    a. markets.   c. target markets.
    b. market segments.   d. buyers.

QUICK QUIZ

1Q.
How does planning create the relationship between an organization and its environment?

1A.
The organization with no plans is the "victim" of its environment; the organization with plans can meet its challenges.

2Q.
What would be an example of a strategy and a tactic for a retail marketer?

2A.
Strategy--A&P closes all stores in six midwestern states to concentrate on developing sunbelt business.

Tactic--A&P drops Reese's Peanut Butter Cups from store #1,532 because they are not selling.

3Q.
The evaluation of organizational strengths and weaknesses in terms of environmental forces is called market oportunity analysis, but, evaluating organizational goals in terms of the environment is called marketing opportunity analysis. Why the difference?

3A.
When the organization compares its abilities to environmental factors, it is seeking to identify markets it can serve right now. Bayer Aspirin can be sold in Florida. When goals are considered, opportunities for marketing in new ways are being identified. If such sales were a Bayer goal, new marketing plans and efforts would be needed.

EXPERIENTIAL ACTIVITIES

3-A. Mission Statements

All organizations should have a mission statement to guide executives in determining objectives and in selecting among strategies. A mission statement provides organizational purpose by defining what an organization does or can do in terms of satisfying basic needs of target markets. Mission statements of two competing corporations are below.

Tire Specialities Companies Mission Statement

The Tire Specialties Companies are a group of related companies which serve the needs of the aftermarket for virtually all forms of transportation through the provision of high quality products and services to consumers, businesses, farmers, and insurance companies via wholesale and retail locations throughout the Midwest.

Mars Tire and Auto Companies Mission Statement

Our mission is to service customer needs in retail, wholesale, and manufacturing, and to be able to open new market areas in the product lines and customer services offered for company growth in the automotive aftermarket and transportation care needs.

Assignment

1. Evaluate these two mission statements.

   Tires Specialties Companies

   _____

   _____

   _____

   _____

   _____

   _____

   Mars Tire and Auto Companies

   _____

   _____

   _____

   _____

   _____

   _____

2. Select the mission statement you prefer. Justify your choice.

   Preferred mission statement: _____

   Justification: _____

   _____

   _____

   _____

   _____

3. Write an improved mission statement for one of these two companies based on your evaluation.

   _____

   _____

   _____

   _____

   _____

3-B. Strategic Gap and Marketing Strategy

You are a new divisional manager for one of the two companies described in experimental activity 3-A. Sales and net profit figures for the last three years are given below.

Year	Net Sales	Net Profit (loss)
1984	$3,953,000	($101,500)
1983	$4,161,000	($38,000)
1982	$4,380,000	$175,000

Gross margin percents are near the industry average. Retail gross margins exceed wholesale gross margins by 50 percent. An analysis of 1984 sales indicates these breakdowns:

	Percent of Net Sales
Tires	75
Auto parts and services	25
Retail	20
Wholesale	80

Gross margins are higher for auto services.

The company's financial objective is to achieve a net profit equal to ten percent of net sales. Net sales for 1989 are forecasted to be $6,880,000.

Assignment

1. Determine the strategic gap that would exist in 1989 if current strategies are not changed.

2. Describe the marketing strategies you would recommend to reduce or eliminate this strategic gap.

ANSWERS TO OBJECTIVE QUESTIONS

MATCHING

1.	L	4.	Q	7.	H	10.	R	13.	T
2.	M	5.	I	8.	J	11.	N	14.	K
3.	O	6.	C	9.	A	12.	E	15.	P

TRUE OR FALSE

1.	T	5.	T	9.	F	13.	T	17.	T
2.	F	6.	T	10.	F	14.	F	18.	T
3.	T	7.	T	11.	T	15.	F	19.	F
4.	F	8.	F	12.	F	16.	F	20.	T

MULTIPLE CHOICE

1.	b	5.	c	9.	c	13.	b	17.	b
2.	d	6.	d	10.	c	14.	c	18.	b
3.	a	7.	a	11.	d	15.	a	19.	d
4.	c	8.	a	12.	d	16.	c	20.	c

CHAPTER 4

MARKET SEGMENTATION

OBJECTIVE

Market segmentation is the process of identifying meaningful market segments. Marketing managers can select one or more of these segments as target markets and then develop a unique marketing mix for each target market. This is the concept of target marketing.

OUTLINE

I. What is a market?

    A. A market is a group of individuals or organizations who may want the product being offered for sale.

    B. In addition, market members must have the authority and willingness to spend their purchasing power to buy the product offered for sale.

II. The major markets: consumer and organizational

    A. Products that are used to satisfy an individual's personal or household needs are sold in the consumer market.

    B. Products that are used to satisfy needs of a manufacturer or other organization (non-profit organization, wholesaler, retailer, or government) are sold in an organizational or industrial market.

    C. Product classification is based on who bought the product and why they purchased the product.

III. Market segmentation

    A. Marketers identify subgroups within total markets.

55

B. The process of dividing a heterogeneous market into smaller more homogeneous markets is market segmentation.

C. A market segment is meaningful if a characteristic distinguishes the segment, the segment has adequate market potential and is accessible, and the segment members respond favorably to a specialized marketing mix.

D. A cross-classification matrix helps to identify precise segments within a market.

E. A marketing manager must match the marketing mix to the target market.

IV. Four strategies for market segmentation

A. An organization uses an undifferentiated marketing strategy when no meaningful segments exist within a market and the organization develops one marketing mix to satisfy all customers within the market.

B. A concentrated marketing approach is used when all of an organization's marketing effort is directed toward one target market segment within a market.

1. Selection of a target market is based on management's perception of a competitive advantage in dealing with this segment.

2. The market potential of the selected target market may be inadequate, i.e., the market segment is too narrow.

3. The 80/20 principle supports concentration on a target market comprised of heavy users.

4. The majority fallacy concept warns that an organization's marketing may be more effective and efficient directed toward a target market that is less attractive to competitors.

C. An organization practices differentiated marketing when it selects more than one target market segment and develops a unique marketing mix for each target market.

1. A differentiated marketing strategy exploits differences between market segments.

2. Large resources are necessary to execute this strategy.

D. A custom marketing strategy is appropriate when each customer has unique needs.

V. Identifying market differences

A. Market segmentation strategy involves identifying differences within total markets on which to base the development of marketing mixes.

B. There are various bases for segmentation.

VI. Bases for market segmentation

A. Geographic factors such as natural boundaries, climatic conditions, political boundaries, and population boundaries are important segmentation bases.

B. Demographic variables are commonly used as a basis to segment consumer markets.

1. Segmentation based on age needs to consider the changing age distribution.

2. Family life cycle is an effective basis for segmentation when product consumption is related to life cycle stage rather than to age directly.

C. Socio-economic factors such as income, occupation, education, and social class can be used to distinguish groups of customers.

D. Psychographic or lifestyle segmentation is related to people's activities, interests, and opinions.

E. Behavioral bases of segmentation are type of store shopped, number of units purchased, shopping frequency, time of purchase, impulse purchase, brand requested, or media habits.

F. Segmentation can be based on consumption patterns such as frequency of use, purchase occasion, brand/store loyalty, heavy or light usage, or ownership of other products.

G. Benefit segmentation identifies groups of customers according to the benefit sought.

VII. "Best" segmentation variable

   A. The "best" segmentation variable is one which identifies meaningful target market segments.

   B. A bundle of segmentation variables may be used to identify a meaningful target market segment.

SUMMARY

<u>Learning Objective One</u>: To define the term "market" and differentiate between consumer and industrial/organizational markets.

   A market consists of a group of individuals or organizations who meet four criteria.

   1. These individuals or organizations must want the product being offered.

   2. Market members must have the purchasing power to buy the product.

   3. Market members must be willing to spend their purchasing power (money or other resources) to obtain the product.

   4. Market members must have the authority to make such expenditures.

   Consumer and industrial/organizational markets are differentiated on the basis of the buyer's intended use of the product. A consumer market is a group of individuals who use products for their personal or household needs. An industrial/organizational market consists of individuals or organizations who use products in the operation of their organization.

<u>Learning Objective Two</u>: To explain the logic underlying the concept of market segmentation.

   Market segmentation is the breaking-down of a heterogeneous market into a number of smaller, more homogeneous submarkets. Market segmentation is based on the premises that: (1) buyers are different; (2) subgroups of people or organizations with similar behavior, values, and/or backgrounds are identifiable; (3) subgroups will be smaller and more homogeneous than the individuals or organizations comprising the total market; and (4) marketing to these smaller submarkets will be more effective and efficient.

Learning Objective Three: To describe the processes of market segmentation and target marketing.

The processes of market segmentation and target marketing involve these steps. The first step is to research the total market and then disaggregate this market. Next, the customers are regrouped into several meaningful segments according to one or more characteristics such as geographic location and buying pattern. A meaningful segment is a group of identifiable customers who can be reached by a marketing mix to which the segment members will respond favorably. The marketing manager then selects at least one of these meaningful market segments as a target market.

Learning Objective Four: To tell why successful segmentation must lead to the identification of meaningful target markets.

The essence of market segmentation is to identify differences in market behavior within a total market on which to base the development of a successful marketing mix. If a segment is not meaningful it has little managerial value as an effective and efficient marketing mix cannot be developed. Effective target marketing is not possible unless meaningful target markets are identified.

Learning Objective Five: To show the relationship between target marketing and the development of effective marketing mixes.

The marketing mix must be matched to the needs of the target market. In the process of target marketing, much information is obtained regarding who comprises the market, behavioral patterns of these individuals or organizations, and what appeals to these customers. Such information aids managers in developing an effective marketing mix to satisfy those members of the target market.

Learning Objective Six: To distinguish between undifferentiated, concentrated, differentiated, and custom marketing segmentation strategies.

Market segmentation strategies are distinguished on the basis of the number of target markets toward which a well prepared marketing mix is directed. When no meaningful segment can be isolated within a total market and individual customers do not require a unique marketing mix, an undifferentiated marketing approach is used in which one marketing mix is directed toward the total market. Custom marketing is appropriate for a disaggregated market where each customer's needs require a unique marketing mix.

A concentrated or differentiated segmentation strategy is followed when meaningful market segments are identified. A concentrated marketing strategy is employed when an organization develops one marketing mix and directs all marketing efforts and resources toward one target market. This approach is appropriate when an organization perceives it has a competitive advantage with the target market segment. An organization practices differentiated marketing when it selects more than one target market segment to serve; and, this organization develops a unique marketing mix for each target market. This multiple market segmentation approach requires more resources to exploit the differences between market segments. This approach maximizes market share.

Learning Objective Seven: To be familiar with the 80/20 principle and the majority fallacy, and their effects on marketing strategy.

The 80/20 principle states that the majority of a product's sales is accounted for by a small percentage of those who use the product. These heavy users constitute an attractive target market. Pursuit of these heavy, most accessible users without consideration of where competitors are directing their marketing efforts is the majority fallacy. Since competitors are likely to pursue this attractive target market of heavy users, the firm's marketing strategy may be less profitable than a strategy directed toward a market segment which is less attractive to competition.

Learning Objective Eight: To describe the many market segmentation variables available to marketing managers, and tell which ones are the better ones.

Segmentation variables can be classified according to geographic, demographic, socioeconomic, psychographic, behavioral patterns, consumption patterns, and consumer predisposition bases. Geographic bases of segmentation are appropriate when product usage is impacted by geographic-related dimensions such as climatic conditions, political boundaries, and population boundaries. A manager uses a demographic basis to segment a market when the need for a product can be attributed to a demographic-related variable such as age, sex, or family life cycle. Market behavior can frequently be explained by socio-economic variables. Social class, income, education, and occupation are socio-economic variables which are commonly employed as a basis of segmentation. Segmentation based on psychographics reflects that individuals' lifestyles differ even though their demographic and/or socio-economic backgrounds are similar. Psychographic segmentation distinguishes market segments in terms of activities, interests, and opinions of the market members. Behavioral bases of segmentation underscore that market members have different shopping habits and patterns in terms of type of store shopped, when they shop, frequency of shopping, size of purchase, and media habits.

The consumption behavior of members of a market can differ in terms of usage, brand loyalty, ownership of other products, and occasion for purchase. Each of these consumption-related factors can provide a meaningful basis of segmentation. Finally, consumer predisposition bases of segmentation acknowledge that individuals differ in terms of product knowledge, reasons for purchase, product and brand beliefs, and product benefits sought.

The better market segmentation variables would be the bundle of segmenting variables that identifies meaningful market segments. This bundle of variables would identify differences between market segments and enable an organization's marketing managers to develop a marketing mix to exploit these differences. The best combination of segmenting variables, however, will vary by the market situation.

VOCABULARY BUILDING

Matching Exercise

Match the following by placing the letter of the concept or term on the blank preceding the phrase which best describes this concept or term. You should use a term or concept only once.

A. Market	M. Majority fallacy
B. Market segmentation	N. Differentiated market
C. Disaggregated market	O. Multiple market segmentation
D. Consumer market	P. Complete segmentation
E. Organizational market	Q. Custom marketing
F. Industrial market	R. Demographics
G. Target market	S. Socio-economic variables
H. Meaningful market segments	T. Family life cycle
I. Cross-classification matrix	U. Psychographics
J. Undifferentiated marketing	V. Lifestyle
K. Concentrated marketing	W. Benefit segmentation
L. 80/20 principle	X. Consumption patterns
	Y. Purchase occasion

_____ 1. Describing the size, composition, and distribution of people.

_____ 2. A group of buyers toward which the organization decides to direct its marketing effort.

_____ 3. Blind pursuit of the largest, most accessible market segment.

_____ 4. Variables which reflect an individual's social position and/or economic standing within a society.

_____ 5. Products used to satisfy personal or household needs are sold in this market.

_____ 6. A market grid which helps isolate precise subdivisions in a market.

_____ 7. Marketing effort typified by an absence of segmentation.

_____ 8. A segmentation approach which distinguishes groups of customers by the benefits they seek.

_____ 9. A group of customers who want a particular product, have the ability and authority to purchase, and are willing to spend their money.

_____ 10. Identifies patterns in the pursuit of life goals.

_____ 11. Process of dividing a heterogeneous market into a number of smaller, more homogeneous submarkets.

_____ 12. Meets the criteria of accessibility, ease of measurement, and adequate size.

_____ 13. Marketing approach required in a disaggregated market.

_____ 14. Bases of segmentation which distinguishes between market segments in terms of usage or loyalty.

_____ 15. Marketing approach which selects one target market, develops an appropriate marketing mix, and directs all marketing effort and resources toward that segment.

VOCABULARY BUILDING

Programmed Learning Exercise

1. Products used to satisfy the needs of a business or other organization are sold in the _____ or _____ market.

                                              [organizational, industrial]

2. _____ buy products for resale to retailers or other businesses.

[Wholesalers]

3. Market segmentation consists of dividing a _____ market into a number of smaller, more _____ submarkets.

[heterogeneous, homogeneous]

4. A _____ market is where the number of market segments equals the number of prospects.

[disaggregated]

5. A target market is a market segment toward which the organization decides to direct its _____ _____ .

[marketing plan or mix]

6. The process of segmentation provides _____ as to how to market to the target markets.

[hints or clues]

7. Target marketing rests on the assumption that the differences among buyers are related to meaningful differences in _____ _____ .

[market behavior]

8. A meaningful market segment must have a _____ _____ of adequate size.

[market potential]

9. Marketers must _____ the marketing mix to the target market.

[match]

10. Market segmentation and target marketing can help tell to whom to appeal and also give hints on _____ to make the appeal.

[how]

11. The four strategies of market segmentation are _____ , _____ , _____ , and _____ marketing.

[undifferentiated, concentrated, differentiated, custom]

12. An organization which appeals to everyone may make this organization extremely vulnerable to _____ .

[competition]

13. A firm concentrates on a single market niche because management believes its company has a _____ _____ .

[competitive advantage]

14. The 80/20 principle refers to the phenomenon that a _____ percent-age of all users of a product accounts for a _____ portion of that product's sales.

[small, large]

15. An organization practices _____ marketing or _____ segmentation when it chooses more than one target market segment and prepares a unique marketing mix for each segment.

[differentiated, multiple market]

16. The essence of market segmentation strategy is to look for _____ within total markets on which to base the development of successful marketing mixes.

[differences]

17. The disadvantage of high marketing costs is associated with _____ marketing strategies.

[custom]

18. _____ _____ Statistical Areas consist of a large urbanized county, or cluster of counties, with strong internal economic and social links.

[Primary Metropolitan (PMSAs)]

19. _____ _____ _____ is a demographic variable that depicts that an individual goes through a series of stages.

[Family life cycle]

20. _____ is reflected in an individual's activities, interests, and opinions.

[Lifestyle]

TRUE OR FALSE STATEMENTS

T F   1. In describing a market, it is important to include the product category.

T F   2. Reseller markets are a type of industrial market.

T F   3. Demand curves for submarkets are similar to the "typical" demand curve presented in "economics textbooks."

T F   4. Market segmentation results from breaking down the relatively homogeneous total market into smaller, more heterogeneous segments.

T F 5. A single marketing company is likely to pursue all possible market segments.

T F 6. A meaningful market segment must meet the criterion of accessibility.

T F 7. Target marketing results from effective market segmentation.

T F 8. A marketer which offers different product versions to each of three different market segments is engaged in custom-marketing.

T F 9. An undifferentiated marketing strategy may result in lower production costs than a differentiated marketing strategy.

T F 10. A major disadvantage of a custom marketing approach is high marketing costs.

T F 11. The "majority fallacy" traps unwary firms into a highly competitive market segment.

T F 12. A multiple market segmentation approach differs from a differentiated marketing approach.

T F 13. Demographic bases of segmentation includes age, sex, occupation, and marital status.

T F 14. Behavior and consumption patterns are bases for market segmentation.

T F 15. Metropolitan Statistical Areas must have an urbanized population of at least 50,000 people.

T F 16. By the year 1990, the largest U.S. age segment will be in the 18-25 age group.

T F 17. Family life cycle is a socio-economic variable.

T F 18. Social class is not an effective socio-economic variable to distinguish groups of customers.

T F 19. Life simplification is a lifestyle trend affecting market planners.

T F 20. Benefits customers seek from products is a consumer predisposition base of segmentation.

MULTIPLE CHOICE QUESTIONS

1. Which one is not a requirement for a market?
    a. Location to buy.
    b. Willingness to spend.
    c. Authority to buy.
    d. Purchasing power.

2. A product is classified as a consumer product if
    a. it has some economic utility.
    b. an organization uses it to make another product.
    c. an individual uses the product to satisfy a household need.
    d. a consumer uses the product to make another product which is sold for a profit.

3. Which one is not an example of an organizational or industrial product?
    a. A pen used to complete a sales order.
    b. A pen used to prepare a resume.
    c. A pen used to sketch a landscape scene by an artist.
    d. A pen used to prepare an examination.

4. A marketer may want to identify smaller, more homogeneous submarkets to
    a. differentiate a product in a market.
    b. develop a more precise marketing mix.
    c. avoid governmental interference.
    d. reduce marketing expenses.

5. The strategy of market segmentation can be used when the total market consists of _____ members.
    a. many
    b. homogeneous
    c. similar
    d. heterogeneous

6. The process of market segmentation involves all but
    a. positioning the firm's product.
    b. selecting a target market.
    c. grouping market members.
    d. disaggregating the total market.

7. A meaningful market segment must be
    a. heterogenous, accessible, and responsive.
    b. measurable, responsive, and heterogeneous.
    c. accessible, measurable, and responsive.
    d. accessible, heterogeneous, and measurable.

8. When little diversity exists among market segments, an organization is likely to use a(n) _____ marketing approach.
    a. concentrated
    b. undifferentiated
    c. custom
    d. differentiated

9. When a marketer matches one marketing mix to the needs of one target market, the organization is following which marketing approach.
   a. Concentrated.
   c. Custom.
   b. Undifferentiated.
   d. Differentiated.

10. The selection of a too narrow target market segment can be a problem with which marketing approach.
    a. Concentrated.
    c. Custom.
    b. Undifferentiated.
    d. Differentiated.

11. The 80/20 principle suggests that
    a. only 80% of the market uses a product.
    b. only 20% of the market uses a product.
    c. a large percentage of a product's users account for a small portion of sales.
    d. a small percentage of a product's users account for the major portion of sales.

12. The "majority fallacy" refers to
    a. a majority of producers concentrating on the same market segments.
    b. a firm targeting a market segment that competitors ignore.
    c. a firm targeting the largest, most accessible market segment.
    d. the heavy competition that one finds in a market.

13. Differentiated marketing is when an organization
    a. selects several target markets and develops one marketing mix for all target markets.
    b. selects one target market and develops several marketing mixes to be directed toward this target market.
    c. selects several target markets and develops a unique marketing mix for each target market.
    d. develops a unique marketing mix for each customer in the market.

14. Which one is not a commonly used segmentation variable?
    a. Lifestyle.
    c. Family life cycle.
    b. Product knowledge.
    d. Gross national product.

15. Which statement is incorrect regarding geographic bases of segmentation?
    a. Political boundaries are better than population boundaries to segment markets.
    b. Climatic conditions can be an effective segmentation for some products.
    c. Metropolitan Statistical Areas can be used to form population boundaries.
    d. Geographic-related variables can be useful in developing a marketing strategy even if other variables are used for market segmentation.

16. All are examples of demographic variables except
    a. age.
    b. income.
    c. marital status.
    d. family size.

17. Socio-economic factors used for segmentation purposes are
    a. lifestyle, occupation, and consumer benefits.
    b. education, occupation, and lifestyle.
    c. occupation, income, and social class.
    d. social class, lifestyle, and education.

18. Compared to other bases for segmentation, psychographics market segmentation
    a. provides little useful information to marketers.
    b. is easy to interpret.
    c. does not reflect lifestyle.
    d. enhances demographic and socioeconomic factors.

19. Which statement is incorrect in terms of segmentation variables?
    a. Consumers vary widely in terms of their beliefs about product brands.
    b. Benefit segmentation is based on consumer problems.
    c. Individuals exhibit different behavior patterns regarding shopping.
    d. Consumption patterns can be a good base for market segmentation.

20. The "best" segmentation variable is one that
    a. divides the market into segments.
    b. groups a large number of people in one segment.
    c. identifies a meaningful market segment.
    d. makes an undifferentiated marketing approach possible.

QUICK QUIZ

1Q.
In the case of the "I Hate the Yankees HANKY" ... What is the target market segment? Where would you sell or promote such a thing?

1A.
The segment is obviously baseball fans, who live in the Cleveland area, and hate the New York Yankees. This suggests selling the product in or near Cleveland Stadium when the Yankees are playing in Cleveland, and/or at the sports shops in the area. It also suggests promotion on area sports shows, which are, of course, heard or seen by fans or local teams.

68

2Q.
Don't all market organizations segment markets and select target markets?

2A.
In a sense, they all do. Everything the marketer does will either attract or repel customers. Thus, if a store remains open all night, certain types of customers will be drawn to that store during evening and early morning hours. The idea is to consciously and carefully select attractive target markets.

3Q.
Can just a few variables in a cross-classification matrix really identify meaningful, market segments and targets?

3A.
Yes. Even one or two variables can account for a great portion of sales. Examples: Most cigars are bought by men over the age of 18; most 45 rpm records are bought by females ages 11 to 14.

4Q.
Should a marketer of hacksaw blades or brass polish not investigate the possibility to segment the market for these products?

4A.
While the best approach may be undifferentiated marketing, the marketer should investigate the possibility. Meaningful segments (e.g., by purchase quantity) may exist. A marketer should not ignore such a powerful tool as segmentation. Its possible benefits should always be considered.

69

5Q.
Can a service marketer practice concentrated marketing as do manufacturers?

5A.
Yes. For example, Leo Burnett is the sixth largest advertising agency yet it has only a very few clients (less than thirty). Burnett focuses its efforts on servicing a small number of well-heeled clients with huge advertising budgets. Specializing seems to work in this volatile business, since more than half of Burnett's clients have been with the agency for more than ten years.

6Q.
Exhibit 4-11 shows the marketing organization attempting to reach customers by means of individual marketing mixes. This is custom marketing. But Exhibit 4-10 shows the Phillip Morris Company reaching customers with different marketing mixes and it's called differentiated marketing. What's the difference?

6A.
Phillip Morris uses several marketing mixes, each designed to please groups of customers (men, women, low-tar smokers, and so on). The industrial robot manufacturer, in Exhibit 4-11, designs a marketing mix for each individual customer.

7Q.
Does being the first to identify and fill a need (as did No More Tangles) guarantee success?

7A.
Probably . . . at least, in the short run. For example, the market for liquid cleaning products of the Janitor-in-a-Drum sort was developed by Lestoil in the 1950s. However, once the product became a regional (East Coast) success, Proctor and Gamble and other biggies brought out their own liquid cleaners and soon left Lestoil's makers "eating their dust."

8Q.
How have colleges and universities been affected by the "baby boom" and the "adult boom?"

8A.
Many schools swelled to great size as the baby boomers reached college age, enjoying twenty or so years of the "education boom." In the 1970s and 1980s, however, the pool of "traditional" students, what we think of college-age kids, dried up. Some colleges closed while others lost enrollments. Schools with declining enrollments considered effective marketing techniques for the first time by developing specialties to attract students or employing market segmentation. Some colleges and universities sought adult students, ran corporate training programs, and attracted "non-traditional" students. Drawing "non-trads" with special courses and nighttime classes is effective marketing segmentation, and it's keeping many schools afloat.

EXPERIENTIAL ACTIVITIES

4-A. Target Marketing

You have recently conducted a study of consumer preferences related to various characteristics of candy. Your research findings indicate:

1. Children differ in fruit-flavor preference. Some like grape flavor while others prefer orange, strawberry, cherry, apple, and peach.

2. Some children prefer multiple pieces of candy while others prefer one large piece for the same price.

3. Some children prefer "hard" candy while others prefer "soft" candy.

71

Based on these findings, management introduced a new mixed fruit-flavored candy. The candy had a "soft" center surrounded by a "hard" exterior and packaged as individual-bite size in the shape of a candy bar.

The sales for this new candy were well below management's expectations. Of those who initially purchased the candy, even fewer purchased the candy a second time.

Assignment

    1. Explain why this new product did not succeed in the marketplace.

    2. Recommend what management should do.

4-B. Target Market Selection

First Republic Savings and Loan recently conducted a probability sample survey of their demand depositors. This sample was two percent of their total demand depositors. The purpose of the study was to determine the demographic profile of various groups of demand depositors. The research findings are summarized in Exhibit 4-1 below in terms of the market segments identified. First Republic has a 25 percent share of the market.

EXHIBIT 4-1

Market Segment	Characteristic of Segment	Number	Average Balance
A	College graduate (75%)[a] Retired (65%) Self-employed (30%) Private income (70%)	43	$3,260
B	Retired (25%) Manager/professional (75%) $15,000 or more annual income (100%) 10-20 years on job (60%) Owns home/no mortgage (100%)	79	1,560
C	College graduate (0%) Retired (55%) Wage/salary (45%) Pension/social security (55%)	153	980
D	Self employed (80%) Manager/professional (100%) Under 20 years on job (90%) $15,000 or more annual income (100%)	118	730
E	Under $15,000 annual income (85%) Manager/professional (81%) Owns home/with mortgage (64%) Rents (36%)	226	580
F	Craft/operative job (60%) Clerical position (29%) Wage/salary (100%) College graduate (0%)	445	390
	Total	1,064	

[a] To be read as a percent of the number in this segment. For example, 75% of Segment A are college graduates.

Assignment

1. Select the target market(s) towards which First Republic Savings and Trust should direct their marketing efforts.

   Target market(s): _____

   _____

2. Explain and apply the criteria you used to select the target market(s).

3. Discuss the marketing strategies you would direct toward each target market.

ANSWERS TO OBJECTIVE QUESTIONS

MATCHING

1.	R	4.	S	7.	J	10.	U	13.	Q
2.	G	5.	D	8.	W	11.	B	14.	X
3.	M	6.	I	9.	A	12.	H	15.	K

TRUE OR FALSE

1.	T	5.	F	9.	T	13.	F	17.	F
2.	T	6.	T	10.	T	14.	T	18.	F
3.	F	7.	T	11.	T	15.	T	19.	T
4.	F	8.	F	12.	F	16.	F	20.	T

MULTIPLE CHOICE

1.	a	5.	d	9.	a	13.	c	17.	c
2.	c	6.	a	10.	a	14.	d	18.	d
3.	b	7.	c	11.	d	15.	a	19.	b
4.	b	8.	b	12.	c	16.	b	20.	c

CHAPTER 5

OVERVIEW OF THE MARKETING RESEARCH PROCESS

OBJECTIVE

Research information contributes to effective marketing decision-making. Marketing research follows a problem-solving process in providing marketing information.

OUTLINE

I.   The place of information in effective marketing

    A.   Marketing information aids the decision-making process.

    B.   Several examples of the value of information are provided.

    C.   Research information reduces uncertainty.

II.   Scope of marketing research

    A.   Marketing research involves the objective and systematic gathering, recording, and analyzing of data for marketing decision-making.

    B.   Unobjective research should be avoided.

    C.   Research information complements managerial judgment.

III.   The process of marketing research

    A.   Marketing research information reduces uncertainty.

    B.   Marketing research is a formal information gathering process.

IV. Classifications of marketing research

    A. Marketing research can be classified according to the purpose of research--exploratory, descriptive, or causal.

    B. Exploratory research clarifies and refines the nature of the problem.

        1. Exploratory research is not conclusive research.

        2. The focus group interview is a common exploratory research technique.

    C. Descriptive research is used to describe the characteristics of a marketing phenomenon.

        1. Descriptive research is conclusive research.

        2. Performance monitoring research is a special kind of descriptive research which provides continuous market feedback.

    D. Causal research seeks to identify cause-and-effect relationships among variables.

    E. The uncertainty associated with the research problem determines if exploratory, descriptive, or causal research is needed (as noted in Exhibit 5-2 in the Zikmund and d'Amico textbook).

V. The stages in the research process

    A. Problem definition is the first stage in the research process.

        1. Problem definition begins with discovery of the existence of a problem or opportunity.

        2. Exploratory research clarifies the problem.

        3. A problem is defined when precise research objectives can be stated.

        4. A research objective can be expressed as a testable hypothesis.

    B. Planning the research design is the second research stage.

        1. The research design is the plan which specifies the techniques and procedures to be used to collect and analyze data relevant to the research problem.

2. The research design specifies which of the four basic research techniques (secondary data, observation, surveys, or experiments) will be used.

3. Survey research involves sampling errors and systematic errors.

4. Survey data collection methods are personal interviews, telephone interviews, and self-administered mail questionnaires.

5. Wording survey questions correctly is an art.

6. Experiments can be conducted in the field or in a laboratory.

7. There is no "best" research design since several designs will provide information relevant to the research problem.

C. Selecting a sample is the third research stage.

1. Most research projects take a sample, rather than a census, of the population.

2. Sampling involves identifying the target population, determining the sample size, and specifying how to select sample members.

3. Sample members may be selected according to probability or nonprobability methods.

4. Probability sampling methods can be used to select simple random samples, stratified samples, and cluster samples.

5. Nonprobability sampling can be employed to select convenience samples, judgment samples, and quota samples.

D. Data collection is the fourth stage in the research process.

1. The researcher should pretest the questionnaire, data collection methods, and data analysis methods.

2. The actual collection of data should be designed to minimize systematic errors associated with the data collection process.

E. Data analysis is the fifth research stage.

1. Data processing involves the editing and coding tasks.

2. Analysis of data can involve statistical and/or qualitative analyses.

F. Drawing conclusions and preparing the report is the sixth research stage.

G. The last or seventh stage in the research process is the follow-up to determine how useful the report was to management.

VI. The value of research

A. Research enables organizations to carry out the marketing concept.

B. Effective marketing management requires research.

SUMMARY

<u>Learning Objective One</u>: To understand the importance of information in effective marketing.

Marketing information enables managers to implement more effectively the philosophy of the marketing concept. A consumer orientation requires timely information about an organization's customers, its environment, and its marketing activities. Marketing information provides a sound foundation for decision-making by reducing the uncertainty surrounding decision areas. Information regarding past events, current events, and predictions of future events enhances the quality of decision-making. Improved decision-making results in more effective marketing.

<u>Learning Objective Two</u>: To explain the contribution marketing research makes to effective decision-making by management.

Marketing research is a major tool of marketing decision-makers. Marketing research is used to complement managerial judgment by providing objective information about marketing phenomena. This objective information reduces the role of intuition in decision-making as well as the uncertainty surrounding marketing phenomena. Better decisions should result.

<u>Learning Objective Three</u>: To understand the exploratory, descriptive, and causal types of research and be able to show their relationship to particular marketing management problems.

Each type of research addresses one of three major purposes of research. These purposes relate to the uncertainty of the problem confronting marketing management. When management is unaware of the problem, exploratory research is conducted to clarify and refine the problem situation. Descriptive research requires that the problem be known to describe the marketing phenomenon. When a researcher has a well constructed, testable hypothesis, the researcher uses causal research to investigate the cause-and-effect relationship.

Learning Objective Four: To describe the general format of the marketing research process and explain the logic of that process.

The marketing research process has seven interrelated stages. These stages are: (1) problem definition, (2) planning the research design, (3) selection of the sample, (4) data collection, (5) data analysis, (6) drawing conclusions and preparing the report, and (7) follow-up. Since marketing research involves a systematic process, one research stage leads to the next stage. In addition, the interrelationships between these seven stages suggest that forward and backward linkages exist between the stages. A forward linkage is when an early research stage impacts on a subsequent stage. For instance, problem definition impacts on each of the other stages. And, planning the research design affects selection of the sample, data collection, and data analysis. Data analysis limits how information can be presented in reports. When an earlier research step is impacted by a later stage, backward linkage exists. For example, techniques of data analysis affect construction of questions and selection of sample members. Successful completion of these seven stages provides management with information to enhance decision-making regarding a management problem or opportunity.

Learning Objective Five: To be familiar with the use of such tools as surveys, experiments, and observation.

Observation, surveys, and experiments are used to collect primary data. Observation records verbal and nonverbal marketing-related behavior as this behavior occurs. Behavioral actions can be recorded visually or mechanically by such devices as the audimeter, eye camera, psychogalvanometer, or a traffic counter. Observation cannot indicate why this behavior occurred, nor can it record intended behavior.

Surveys use well constructed, pretested questionnaires to gather primary marketing information from a sample. Surveys can provide information regarding the who, what, when, where, and how of marketing behavior. Designs for survey research can be adapted to most marketing situations. Survey research, however, needs to be well planned and well executed to minimize systematic research errors or biases.

Field and laboratory experiments are conducted to find causes of marketing behavior. Experiments are appropriate when a problem is well defined and states a cause-and-effect relationship among marketing variables.

Learning Objective Six: To discuss the importance of communication between the researcher and the marketing decision-maker.

Marketing research has little value unless it provides the information necessary to reduce the uncertainty associated with management's problem. Communication between the researcher and decision-maker involves more than oral and physical reports provided to decision-makers. Both the researcher and the decision-maker need to agree: (1) that the correct problem has been defined; (2) that the research design is appropriate for the problem, resources, and the decision-maker's decision time frame; (3) on how to report the findings; and (4) to follow-up the study to improve the value of research to decision-makers. In essence, little communication between these individuals will result in untimely and improper research information.

VOCABULARY BUILDING

Matching Exercise

Match the following by placing the letter of the concept or term on the blank preceding the phrase which best describes the concept or term. You should use a term or concept only once.

A. Marketing research
B. Exploratory research
C. Descriptive research
D. Causal research
E. Problem definition
F. Research design
G. Secondary data
H. Primary data
I. Survey
J. Experiment
K. Sample

L. Census
M. Probability sample
N. Nonprobability sample
O. Simple random sample
P. Stratified sample
Q. Cluster sample
R. Convenience sample
S. Judgment sample
T. Quota sample
U. Editing
V. Coding

_____ 1. Purpose is to ensure completeness, consistency, and reliability of data.

_A_ 2. Systematic and objective process of gathering, recording, and analyzing data for marketing decision making.

_____ 3. Data gathered and assembled specifically for the project at hand.

_K_ 4. Part of a larger population.

82

_____ 5. Primary sampling unit is <u>not</u> the individual element in the population.

_____ 6. Specifies methods and procedures for collecting and analyzing needed information.

_____ 7. Type of sampling where sample units are selected on the basis of convenience or personal judgment.

_____ 8. Sampling method where an experienced individual selects the sample based upon some appropriate characteristic of the sample members.

_____ 9. Assures that each population element has an equal chance of being included in the sample.

_____ 10. A sample in which every population element has a known, nonzero probability of selection.

_____ 11. Uses a questionnaire to gather information from a sample of people.

_____ 12. Research conducted to clarify the nature of the problem.

_____ 13. A basic research technique for investigation where conditions are controlled so that one or more variables can be manipulated.

_____ 14. Process of identifying and classifying each answer with a numerical score or other character symbol.

_D__ 15. Type of research conducted to identify cause-and-effect relationships.

VOCABULARY BUILDING

Programmed Learning Exercise

1. Marketing research should yield _____ that helps managers make decisions.
   [information]

2. Providing conclusions is not the purpose of _____ research.
   [exploratory]

3. Causal relationships are impossible to _____ absolutely.
   [prove]

4. The stages in the marketing research process are highly _____.
   [interrelated]

83

5. The _____ associated with the research problem determines the research methodology.

    [uncertainty]

6. The problem definition stage should culminate in a clear understanding of the _____ of the research.

    [objectives]

7. A _____ is an unproven proposition or possible solution to the problem.

    [hypothesis]

8. _____ data are those data previously collected and assembled for some purpose other than the project at hand.

    [Secondary]

9. Sampling errors are a _____ phenomenon.

    [statistical]

10. _____ errors are those which occur in the design or execution of the research.

    [Systematic or nonsampling]

11. A mail questionnaire requires a highly _____ format.

    [standardized]

12. The wording of questions should be _____ and _____ .

    [simple, unambiguous]

13. _____ _____ are utilized to measure consumers' attitudes.

    [Rating scales]

14. A survey of all members of a population is called a _____ .

    [census]

15. A crucial aspect of sampling is identifying the _____ population.

    [target]

16. Whatever data collection method is used, the researcher's task is to _____ errors in the process.

    [minimize]

17. A _____ should precede the actual data collection.

    [pretest]

18. Numerical codes are especially useful when _____ analysis of the data is to be employed.

[computer]

19. The culmination of the research process must be a _____ that usefully communicates research findings to management.

[report]

20. In tales of marketing success, the common element is the stress placed on _____ satisfaction.

[consumer]

TRUE OR FALSE STATEMENTS

T F   1. Marketing research tools and techniques are many and varied.

T F   2. Failure to collect adequate information can lead to marketing failure.

T F   3. A good example of marketing research is overhearing a conversation about a competitor's new product while waiting in a dentist's office.

T F   4. Good marketing research is an effective substitute for managerial judgment.

T F   5. Exploratory research is often necessary as a first step before moving to more specific types of research.

T F   6. Causal research provides a continuous flow of information.

T F   7. Causal research requires a clearly defined problem.

T F   8. Some problems that market researchers face may be viewed as opportunities.

T F   9. A disadvantage of secondary data is that secondary data are more expensive than primary data.

T F   10. Secondary data are specifically gathered and assembled for the project at hand.

T F   11. The greatest strength of observation is that the observer records why the observed behavior occurred.

T F   12. Statistical errors are possible even if you have a technically proper random probability sample.

85

T F 13. Systematic errors differ from non-sampling errors.

T F 14. Personal interviewers elicit better respondent cooperation than telephone interviewers.

T F 15. Personal interviewers influence interviewer's answers more than telephone interviewers do.

T F 16. A semantic differential attitude scale requires respondents to indicate their degree of agreement with a statement.

T F 17. A cluster sample is a nonprobability sample since clusters of people are conveniently selected.

T F 18. Interviewers need to be selected and trained carefully to collect data.

T F 19. Coding involves checking for omissions on the data collection form.

T F 20. Marketing research findings should be communicated to top management via a report which emphasizes technical and statistical detail.

MULTIPLE CHOICE QUESTIONS

1. In terms of an identified marketing problem or opportunity, which statement is _incorrect_ regarding the information needs of an effective marketer?
   a. Information is needed to understand past events.
   b. Information is needed to identify what is occurring now.
   c. Information is needed to try to predict what might occur in the future.
   d. Information is not needed for an identified problem.

2. Which one of the following is _not_ an appropriate use for marketing research?
   a. Experiment with different price levels.
   b. Prove to other managers that your views are correct.
   c. Test different promotional themes.
   d. Investigate new product opportunities.

3. Which statement regarding marketing research is _incorrect_?
   a. Marketing research information should help managers make decisions.
   b. Research is intended to replace managerial judgment.
   c. Marketing research is not restricted to advertising research.
   d. A manager has a responsibility to study research findings.

4. If a marketing manager realizes a problem exists, but does not understand the nature of the problem, the appropriate type of research would be
   a. experimental research.
   b. descriptive research.
   c. exploratory research.
   d. causal research.

5. The focus group technique is most often used in
   a. exploratory research.
   b. conclusive research.
   c. causal research.
   d. descriptive research.

6. Which is not an example of an appropriate research objective for descriptive research?
   a. To determine if advertising increases product awareness.
   b. To determine a demographic profile of heavy users.
   c. To determine how many people read an advertisement.
   d. To determine what hours customers prefer shopping.

7. Performance monitoring research is classified as
   a. causal research.
   b. experimental research.
   c. exploratory research.
   d. descriptive research.

8. Which one of the following is not a stage in the marketing research process?
   a. Drawing strategic conclusions.
   c. Data generation.
   b. Data analysis.
   d. Planning the research design.

9. The selection of a marketing research method is most affected by
   a. time, money, and personnel.
   b. money, personnel, and environment.
   c. personnel, environment, and time.
   d. environment, time, and money.

10. Exploratory research is most useful in the _____ stage of the marketing research process.
    a. drawing conclusions
    b. problem definition
    c. data generation
    d. data collection

11. Published census tract information is an example of
    a. primary data.
    b. observation data.
    c. secondary data.
    d. survey data.

12. What kind of data is provided by survey research?
    a. Primary data.
    b. Observation data.
    c. Secondary data.
    d. Survey data.

13. Which one is not a problem associated with survey research?
    a. Poor wording of questions.   c. Sampling errors.
    b. Misinterpretation of results.   d. Few possible applications.

14. When comparing typical characteristics of mail, telephone, and personal survey methods, lowest cost is associated with the _____ survey method.
    a. mail   c. personal
    b. telephone   d. all are equally costly

15. Which represents the "best" research design?
    a. Secondary data.   c. Observation.
    b. Surveys.   d. Depending on the situation, any can be "best".

16. Sampling involves asking each of these questions except
    a. how big should the sample be?
    b. who is to be sampled?
    c. why sample?
    d. who should be included in the sample?

17. Which is not a method for drawing a probability sample?
    a. Cluster sample.   c. Stratified sample.
    b. Quota sample.   d. Simple random sample.

18. Data collection methods include all but the use of a(n)
    a. psychogalvanometer.   c. eye camera.
    b. audisound bite.   d. pantry audit.

19. Which statement is correct regarding data analysis?
    a. Data analysis involves only statistical analysis.
    b. Editing involves determining meaningful categories.
    c. Data processing includes editing and coding.
    d. Data analysis involves drawing conclusions.

20. Marketing research can aid marketers by
    a. reducing uncertainty.
    b. identifying courses of actions.
    c. predicting future environment conditions.
    d. doing all of the above.

QUICK QUIZ

1Q.
What would be an example of a marketing problem "suggesting" the use of a specific marketing research tool?

1A.
For example, if we wanted to know if consumers read the information on the backs of soup can labels in stores before buying, we would probably use observation. Researchers would simply <u>observe</u> shoppers to see if they read the labels before placing the cans in their shopping carts.

2Q.
Was the study that described the Tampa Bay Rowdies' female fans based on exploratory research?

2A.
Yes, though likely it was quite informal. The team's marketing director may have noticed "a lot" of women in the stands and may have checked if this opinion was shared by ticket-takers and ushers. A pilot study, for example counting women at one stadium entrance, probably was completed before the "big" descriptive study was planned.

3Q.
Would a marketing manager ever choose a research method or "path" known to be less accurate than other possible methods?

3A.
Yes. Constraints may mean that the more accurate but time-and-resource-consuming methods would have to yield to the "quick and dirty" methods. Occasionally, the marketing decision-maker makes choices based on experience and hunches rather than on research.

		An
	<u>time and money</u> ·	Answer
Problem·		
	Three times the	"Best"
	<u>time and money</u> ·	Answer

4Q.
Can you make-up a survey question that will be unlikely to get the respondent's true opinion or belief about a candidate for President of the United States?

4A.
A commonly used question is "If the election were today, for whom would you vote?" A "bad question would be "Don't you think you want to vote for Senator Jones for President?"

EXPERIENTIAL ACTIVITIES

5-A. Planning the Research Design

Rental Town, Inc. is a large rental store in a city of 120,000 residents. Even though their rental business is good, a major competitor has a larger share of the market. Management of Rental Town, Inc. wants to improve their market position in the consumer market. To do so management feels that they need to have additional information about their market, which types of people rent household-related items, peoples' perception toward Rental Town, Inc., and the impact of their advertising.

Assignment

1. Plan a research design to provide the information that management needs. Your research design should state the research objectives for the study, type of research, basic technique(s) to collect data, types of information needed, sample design, data analysis methods, and method(s) of reporting findings to management.

   Research objectives: _____

   _____

   _____

   _____

   _____

   _____

   Research type or classification: _____

   _____

   Data collection method: _____

   _____

90

Data collection techniques(s): _____

_____

Sample design: _____

_____

_____

Data analysis: _____

_____

_____

Data presentation: _____

_____

2. Develop a questionnaire to collect the needed information.

5-B.   Data Analysis and Drawing Conclusions

Assume you have completed a telephone survey of 501 households regarding their behavioral patterns, beliefs, and perceptions toward renting infrequently-used household products and garden-related items.   Tabulations of selected questions are below.

		Frequency	Percent
A. Major Rental Influences			
	Male Spouse	186	37
	Female Spouse	94	19
	Both Spouses	192	38
	Other	29	6
		501	
B. Attitude Toward Owning Infrequently Used Equipment			
	Strongly Agree	21	4
	Agree	243	49
	Neither Agree or Disagree	103	21
	Disagree	130	26
	Strongly Disagree	4	1
		501	
C. Rented Equipment Within the Last Two Years			
	Yes	343	68
	No	158	32
		501	
D. Satisfaction with Rental Experience			
	Yes	325	65
	No	18	4
	Don't Rent	158	32
		501	
E. Who Picks Up Rental Equipment			
	Husband	202	40
	Wife	75	15
	Delivery	10	2
	Other	56	11
	Don't Rent	158	32
		501	

93

	Frequency	Percent

F. **Where Rent Equipment**

	Frequency	Percent
Handy's Place	197*	39
Rental Town	163	33
Miller's	23	5
Other	87	17

[*Over the two year period, one could
rent from several rental stores.]

G. **Awareness of Rental Stores**

	Frequency	Percent
Handy's Place	443*	88
Rental Town	373	74
Miller's	36	7

[*Respondents could be aware of
more than one rental store.]

H. **Ages of Respondents**

	Frequency	Percent
18-24 Years	91	18
25-34 Years	125	25
35-49 Years	115	23
50-64 Years	100	20
65 Years and Older	65	13
Refusal	5	1
	501	

I. **Annual Family Income**

	Frequency	Percent
Under $5,000	40	8
$ 5,000 - $ 9,999	75	15
$10,000 - $14,999	110	22
$15,000 - $24,999	150	30
$25,000 and Over	66	13
Refusal	60	12
	501	

	Frequency	Percent
J. **Occupational Class of Head of Household**		
Professional	120	24
Skilled and unskilled labor	110	22
Retired	86	17
Managers and owners	55	11
Service	35	7
Sales	30	6
Student	30	6
Clerical and secretarial	25	5
Unclassified	10	2
	501	

Assignment

1. Calculate the percentages for each table above and record these percentages in the space provided.

2. State the conclusions that one can draw from these tables. What are the managerial implications of these conclusions?

Conclusion number 1: _____

_____

Conclusion number 2: _____

_____

Conclusion number 3: _____

_____

Conclusion number 4: _____

_____

Conclusion number 5: _____

_____

Conclusion number 6: _____

_____

Conclusion number 7: _____

_____

Conclusion number 8: _____

_____

Managerial implications: _____

_____

_____

_____

_____

_____

_____

_____

_____

_____

_____

3. Identify what additional information you would find useful to management.

   a. _____

   _____

   b. _____

   _____

   c. _____

   _____

   d. _____

   _____

   e. _____

   _____

ANSWERS TO OBJECTIVE QUESTIONS

MATCHING

1. U	4. K	7. N	10. M	13. J
2. A	5. Q.	8. S	11. I	14. V
3. H	6. F	9. O	12. B	15. D

TRUE OR FALSE

1. T	5. T	9. F	13. F	17. F
2. T	6. F	10. F	14. T	18. T
3. F	7. T	11. F	15. T	19. F
4. F	8. T	12. T	16. F	20. F

MULTIPLE CHOICE

1. d	5. a	9. a	13. d	17. b
2. b	6. a	10. b	14. a	18. b
3. b	7. d	11. c	15. d	19. c
4. c	8. c	12. a	16. c	20. d

CHAPTER 6

THE MARKETING INFORMATION SYSTEM AND SALES FORECASTING METHODS

OBJECTIVE

Marketing information needs to be managed systematically to provide decision-makers with accurate, pertinent, and timely information.

OUTLINE

I. Marketing information systems

A. Computer technology continues to have a major impact on information systems.

B. The primary sources of marketing information are marketing research, marketing intelligence, and informally gathered information.

C. Marketing information represents all the facts, data, and guesses with which the marketer works.

D. Marketing intelligence provides information concerning markets and competitors.

II. The scope of marketing information systems

A. A marketing information system (M.I.S.) manages systematically timely information flows to managers.

B. A M.I.S. involves a continuing and interacting structure of people, equipment, and procedures.

C. Three subsystems within a M.I.S. are a marketing research system, informally gathered information, and a marketing intelligence system.

D. Analysis is an important M.I.S. function as the system transforms raw data into information.

III. Sales forecasting

A. Sales forecasting involves predicting an organization's sales totals over some specified future time period.

B. An organization may forecast general economic conditions, industry sales, and market potential as well as their own sales.

C. Three levels of forecasting are market potential, sales potential, and sales forecast.

   1. Market potential is the maximum industry demand expected during a given time period.

   2. Sales potential refers to the company's maximum share of the market during a given time period.

   3. Sales forecast is the company's expected sales volume for a given time period.

D. Conditional forecasting involves making an optimistic forecast, a pessimistic forecast, and a most likely forecast for anticipated economic conditions.

E. Forecasts are made for short term (one year or less), long term (five or more years), and intermediate term (one to five years).

F. Uncertainty increases as forecasting time frames increase.

G. Common forecasting methods are executive opinion, sales force composite, survey of customers, projection of trends, analysis of market factors, and using market factor indexes such as Sales Management Buying Power Index.

SUMMARY

Learning Objective One: To show how various formal and informal sources of data contribute to management's decision-making processes.

An aura of uncertainty is created by dynamic environmental forces with which marketing managers must cope. Formal and informal sources of data, when analyzed properly, provide marketing information. This information improves the quality of decision-making by reducing the uncertainty related to an impending decision. Routine or day-to-day decisions require a continuous flow of relevant marketing information generated primarily from internal records. Nonroutine decisions use data gathered primarily by formal marketing intelligence systems and marketing research studies. Informally gathered information from news stories, rumors, and conversations alert managers to potential or actual changes in marketing's environment. Management of these various data sources provides relevant and timely information for more effective decision-making pertaining to marketing planning, execution, and control activities, especially when combined with managerial judgment.

Learning Objective Two: To describe the nature and functions of a Marketing Information System.

A marketing information system (M.I.S.) is the systematic management of information obtained from formal and informal sources of data. This information management involves a continuing and interacting structure of people, equipment, and procedures. The functions of a M.I.S. are to gather, sort, analyze, evaluate, and distribute pertinent, timely, and accurate information to marketing managers. The subsystems of a M.I.S. are marketing research, marketing intelligence, and informally gathered information.

Learning Objective Three: To discuss the purposes of the sales forecast and be familiar with what forecasting involves.

Sales forecasting involves predicting an organization's expected sales totals over a specified time period. In addition to forecasting expected sales, managers can forecast economic conditions, market potential, and company sales potential. The company's sales forecast is used by managers in the planning and control of production, distribution, and promotion activities. Operational planning keys on the sales forecast while the control function uses the sales forecast as a performance standard. Planning and control are improved when the forecaster does conditional forecasting and makes forecasts for the short term, the intermediate term, and the long term. Forecasting can employ such methods as executive opinion, sales force composite, customer expectations, projection of trends, and analysis of market factors.

VOCABULARY BUILDING

Matching Exercise

Match the following by placing the letter of the concept or term on the blank preceding the phrase which best describes the concept or term. You should use a term or concept only once.

A. Marketing information	H. Information
B. Marketing intelligence	I. Sales forecasting
C. Marketing information system	J. Market potential
D. Raw data	K. Sales potential
E. Marketing research system	L. Sales forecast
F. Marketing intelligence system	M. Market factor
G. Internal records	N. Market factor index

_____ 1. Estimate of a company's maximum share of the market.

_____ 2. Key market information emphasizing competitors.

_____ 3. Set of sources and procedures which provides everyday information about development in the external marketing environment.

_____ 4. Expected actual sales volume for a brand during a given time period.

_____ 5. A variable which reflects an association with sales.

_____ 6. Continuing and interacting system of people, equipment, and procedures.

_____ 7. Recorded measures of certain phenomena.

_____ 8. Data, facts, rumors, news stories, and research reports with which a marketing manager works.

_____ 9. Upper limit of industry demand.

_____ 10. Process of predicting an organization's expected sales totals over a specified time span.

VOCABULARY BUILDING

Programmed Learning Exercise

1. Computers enable managers to play _____ games with figures to see how changes in marketing strategies and/or marketing tactics could affect results.

   [what-if]

2. An important source for marketing intelligence is the organization's _____ _____.

   [sales force]

3. _____ should be managed systematically.

   [Information]

4. Internal records are part of the _____ _____ subsystem.

   [marketing research]

5. _____ refer to the exposure of the product on a retailer's shelf.

   [Shelf-facings]

6. _____ transforms raw data into information.

   [Analysis]

7. Operational planning is highly dependent on the _____ _____.

   [sales forecast]

8. Sales forecasts focus on _____ sales.

   [company]

9. Conditional forecasting involves making _____ forecasts, _____ forecasts, and _____ forecasts.

   [optimistic, most likely, pessimistic]

10. Conditional forecasting distinguishes between what is actually _____ and what is _____.

    [predicted, possible]

11. _____ increases as forecasting time frames increase.

    [Uncertainty]

12. Asking each salesperson to project his/her sales for the upcoming period is called the _____ method.

    [sales force composite]

13. _____ should not be blindly extrapolated.

[Trends]

14. Sales Management Buying Power Index is an example of a _____ _____ index.

[market factor]

15. _____ is necessary for effective marketing management.

[Information]

TRUE OR FALSE STATEMENTS

T F 1. The technologies embodied in executive computer work stations are used by a majority of marketing managers today.

T F 2. Information support systems are becoming more accessible to marketing personnel.

T F 3. Managers can receive too much information.

T F 4. The existence of a M.I.S. requires a computer and related software (programs).

T F 5. A firm's sales force may be a good source of marketing intelligence.

T F 6. The M.I.S. is part of the marketing research system.

T F 7. The "break-down method" of forecasting typically starts with the industry forecast.

T F 8. Sales potential reflects expected sales volume.

T F 9. For conditional forecasting, the "most likely" forecast is the midpoint between optimistic and pessimistic forecasts.

T F 10. Sales forecasting facilitates marketing planning and control.

T F 11. The survey of customers sales forecasting method is most effective when forecasting expected sales for established products.

T F 12. The projection of trends is not a common method to forecast sales because the dynamic marketing environment causes market trends to fluctuate too rapidly.

T F 13. If an association exists between sales and another variable, the market factor method may be used to forecast sales.

T F 14. An example of a market factor index is the <u>Sales Management Buying Power Index</u>.

T F 15. <u>Sales Management's Survey of Buying Power</u> provides the median age of population by county.

MULTIPLE CHOICE QUESTIONS

1. Which one is <u>not</u> a source of marketing information?
    a. Marketing research.
    b. Articles in business publications.
    c. Rumors.
    d. Contrary to the question, all may be sources of marketing information.

2. Which type of information would most likely come to the manager on an unscheduled basis?
    a. Consumer survey results.
    b. Informally gathered information.
    c. Analysis of competitors' advertising.
    d. Daily sales figures.

3. Which one is <u>not</u> a necessary component of a marketing information system?
    a. Procedures.   c. Money.
    b. People.   d. Equipment.

4. All are subsystems of a marketing information system <u>except</u>
    a. marketing research.
    b. informally gathered information.
    c. marketing planning.
    d. marketing intelligence.

5. Which one is <u>not</u> an example of regularly kept internal records?
    a. Conversations.   c. Sales reports by territory.
    b. Back-orders.   d. Inventory statements.

6. To the marketing decision-maker, analyzed facts in a form suitable for use represent
    a. sales forecasts.   c. research.
    b. information.   d. raw data.

7. All are characteristics of a successful M.I.S. <u>except</u>
    a. current data bases.
    b. procedures to expedite information flow.
    c. availability of irregular information.
    d. structured communication formats.

8. An accurate sales forecast can be helpful in all <u>but</u>
   a. scheduling production.
   c. executing operational plan.
   b. planning distribution.
   d. determining strategic gap.

9. _____ reflects the market's ability to absorb a type of product.
   a. Sales forecast
   c. Sales potential
   b. Market forecast
   d. Market potential

10. While relevant time periods vary, forecasters agree that short term forecasts cover a period of
    a. one to three years.
    c. three months or less.
    b. one year or less.
    d. one month or less.

11. The executive opinion method of forecasting may be described as a(n) _____ way to forecast.
    a. convenient
    c. scientific
    b. expensive
    d. impractical

12. Which sales forecasting method works best in stable, mature markets?
    a. Sales force composite.
    c. Projection of trends.
    b. Survey of customers.
    d. Analysis of market factors.

<u>QUICK QUIZ</u>

1Q.
Does every organization need an
M.I.S.?

1A.
Leaving aside the possibility that an organization can conceivably survive, at least over the short run, on blind luck, the fact is that all organizations <u>have</u> a M.I.S. This is, all managers use information, in <u>some</u> way, to make decisions. The "bottom line" of the M.I.S. is this: The manager has <u>some</u> "system" in place so why <u>not</u> try to make it a well-organized, properly operating one?

106

2Q.
The definition of a sales forecast stated that it predicted sales over some specific period of time? Why must "time" be included?

2A.
A forecast sets up a goal or a sales total to shoot for. If, as is also the case when other objectives are set for an organization, no time frame or limit is set, the organization would seem to be allowed "forever" to achieve that objective.

3Q.
It is common to use a "break-down" approach to arrive at a sales forecast. Is there a "build-up" approach as well?

3A.
Yes. Some forecasters, who have good data relating to, for example, likely sales in individual sales territories, can "add up" or "build up" that data to achieve a total sales forecast. Some argue that this is the better approach since errors in forecasting sales for limited areas divide the forecasting into smaller parts wherein only small mistakes will be made. If data are available, a forecaster could use both "break- down" and "build-up" approaches, using each as a check against the other.

4Q.
How many sales forecasts does a company or other organization make each year.

4A.
Obviously, some managers might claim to make "no" forecasts. In fact, even these managers probably do have rough "guesses" or even "hopes" as to what lies ahead. Other's may have to make a great number of estimates. A manufacturer of hundreds of products is likely to develop a sales forecast for each product. Most common, however, are quarterly.

107

EXPERIENTIAL ACTIVITIES

6-A. Sales Forecasting

You accepted a position with a major bicycle manufacturer after graduation from college. One of your earliest assignments is to forecast next year's sales. The company's sales for the most recent five years are listed below.

Year	Unit Sales (in 000)
1982	1,005
1981	955
1980	870
1979	825
1978	660

In 1982, your company had a market share [company sales divided by industry sales] of 15 percent. Industry sales have been relatively flat for several years.

Assignment

1. Forecast expected sales for 1983 using the straightline trend extension method. This approach requires that you complete the four steps below.

   a. Plot the company's sales for the years of 1978 to 1982 on the graph below.

   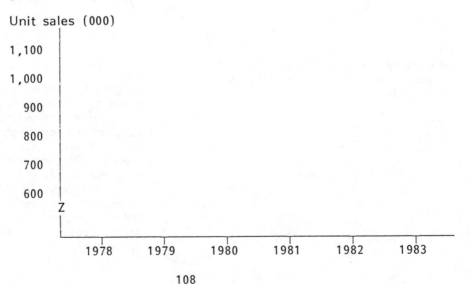

   Unit sales (000)

b. Fit a freehand straightline that "best fits" these data.

c. Extend your line to 1983 for your forecast.

d. 1983 company sales forecast: _____ bicycles.

2. The marketing manager is also interested in a sales forecast for Tucson, Arizona. Annual sales were 1,320, 1,300, 1,330, 1,340, and 1,400 units for 1978 to 1982 respectively.

   a. Forecast expected sales for 1983 using the straightline trend extension method.

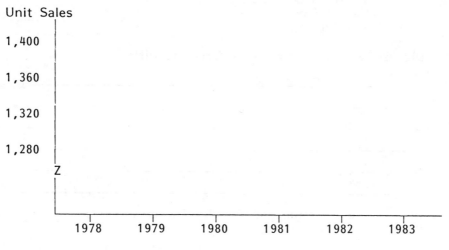

   1983 Tucson sales forecast: _____ bicycles.

3. You decide to use the market factor method to forecast Tucson's sales. You recall that the Sales Management Buying Power Index is judged to be an excellent multiple market factor index by many researchers. You conclude that the Buying Power Index (BPI) is appropriate for bicycles.

   a. Referring to Exhibit 6-6, pages 168-169 in the Zikmund and d'Amico textbook, the BPI for Tucson is _____.

b. Calculate the 1983 sales forecast for Tucson using the BPI as your market index. This method requires these steps.

(1) Multiply industry sales by the BPI for Tucson.

Industry sales: _____ bicycles
Tucson's BPI: _____
Tucson's market potential: _____ bicycles

(2) Multiply Tucson's market potential by the firm's market share percentage.

Tucson's potential: _____ bicycles
Market share: _____
Sales forecast: _____ bicycles

4. Discuss why these two sales forecasts differ.

_____

_____

_____

_____

_____

_____

5. What is the strategic gap for the Tucson market? _____ bicycles
Please show your work.

6-B. Type of Information

For each situation you should indicate the type of information--marketing research, marketing intelligence, informally gathered information, or not information--for this situation. Please justify your decision.

1. A librarian determines through a review of records that approximately two percent of the books checked out are not returned.

   Type of information: _____

   Justification: _____ _____

   _____

   _____

   _____

2. An officer of a student marketing club hears that business professors at another university do less research than professors at her school.

   Type of information: _____

   Justification: _____ _____

   _____

   _____

   _____

3. A marketing manager, while reviewing a sales report, discovers that a competitor has been asking customers about a different price discount schedule.

   Type of information: _____

   Justification: _____ _____

   _____

   _____

   _____

4. A marketing manager reviews a survey regarding customer's perceptions toward price discounts.

   Type of information: _____

   Justification: _____

   _____

   _____

   _____

5. The administrator of a local hospital reads an article that more influenza is expected this year.

   Type of information: _____

   Justification: _____

   _____

   _____

   _____

ANSWERS TO OBJECTIVE QUESTIONS

MATCHING

1. K	3. F	5. M	7. D	9. J
2. B	4. L	6. C	8. A	10. I

TRUE OR FALSE

1. F	4. F	7. F	10. T	13. T
2. T	5. T	8. F	11. T	14. T
3. T	6. F	9. F	12. F	15. T

MULTIPLE CHOICE

1. d	4. c	7. d	10. b
2. b	5. a	8. c	11. a
3. c	6. b	9. d	12. c

CHAPTER 7

SOCIOLOGICAL FACTORS IN CONSUMER BEHAVIOR

OBJECTIVE

Individual buyer behavior is strongly influenced by sociological factors. An effective marketer develops marketing strategies and tactics that incorporates knowledge about these sociological influences.

OUTLINE

I.   A simple start

    A.   Consumer behavior is a subset of human behavior.

    B.   Behavior results when a person interacts with the environment through physical, sociological, and psychological encounters.

    C.   Consumer behavior involves activities and decision processes that influence the buying and using of products.

    D.   An individual buying event consists of a consumer's decision-making process and the situational influence occurring at the time of the purchasing decision.

II. Social forces

    A.   Culture, subculture, social class, reference groups, family, and role are sociological influences on an individual buying event.

    B.   Culture is learned patterns of thought and behavior.

        1.   Cultural values and associated symbols vary according to a particular society.

        2.   Marketing activities must be consistent with cultural values to be effective.

C. Subcultures are segments of a culture with behavioral differences and language variations.

II. Social institutions

A. Each social institution has its values, norms, roles, and statuses.

B. The political, legal, and economic systems, science, education, religion, and family are examples of major social institutions.

C. One's daily behavioral patterns, life style, and consumer behavior are affected by norms (goals reflecting a society's moral order) and values (rules of conduct).

D. Roles (behaviors associated with a social-related position) and status (socially defined position that one may hold) help define customary marketplace behavioral patterns.

III. Social class

A. A social class is a group of people with similar levels of prestige, power, and wealth who share a set of related beliefs, attitudes, and values.

B. The American class system includes an upper class, an upper-middle class, a lower-middle class, a working class, and a lower class.

C. Social class impacts on shopping patterns, such as when and where one shops and the products purchased.

D. Conspicuous consumption refers to consumption of certain products to express one's social class status.

IV. Groups

A. Each individual belongs to small intimate primary groups (family, close friends) and to larger, more impersonal secondary groups (business students, American Marketing Association).

B. Groups which influence an individual are referred to as reference groups.

1. Reference groups serve as a point of comparison.

2. An individual can be a member of a group (membership group) or aspire to be a member of a group (aspirational group).

3. Reference groups are more influential for conspicuous products and/or brands.

4. Opinion leaders or group leaders are individuals from whom one seeks informational cues concerning a particular product.

V. Family

A. The family performs the consumer socialization process.

B. Single-parent households and one member households are increasing in America today.

C. Implications related to the increasing percentage of working women will continue to impact on marketing activities.

D. Marketers need to determine if joint decision-making occurs, and then if the purchasing decision is syncretic or involves a dominant role.

VI. The three roles in the decision

A. The decision-making process involves roles related to buyer, consumer, and decision-maker.

B. The decision-maker may perform a gatekeeper function.

SUMMARY

Learning Objective One: To describe buyer behavior in terms of human interaction with the surrounding environment.

Buyer behavior, a specific type of human behavior, involves activities and decision processes that influence the buying and using of products. Interactions with physical, psychological, and social factors encountered in the environment trigger buyer behavior. For example, during the behavior of brushing teeth, one notices that the toothpaste is almost gone (a physical encounter) and decides to purchase the same brand (learning, a psychological factor) because other people have commented on beautiful teeth (a social influence). An individual buying event occurs when this person purchases this brand of toothpaste. The act of buying was influenced by interactions with the surrounding environment.

<u>Learning Objective Two</u>:   To describe how culture affects the behavior of individuals.

Culture affects human behavior by determining acceptable behaviors within a particular society. Thus, culture has a broad sociological influence on what, when, where, and how products are consumed.

<u>Learning Objective Three</u>:   To define the terms role, status, values, and norms as they apply to buyer behavior.

Social institutions impact on buyer behavior by influencing activities and decision processes that affect buying and using products. Roles, statuses, values, and norms are associated with each social institution. Roles are customary behaviors associated with a socially-defined position (status) while norms refer to rules of conduct. Values are goals that reflect a society's moral views. Buyers and sellers are expected to perform certain activities (roles) according to acceptable norms. Both buyers and sellers adjust their roles according to the perceived prestige (status) of the other party. Marketing activities are more effective if these activities reflect a society's values.

<u>Learning Objective Four</u>:   To discuss the different social classes in the United States.

Social institutions impact on buyer behavior by influencing activities and decision processes that affect the buying and using of products. Each social institution has its own values, norms, roles, and statuses.

According to one view, five social classes exist in the United States. Overall, these classes differ relative to income, property, occupation, education, and personal and family life. For example, lower class members (around 20% of the population) have a poverty level income, no savings, high unemployment, high illiteracy rate and little interest in education, lower life expectancy, and poorer health (mental and physical) than those in the working class (40% of the population), the lower-middle class (30% of the population), and the upper class (about 1% of the population).

Those of the working class have a low income level earned from a skilled or unskilled labor position, some savings, some high school, possibly vocational training, unstable family life, and conformist personality. Members of the lower-middle class earn a modest income from a small business, or farm, or a sales or clerical position. These individuals are likely to have some college education and a longer life expectancy than those in the working class.

118

Upper-middle class members have high incomes, property, graduate training, better physical and mental health, and a professional or managerial position. Upper class families have very high incomes, old wealth, liberal arts education, high civil or military or corporate heads positions, and stable family life.

Social class membership can affect shopping patterns and brands and/or products purchased. Consumption patterns are symbols of class membership.

Learning Objective Five: To analyze the impact groups have on the individual buyer.

Primary and secondary groups exert a major influence on an individual buyer's behavior. Primary groups, especially the family, pass on cultural values to the individual through the socialization process. Culture has a broad influence on products consumed. Individuals use reference groups (membership and aspirational) as a point of comparison to evaluate a buying event as conforming to group values and behaviors. Reference groups exert more influence for products and/or brands which are more conspicuous. Opinion leaders serve as an informal source of information and through their word-of-mouth, recommendations are very influential. An organization's communication concerning a product and/or brand may encode reference group cues.

Learning Objective Six: To identify the three roles played in the consumer decision-making process and to tell which of these is the most significant in terms of buyer choice.

The consumer decision-making process involves buyer, consumer, and decision-maker roles. The decision-maker is the most significant in terms of buyer choice and should be a prime target. The decision-maker performs a gatekeeper function. If this "gate" is closed, buyer and consumer roles cannot be executed.

VOCABULARY BUILDING

Matching Exercise

Match the following by placing the letter of the concept or term on the blank preceding the phrase which best describes the concept or term. You should use a term or concept only once.

A. Consumer behavior
B. Culture
C. Subculture
D. Values
E. Norms
F. Roles
G. Status
H. Prestige
I. Social class
J. Primary group

K. Secondary group
L. Reference group
M. Opinion leaders
N. Socialization process
O. Joint decision-making
P. Buyer
Q. Consumer
R. Decision-maker
S. Syncretic decision
T. Gatekeeper

___F___ 1. Socially defined positions that an individual may hold.

___R___ 2. Role of the person who decides which brand or product to buy.

___A___ 3. Purchasing activities and decision processes that precede and determine the acts of buying and selling products.

___M___ 4. Individuals in a group who provide informational cues to other group members.

___E___ 5. Rules of conduct to be followed in particular circumstances.

___P___ 6. Role of the individual responsible for the actual purchasing decision, but not involved in the use of a product.

_____ 7. Learned behavioral patterns of a particular society.

___L___ 8. A group of people which has an influence on an individual because that individual is a member of the group or aspires to be a member.

___N___ 9. Transmittal of cultural values and norms of a society to its members.

___Q__10. Person who uses the product.

___O__11. Decisions made by both spouses together.

_____12. Appropriate behavior patterns associated with a position in a social setting.

120

_J_ 13. A group where face-to-face contact endures over time.

_I_ 14. A group of people with similar levels of prestige and wealth who share a set of related beliefs, attitudes, and values in their thinking and behavior.

_D_ 15. Goals that society views as important.

VOCABULARY BUILDING

Programmed Learning Exercise

1. A study of consumer behavior is essential because the _____ is the focal point about which all marketing activities revolve.

    [consumer/buyer]

2. Consumers are members of many _____.

    [groups]

3. Behavior is a function of the interaction between the _____ and the _____.

    [person, environment]

4. An _____ _____ event consists of the individual consumer's decision-making process and the situational influence occurring at the time of the purchasing decision.

    [individual buying]

5. Culture _____ from place-to-place and affects the success of marketing worldwide.

    [varies]

6. A _____ reflects cultural differences and language variations of segments of a culture.

    [subculture]

7. Each social institution develops a series of _____, _____, _____, and _____ to fulfill its central purpose.

    [values, norms, roles, statuses]

8. _____ reflect the moral order of a society and give meaning to social life.

    [Values]

121

9. _____ is the assignment of value judgments about a status or role.

[Prestige]

10. Members of different social classes know which _____ and products are for people of their social class.

[stores]

11. A larger, more impersonal group is called a _____ group.

[secondary]

12. Membership groups exert strong _____ _____ on individual members to conform.

[peer pressure]

13. An _____ group is a group of people to which an individual hopes to join.

[aspirational]

14. Reference groups may influence the type of _____ consumed and/or _____ purchased.

[product, brand]

15. For some marketers, their target market is the _____ rather than the individual.

[household/family]

16. The major growth in the work force is due to an increase in the number of _____ entering the work force.

[women]

17. _____ decision-making connotes the discussion of consumer decisions among all individuals in a group.

[Joint]

18. The _____ _____ in group decision-making is commonly taken by a particular group member when particular purchases are the topic of discussion.

[dominant role]

19. Three roles in the decision to buy are the roles of _____, _____, and _____.

[buyer, decision-maker, consumer]

20. The _____ is the person who goes to the store and actually purchases the product.

[buyer]

TRUE OR FALSE STATEMENTS

T F 1. Marketers advocate developing a product and then convince customers they need the product.

T F 2. Consumer behavior is a function of the interaction between a buyer and a seller.

T F 3. An individual buying event is influenced by physical, sociological, and psychological factors.

T F 4. Culture is learned.

T F 5. The success of a product in France assures this product's success in the United States.

T F 6. Subcultures are variations in culture and language which are found between different countries.

T F 7. Values reflect a society's moral order.

T F 8. Values are more situation specific than norms.

T F 9. Norms prescribe what ought to be done to preserve basic values.

T F 10. A social institution provides an established pattern of behaviors that offers a solution to recurrent problems.

T F 11. Status varies according to the individual judging the role.

T F 12. Social classes have a somewhat small influence on shopping patterns or products purchased.

T F 13. The working class has a modest income usually earned in a sales-related position.

T F 14. Members of a social class are likely to shop in similar stores.

T F 15. Examples of conspicuous consumption are infrequent.

T F 16. Reference groups may serve as a standard for comparison.

T F 17. A social class is a reference group.

T F 18. Opinion leaders and gatekeepers are the same individual for a product-specific situation.

T F 19. The increase of non-traditional households in the United States has an impact on marketing activities.

T F 20. Most purchases are dominated by one group member.

MULTIPLE CHOICE QUESTIONS

1. Decision-making processes and actions of obtaining and using products is referred to as
   a. organizational behavior.
   c. consumer behavior.
   b. human behavior.
   d. purchasing.

2. Sociology is a discipline which investigates
   a. human behavior by studying social institutions and their interrelation-ships.
   b. individual behavior by studying roles and norms.
   c. buyer behavior by studying the impact of the social institutions of marketing and economics systems.
   d. consumption behavior by studying the interrelationships of situational influences on human behavior.

3. Which statement regarding culture is incorrect?
   a. Culture is that complex whole which includes knowledge and other capabilities and habits acquired by one as a member of a society.
   b. Culture is innate.
   c. Culture is man made.
   d. Culture is the acquired knowledge that people use to interpret experience.

4. A product may fail in the marketplace because
   a. it does not challenge cultural beliefs and attitudes.
   b. it is targeted too precisely.
   c. it is differentiated from competitive products.
   d. it is not consistent with cultural beliefs and attitudes.

5. Marketers in developing an effective marketing mix must
   a. discriminate between product markets.
   b. not adjust to subculture values and norms.
   c. recognize subculture differences.
   d. not advertise on the basis of cultural differences.

6. The fact that capitalistic economic institutions are to make a profit is an example of a
   a. value.
   c. role.
   b. norm.
   d. status position.

7. Social institutions respond to a society's needs. Which social need is addressed by the economic system?
   a. Minimize governmental regulation.
   b. Maximize profits.
   c. Free enterprise.
   d. Produce and distribute products.

8. Which statement is correct regarding roles and status?
   a. An individual buying event is affected by the perceived status of the seller.
   b. Roles and status are of little importance to marketers.
   c. Status is invariant for a particular role.
   d. Role operates independently of status.

9. A social class is a group of people with
   a. heterogeneous beliefs and homogeneous attitudes.
   b. similar beliefs but vary tremendously in their buying behavior.
   c. similar levels of prestige, power, and wealth who have common values and behavior.
   d. common social institutions who purchase different products.

10. Which would not be a characteristic of an individual being a member of the upper-middle class?
    a. Graduate training.   c. Corporate head.
    b. Property accumulation.   d. High income.

11. A single 35 year old person who earns $40,000 annually is a member of which social class?
    a. Working class.
    b. Lower-middle class.
    c. Upper-middle class.
    d. Contrary to the question, social class cannot be determined based on age, marital status, and income.

12. Which statement is inaccurate when referring to people from the same social class?
    a. They have similar life styles.
    b. They have different buying behavior.
    c. They shop at similar stores.
    d. They live in neighborhoods with others from the same social class.

13. When an upper class member expresses achievements by possessing an expensive car and house, this person is engaged in _____ consumption.
    a. emotional   c. expensive
    b. conspicuous   d. durable goods

14. Which statement regarding primary groups is incorrect?
    a. Primary groups do not perform a socialization process.
    b. Primary groups involve face-to-face contact.
    c. The influence of primary groups is enduring.
    d. Primary groups are reference groups.

15. Reference groups serve all of these purposes except as
    a. a point of comparison.   c. an aspirational model.
    b. an information source.   d. a market segment.

16. Opinion leaders are
    a. selected by all group members.
    b. people whose opinion is sought in buying decisions.
    c. the same for all products.
    d. easy to identify and target a marketing mix toward.

17. The family serves as an important reference group and social institution because families
    a. provide purchasing power.
    b. are most knowledgeable of products offered in the market.
    c. are increasing in average size.
    d. perform the consumer socialization process.

18. Which change in the marketplace is not due to an increasing number of working women?
    a. Extended store hours on weekends and evenings.
    b. More health foods and fitness centers.
    c. More easily prepared products.
    d. Popularity of take-out food.

19. Joint decision-making implies that
    a. only parents are involved in the decision to buy.
    b. these are syncretic decisions.
    c. some decisions to buy are decided by groups of two or more persons.
    d. no dominant role exists.

20. The gatekeeper function is performed by
    a. the buyer.   c. the decision-maker.
    b. the consumer.   d. an influential.

QUICK QUIZ

1Q.
When we say that marketers are striving to develop theories of consumer behavior so as to be able to predict consumer actions, are we saying that marketers hope to be able to treat consumers "mechanically," predicting what each consumer will do in every buying situation?

1A.
No. Marketers, more than anyone, are aware that each buyer may behave differently in similar buying situations. In fact, if someone created a model which predicted all behaviors in all situations, allowing for "every" variable and circumstance, the model has to be unwieldy and unusable. What students of consumer behavior are striving for are general theories and models, guidelines that may predict how many buyers might act in given situations, not all-inclusive theories that cover every single case.

2Q.
What is "class"?

2A.
As we've seen in our discussions, "class" is somewhat difficult to define. But, people have perceptions of "class." For instance, class is reflected when sales clerks wait on well-dressed persons first or when people look down on others because of their dress, where they live, or who their parents and friends are. Social class is more than money -- it is reflective of source of income, occupation, educational attainment, and type and place of residence.

3Q.
In appealing to mothers who buy baby food rather than the babies who eat it, do manufacturers of baby food add spices to the food to make it taste good to the mothers rather than to make it as "pure" as possible for the baby?

3A.
Before the possible dangers of salt, sugar, and other additives were clearly understood, yes they did make the food to the mother's taste. In recent years, these substances have been removed from the product formulations. Even at that, a good portion of that change is due to changes in the mothers' tastes, not the babies'. It is, after all, the mothers who want these additives out, not the babies. Thus, the importance of the mother as gate-keeper is, in fact, maintained.

EXPERIENTIAL ACTIVITIES

7-A. Sociological Influences on Buyer Behavior

As part of your second interview with an advertising agency, you have been asked to recommend which sociological influence(s) would be appropriate for use in an advertisement to communicate with a particular type of consumer. Two brief consumer profiles are presented below. Following each profile is a list of five products the consumer might purchase. For each consumer type, indicate the sociological influence(s) (culture, subculture, social class, reference group, family, or role) you would use in an advertisement designed to communicate with this type of consumer. You will need to justify your recommendation.

PROFILE A

A thirty-five year old career woman, Mrs. Solon, a graduate of Rice University, is vice-president of marketing for a medium-size industrial supplier located in Houston. She and her husband live in a six room high rise apartment in downtown Houston. They have no children. Their combined annual income is $75,500.

Product	Sociological Influence	Justification
Prepared frozen dinners	_____	_____ _____
Physical fitness center	_____	_____ _____
Dining room furniture	_____	_____ _____
Tennis shoes	_____	_____ _____
Games	_____	_____ _____

PROFILE B

Mrs. Roberts is a thirty-five year old mother of three children, ages 5, 7, and 11 years. She works within her own home without pay while her husband operates a heating and air conditioning business. The family lives in a four-bedroom bi-level house in the suburbs of Louisville, Kentucky. Their annual family income is $21,700.

Product	Sociological Influence	Justification
Prepared frozen dinners	_____	_____ _____
Physical fitness center	_____	_____ _____

129

Dining room
furniture   _____   _____

                                          _____

Tennis shoes   _____   _____

                                          _____

Games   _____   _____

                                          _____

7-B.   Identifying the Decision-Maker

    The decision-maker needs to be targeted for marketing to be effective.
For products involving some degree of joint decision-making, the marketer
needs to determine the influence of each spouse in the purchase decision.
Spousal influence regarding a purchase decision can be classified as:

        ° syncretic (made by spouses together);
        ° wife-dominant;
        ° husband-dominant; and
        ° autonomic (independent, autonomous).

For the products below classify the relative spousal influence regarding a purchase decision. Explain why you made this classification.

Product	Type of Spousal Influence	Explanation
1. Life insurance	_____	_____
		_____
2. Cleaning products	_____	_____
		_____
3. Vacation	_____	_____
		_____
4. Non-prescription drugs	_____	_____
		_____

130

5. Automobiles _____   _____
                                    _____

6. Scotch whisky _____   _____
                                      _____

7. Cereal _____   _____
                               _____

8. Garden tools _____   _____
                                     _____

9. Small kitchen _____   _____
    appliances   _____

10. Automobiles _____   _____
                                    _____

ADDITIONAL COMMENTS

ANSWERS TO OBJECTIVE QUESTIONS

MATCHING

1.	G	4.	M	7.	B	10.	Q	13.	J
2.	R	5.	E	8.	L	11.	S	14.	I
3.	A	6.	P	9.	N	12.	F	15.	D

TRUE OR FALSE

1.	F	5.	F	9.	T	13.	F	17.	T
2.	F	6.	F	10.	T	14.	T	18.	F
3.	T	7.	T	11.	T	15.	F	19.	T
4.	T	8.	F	12.	F	16.	T	20.	T

MULTIPLE CHOICE

1.	c	5.	c	9.	c	13.	b	17.	d
2.	a	6.	a	10.	c	14.	a	18.	b
3.	b	7.	d	11.	d	15.	d	19.	c
4.	d	8.	a	12.	b	16.	b	20.	d

CHAPTER 8

PSYCHOLOGICAL INFLUENCES IN CONSUMER BEHAVIOR

OBJECTIVE

Effective marketers must understand how psychological factors impact on consumer decision-making. Psychological influences on consumer behavior include motivation, perception, learning, and attitudes. The consumer decision-making process can be represented by a five-step model. Each step provides marketers with opportunities to adjust their marketing mixes to achieve customer satisfaction.

OUTLINE

I. Consumer behavior: the stimulus-response concept

    A. Consumers respond psychologically to cues or stimuli in their environment.

    B. The "black box" model of consumer behavior is a representation of the psychological processes affecting consumer choice and behavior.

        1. Marketers cannot describe exactly an individual's psychological processes.

        2. Marketers draw inferences about consumer behavior based on inputs (stimuli) and outputs (response) of the "black box."

        3. Five models of consumer behavior proposed to explain the "black box" are the Marshallian economic model, Pavlovian learning model, Freudian psychoanalytic model, Veblenian socio--psychological model, and Hobbesian organizational-factors model.

II. Psychological theory and consumer needs

    A. Essential to the understanding of consumer behavior concepts is using a scientific vocabulary.

III. Motivation

    A. Motivation refers to a consumer's psychological internal drive which initiates goal-directed behavior.

    B. A motive is an aroused need (innate desire, basic to human beings).

    C. An unfulfilled motive becomes a drive (internal stimulus) which energizes behavior to search for a response to satisfy an aroused need.

    D. Satisfaction or dissatisfaction may result from the response behavior.

    E. Needs can be classified as physiological (needs stemming from one's biological mechanisms) or social and psychological (needs resulting from one's interaction with the social environment).

    F. Maslow's hierarchy of needs model is used by many marketers.

        1. The ordered categories of needs are physiological needs (most basic needs), safety needs, social or love needs, self-esteem needs, and self-actualization needs (highest needs).

        2. Lower-order needs must be satisfied before higher-order needs.

    G. Motives can be classified as rational or emotional.

IV. Cognitive processes

    A. Cognitive processes connote those mental activities which interpret stimuli and organize thoughts and ideas.

    B. These mental activities include perception, learning, and attitude formation.

V. Perception

    A. Perception is the process of interpreting sensations and giving meaning to stimuli.

    B. Selective perception refers to the individual tendency to screen out certain stimuli and to interpret other stimuli with meanings drawn from personal backgrounds.

        1. Selective perception affects the effectiveness of marketing activities.

2. Marketers can use the principle of closure in their communications.

C. The screening process of selective perception involves selective exposure, selective attention, selective interpretation, and selective retention.

D. Brand image refers to the complex of symbols and meanings associated with a brand.

VI. Learning

A. Learning involves a change in behavior or cognitions based on experience.

B. The operant conditioning theory of the consumer learning process stresses functional and/or symbolic reward to reinforce the stimulus-response process.

C. The attribution theory of learning stresses attributing rewards to one's actions.

D. Learning theories are compatible with marketing activities and the marketing concept.

1. In terms of the evoked set concept, marketers must first have their product/brand in the awareness set.

2. For those products in the awareness set, marketers' goal is to have their product/brand in the evoked set (favorable response set) rather than the acceptable and unacceptable sets.

VII. Attitudes

A. An attitude is a learned predisposition to respond in a consistently favorable or unfavorable manner with respect to a given object.

B. Attitudes are enduring and situational.

C. An attitude has an affective (emotional) component, a cognitive (knowledge) component, and a behavioral (conative) component.

D. Attitude change may occur by raising doubts about an existing attitude, showing how a new attitude answers existing doubts, and finally, solidifying a new attitude by showing reward associated with the new attitude.

VIII. The decision-making process

    A. Decision-making is a cognitive process that combines memory, thinking, information processing, and making evaluative judgments.

    B. Decision-making spans a continuum from routine or habitual decision-making to extensive decision-making.

    C. The steps in the decision-making process are (1) problem recognition, (2) search for alternative solutions and information, (3) evaluation of alternatives, (4) purchase decision, and (5) postpurchase evaluation.

        1. Problem recognition/awareness is the process of determining that an aroused need is not satisfied.

        2. The search for alternative solutions and information is observed more readily for extensive decision-making where perceived risk is greater.

        3. Evaluation of alternatives is based on choice criteria or those critical attributes utilized to evaluate a brand.

        4. The purchase decision involves the decision to buy or not to buy.

        5. Postpurchase evaluation concerns the satisfaction, dissatisfaction, or cognitive dissonance associated with the decision to buy.

    D. The flow of events and the effects of personal and nonpersonal variables in the consumer decision-making process are summarized in Exhibit 8-10, page 221, in the Zikmund and d'Amico textbook.

IX. Personality and self-concept theories

    A. Personality is the underlying dispositions or dominant characteristics of individuals.

        1. Freud's personality theory is based on conflict between the personality components of the id, the ego, and the superego.

        2. Freudian theory stresses the symbolic and the unconscious.

    B. Self-concept is an individual's appraisal of herself or himself.

1. Self-concept involves the way one sees oneself and how one thinks others behave and see the person.

2. Self-concept influences purchase decisions.

SUMMARY

Learning Objective One: To show that buyer behavior is, in fact, a response to stimuli.

Consumers respond psychologically to cues or stimuli. A stimulus acts upon a consumer's basic need, thus creating a motive. This motive energizes behavior to search for a satisfying response to the aroused need. A behavioral response results, yielding either satisfaction or dissatisfaction. For example, a coupon for three dollars off a large pizza may arouse a hunger motive which results in the purchase of a pizza for dinner.

Learning Objective Two: To explain why much of the buyer decision-making process is described as being hidden in a "black box."

Marketers are unable to observe directly the decision-making process within the consumer. The fact that these cognitive processes are hidden from analysis explains the use of the black box model. Marketers can draw inferences about buyer behavior through the observation of inputs influencing the black box and the outputs which result.

Learning Objective Three: To be familiar with Maslow's needs hierarchy and with the importance of both rational and emotional motives.

Maslow's needs hierarchy categories are (1) physiological needs, (2) safety needs, (3) social or love needs, (4) self-esteem needs, and (5) self-actualization needs. According to Maslow's theory, the most basic needs must be satisfied before individuals are motivated by higher-level needs. Marketers can position products, such as food items or automobiles, to appeal to different needs in Maslow's hierarchy. In fact, individuals are motivated by both rational and emotional needs and effective marketing incorporates both types of needs.

Learning Objective Four: To discuss how self-concept and personality affect purchase behavior.

Personality reflects one's dominant behavioral characteristics; whereas, self-concept refers to one's perception and appraisal of herself or himself. Thus, personality and self-concept can be influences on why an individual does or does not purchase a particular product and/or brand. Products, and their symbolic associations, are used to express one's personality and self-concept.

Learning Objective Five: To have an understanding of learning models and the evoked set concept.

Learning models enhance the basic stimulus-response concept by focusing on rewards (or dissatisfaction) associated with a behavioral action. Rewards may be functional or symbolic. According to the operant conditioning learning model, reinforcement (degree of satisfaction or reward) leads to repeating the behavioral action. For example, if an external cue such as an advertisement results in the purchase of a product which subsequently provides satisfaction, the symbolic and functional rewards serve to reinforce the stimulus-response process. The attribution theory of learning stresses that consumers must attribute the reward to their behavioral action.

The evoked set concept suggests that marketers need to get their products first in the target customer's awareness set, and then in the customer's evoked set for a particular problem. Only products in the evoked set are purchased.

Learning Objective Six: To know how and why perceptions differ among individuals, and be familiar with selective perception.

Perceptions differ among individuals because each individual interprets and organizes sensations according to his or her unique background, knowledge, moods, personality, and other attributes such as the content in which the stimuli were encountered. Each of us views reality from a different perspective.

Selective perception is a process which refers to an individual's tendency to screen out certain stimuli and to interpret other stimuli with meanings drawn from personal backgrounds. This process involves selective exposure, selective attention, selective interpretation, and selective retention. Each stage of selective perception reduces the number of stimuli to which an individual responds.

Learning Objective Seven: To describe the three components of an attitude-- affective, cognitive, and behavioral.

Each attitude has an affective component, a cognitive component, and a behavioral component. The affective or emotional component reflects an individual's feelings toward a given object, for example, fast food outlets. Knowledge about this given object or the individual's beliefs comprise the cognitive component. The behavioral component is a predisposition to action as it reflects the intended and actual behaviors toward the object.

Learning Objective Eight: To describe the five step "decision-making process," and tell why the outcome may be dissatisfaction as well as satisfaction.

The five decision-making steps are (1) problem recognition, (2) search for alternative solutions and information, (3) evaluation of alternatives, (4) purchase decision, and (5) postpurchase evaluation. An individual recognizes that a problem exists when an aroused need is unfulfilled. The stages related to the search for alternative solutions and their evaluations are more critical for extensive decision-making than routinized or habitual decision-making. More perceived risk is associated with extensive decision-making. Individuals will search for alternatives and information to reduce this risk. A prospective buyer evaluates alternatives on the basis of choice criteria (critical attributes). Based on alternative evaluations, the prospective buyer makes a decision to buy or not to buy the product. If the decision is to buy, the decision-maker must make a series of decisions related to the "act of purchasing," such as size, style and color, where and when to purchase, and payment. The satisfaction or dissatisfaction resulting from the purchase is determined during the postpurchase evaluation step. Dissatisfaction can occur if the buyer recognizes an incorrect problem, conducts an inadequate search for alternatives and information, makes a wrong decision, or enters a state of cognitive dissonance.

Learning Objective Nine: To understand the importance of the phenomenon known as cognitive dissonance to marketing success.

Cognitive dissonance refers to an individual's anxiety associated with the uncertainty that an erroneous purchase decision was made. Such dissonance can result in dissatisfaction and unfavorable word-of-mouth recommendations. Buyers look for reinforcement that a correct decision was made from friends and from others. Marketers through their communications to target customers and to buyers can reinforce that a correct decision was made.

VOCABULARY BUILDING

Matching Exercise

Match the following by placing the letter of the concept or term on the blank preceding the phrase which best describes the concept or term. You should use a term or concept only once.

139

A. Stimulus (input)	K. Perception
B. Response (output)	L. Selective perception
C. Motivation	M. Selective exposure
D. Need	N. Selective attention
E. Motive	O. Selective interpretation
F. Drive	P. Brand image
G. Cognitive process	Q. Attitude
H. Learning	R. Cognitive dissonance
I. Reinforcement	S. Personality
J. Black box	T. Self-concept

_____ 1. A theory explaining the uncertainty and tension felt by individuals that a decision was erroneously made.

_____ 2. A representation of the psychological processes affecting consumer choice and behavior.

_____ 3. The individual tendency to screen out certain stimuli and to interpret other stimuli with meanings drawn from personal backgrounds.

_____ 4. A learned predisposition to respond in a consistently favorable or unfavorable manner with respect to a given object.

_____ 5. The range of mental activities involving the interpretation of stimuli and the organization of thoughts and ideas.

_____ 6. An innate desire, basic to humans.

_____ 7. A reward that strengthens the stimulus-response model.

_____ 8. An internal stimulus arising from an unfulfilled motive.

_____ 9. The process of interpreting sensations and giving meaning to stimuli.

_____ 10. A consumer's psychological internal drive state which causes the initiation of behavior.

_____ 11. A behavioral action induced by a stimulus.

_____ 12. Perceptual defenses which operate because a newly encountered message is incompatible with an individual's established values or attitudes.

_____ 13. An individual's perception and appraisal of himself or herself.

_____ 14. Any change in behavior or cognitions as a result of experience.

_____ 15. An aspect of the environment that triggers a behavioral response in a subsequent time period.

VOCABULARY BUILDING

Programmed Learning Exercise

1. The _____ _____ model posits that human behavior is largely a learned, associative process.

    [Pavlovian learning]

2. A _____ is a stimulated need.

    [motive]

3. Needs resulting from an individual's interaction with the social environment can be classified as _____ needs and _____ needs.

    [social, psychological]

4. Food, water, and sex are examples of _____ needs.

    [physiological]

5. Motives can be classified as _____ or rational.

    [emotional]

6. The aspect of perception where one mentally finishes incomplete stimuli is referred to as _____.

    [closure]

7. The process of selective perception includes the stages of selective _____, selective _____, selective _____, and selective _____.

    [exposure, attention, interpretation, retention]

8. A _____ _____ is a complex interaction of symbols and meanings associated with a brand.

    [brand image]

9. _____ perception refers to perception of stimuli without conscious awareness.

    [Subliminal]

10. The _____ theory of learning stresses that consumers must attribute the obtained reward to their actions.

[attribution]

11. An _____ _____ consists of products developed by people as a response to the presence of a particular stimulus.

[evoked set]

12. An attitude has an _____ component, a _____ component, and a _____ component.

[affective, cognitive, behavioral]

13. _____ is a cognitive process that combines memory, thinking, information processing, and the making of evaluative judgments.

[Decision-making]

14. The process of determining, as a result of stimuli, that a need is not completely satisfied is referred to as _____ _____.

[problem awareness]

15. The perception of consumers that an action will produce consequences that are unexpected and undesirable is called _____ _____.

[perceived risk]

16. _____ _____ are critical attributes utilized by consumers to evaluate a brand.

[Choice criteria]

17. If the decision is made to purchase a product, the _____ of the purchase must be completed.

[mechanics]

18. Purchase satisfaction or dissatisfaction occurs during the _____ _____ step of the consumer decision-making process.

[postpurchase evaluation]

19. _____ is the underlying dispositions or dominant characteristics of individuals.

[Personality]

20. The _____ represents socially acceptable codes of behavior in Freudian personality theory.

[superego]

TRUE OR FALSE STATEMENTS

T F 1. Internal tension from aroused needs increases attention to external stimuli.

T F 2. Hobbesian organizational-factors model focuses on the corporate person in his/hers attempts to satisfy both personal and organizational needs and goals.

T F 3. Marketing creates needs.

T F 4. An example of a self-esteem need is becoming increasingly like one is capable of becoming.

T F 5. Individuals receive information through their senses.

T F 6. People pay more attention to commercials for products they do not use than products they use.

T F 7. Selective interpretation may be overcome with stimulus factors such as color advertisements.

T F 8. Product distinctions exist only in the products themselves and not in the minds of the consumers.

T F 9. Organizations provide samples of their products to enable consumers to learn about their products.

T F 10. Since learning occurs as a result of experience, observation seldom plays a part in the learning process.

T F 11. Buyers may receive functional and/or symbolic rewards.

T F 12. Consumer satisfaction leads to repeat purchases.

T F 13. According to the evoked set concept, the list of products appropriate for an aroused need does not change.

T F 14. Attitudes are innate predispositions to response in a consistent way to a given object.

T F 15. It is difficult to predict a specific behavior from an attitude toward a single object.

T F 16. Attitudes, in general, are easily changed by a marketer.

T F 17. Only extensive decision-making involves the five stages of the decision-making process.

T F 18. People, in general, prefer to deal with established companies or buy established products because they may want to reduce or avoid any related perceived risk.

T F 19. During postpurchase evaluation, a buyer may mentally downgrade the unselected alternatives.

T F 20. Situational expectations can influence the decision-making process.

MULTIPLE CHOICE QUESTIONS

1. Which model of consumer behavior posits that buying behavior is strongly influenced by group membership?
   a. Fruedian psychoanalytic model.
   b. Pavlovian learning model.
   c. Jameson group membership model.
   d. Veblenian social-psychological model.

2. Which statement best represents the "black-box" concept?
   a. The "black box" refers to the biological functioning of a human being.
   b. The "black box" refers to an individual's physiogenic processes.
   c. The "black box" refers to an individual's psychological processes.
   d. Marketers can observe what occurs inside the black box.

3. Which statement is <u>incorrect</u> regarding a simple model of motivated behavior?
   a. Stimuli act upon motives directly.
   b. Internal tension from aroused needs increases attention to external stimuli.
   c. An unfulfilled motive serves as an internal stimulus or drive.
   d. A need is an innate desire.

4. According to Maslow's needs hierarchy, which statement is correct?
   a. An example of a first level need is the need for protection.
   b. The existence of an individual's lower concerns does not obviate the power of the other needs.
   c. Self-actualization needs arise from a person's need for achievement and to gain respect of others.
   d. A satisfied need continues to be a motivator.

144

5. The correct order of needs for Maslow's hierarchy is
    a. physiological, social, safety, self-actualization, self-esteem.
    b. physiological, safety, social, self-esteem, self-actualization.
    c. safety, physiological, social, self-actualization, self-esteem.
    d. safety, physiological, social, self-esteem, self-actualization.

6. Cognitive activities include all but
    a. learning.   c. attitude formation.
    b. thinking.   d. eating.

7. Which statement is inaccurate regarding perception?
    a. Perception is one's interpretation of reality.
    b. Individuals perceive an advertisement similarly.
    c. Perception uses one's past experience.
    d. Perception is an aspect of a consumer's cognitive processes.

8. Selective perception occurs when an individual
    a. pays equal attention to all advertisements.
    b. interprets all advertisements.
    c. retains information from all advertisements.
    d. screens out certain advertisements.

9. What occurs when a newly encountered message is incompatible with the individual's established values or attitude?
    a. Selective exposure.   c. Selective interpretation.
    b. Selective attention.   d. Selective retention.

10. Which statement regarding learning is incorrect?
    a. Learning is innate.
    b. Learning occurs as a result of experience.
    c. Learning can occur by observation.
    d. Learning is a change in behavior or cognitions.

11. The operant conditioning theory of learning stresses that
    a. consumers attribute obtained rewards to their actions instead of the product.
    b. functional rewards should be the basic appeals for advertisements.
    c. rewards must be tangible.
    d. repeated satisfaction creates buying habits and loyal customers.

12. If a marketer finds that the organization's product is not included in target customer's evoked set, the marketer could
    a. increase distribution to make the product easier to find.
    b. alter the product to achieve greater appeal.
    c. adjust price to make the product more attractive.
    d. do any of the above.

13. Which statement regarding an individual's attitude is <u>incorrect</u>?
    a. An attitude is easily changed.
    b. An attitude contains positive and negative elements.
    c. An attitude is learned.
    d. An attitude is directed toward some object.

14. Which component of an attitude involves knowledge about products?
    a. Rational.   c. Affective.
    b. Cognitive.   d. Behavioral.

15. The five-step decision-making process does <u>not</u> include
    a. postpurchase evaluation.
    b. problem awareness.
    c. search for and evaluation of alternative solutions.
    d. attitude formation.

16. Which statement regarding the consumer decision-making process is <u>incorrect</u>?
    a. Buyers employ choice criteria to evaluate a brand.
    b. Problem awareness is the result of stimuli.
    c. Perceived risk is greater for routine decision-making than for extensive decision-making.
    d. Purchase decision may be not to buy an alternative in one's evoked set.

17. Marketers can employ all of these marketing activities to reduce cognitive dissonance <u>except</u>
    a. broadcast advertising.   c. word-of mouth recommendations.
    b. newsletters.   d. toll-free "hot-line" number.

18. Which statement regarding consumer dissatisfaction is <u>incorrect</u>?
    a. Dissatisfaction does not occur for routine decision-making.
    b. Dissatisfaction occurs if a buyer enters a state of cognitive dissonance.
    c. Dissatisfaction occurs if a buyer seizes on the wrong problem.
    d. Effective marketers adjust their marketing mixes to head-off dissatisfaction.

19. Freudian personality theory suggests that marketers
    a. use personality traits to develop marketing strategy.
    b. base their marketing strategies on personality considerations only.
    c. incorporate symbolic associations in their marketing activities.
    d. do all of the above.

20. Which statement regarding self-concept is <u>incorrect?</u>
  a. Self-concept influences why one buys or does not buy a product.
  b. Self-concept involves an individual's perception of others.
  c. Self-concept is reflected in the way others behave toward an individual.
  d. Self-concept involves roles, statuses, norms, and values.

QUICK QUIZ

1Q.
What is the difference between a need and a motive?

1A.
A need is an innate desire, basic to human beings. Hunger or a desire to have friends are <u>needs</u>. But these needs are not <u>always</u> "activated." That is, they are always within the individual but do not always cause the person to act. When, by whatever means, the need is "activated," it becomes a motive. Thus, the individual is led to action by the motive of hunger or the motive of loneliness. These motives are the aroused needs for food and for companionship.

2Q.
Do learning, perception, attitudes, and all the things done by the individual have application for marketers considering a society--wide phenomena such as Christmas?

2A.
Yes. Society's behavior is, in fact, the summation of individual behaviors. However, the behavior of small groups in the society may differ, though it often goes unnoticed. The Christmas rush is, for many retail marketers, a great demonstration of society's behavior, and accounts for more than 25 percent of annual sales and 35 to 45 percent of yearly earnings. Each sale, of course, is made to an individual who has learned and

developed attitudes about the holiday from "society."

3Q.
Why should a manufacturer of a product be concerned with consumer patronage motives? As long as the product is bought, why is the manufacturer concerned with where it is bought?

3A.
The manufacturer is concerned with patronage motives for a number of reasons. First, the manufacturer needs to know where target customers will want to buy the product, otherwise the product may not be distributed to the proper stores. Second, one needs to know how the retailers stocking the goods will attract and treat the target customer. Perhaps assistance from the manufacturer in the form of advertising money, sales training, or in-store demonstrations will be appropriate. The retailer is a part of the distribution system that manufacturers cannot afford to ignore.

EXPERIENTIAL ACTIVITY

8-A. The Consumer Decision-making Process

A toy manufacturer has developed a self-destruct board game dealing with "College Life at State University." This game is targeted to college students and available in most cities.

Assignment

1. Develop a flow diagram which identifies all alternative (potential) decisions facing a buyer. [Note: This diagram should be structured around the five-step decision-making model.]

2. In the above diagram, identify the decision route one must follow to purchase "College Life at State University" and to become a loyal consumer.

8-B. Product Usage

All organizations need to understand how their products are used in order to be more effective marketers. A soft drink manufacturer is interested in finding out how people use soft drinks.

Assignment

1. Describe how you use soft drinks.

    _____
    _____
    _____
    _____
    _____
    _____
    _____
    _____
    _____

2. Based on your product usage, explain the changes (improvements) that you would recommend to the soft drink manufacturer.

    _____
    _____
    _____
    _____
    _____
    _____
    _____
    _____
    _____

ANSWERS TO OBJECTIVE QUESTIONS

MATCHING

1.	R	4.	Q	7.	I	10.	C	13. T
2.	J	5.	G	8.	F	11.	B	14. H
3.	L	6.	D	9.	K	12.	O	15. A

TRUE OR FALSE

1.	T	5.	T	9.	T	13.	F	17. F
2.	T	6.	F	10.	F	14.	F	18. T
3.	F	7.	F	11.	T	15.	T	19. T
4.	F	8.	F	12.	T	16.	F	20. T

MULTIPLE CHOICE

1.	d	5.	b	9.	c	13.	a	17. c
2.	c	6.	d	10.	a	14.	b	18. a
3.	a	7.	b	11.	d	15.	d	19. c
4.	b	8.	d	12.	d	16.	c	20. b

CHAPTER 9

THE ELEMENTS OF PRODUCTS AND SERVICES

OBJECTIVE

An organization's product is a bundle of satisfactions providing tangible and intangible benefits to buyers. This market offering is enhanced by auxiliary dimensions such as brand name, package, label, and warranty.

OUTLINE

I. Understanding product concepts

    A. A product is a bundle of satisfactions that includes tangible and intangible benefits--a customer-oriented definition.

    B. The total product consists of a broad spectrum of tangible and intangible benefits that might be gained from a product by a buyer.

    C. Services differ from physical goods in that services are intangible, vary in quality, and cannot be stored nor separated from their producers.

II. Product strategy

    A. A product's auxiliary dimensions (package, label, brand name, warranty, and other things that augment a product) provide supplementary benefits to the buyer.

    B. The product concept is a basic idea which emphasizes a particular set of customer benefits.

    C. Product strategy involves planning and developing the product concept's mix of product attributes.

D. Competition needs to be viewed in terms of product class (groups of items which perform a similar task), product category (product class subset), and product brand (marketer's individual property).

E. Product categories contain major competitors.

III. Classification of consumer goods

A. Consumer products can be classified as convenience goods, shopping goods, and specialty goods.

B. Convenience goods are relatively inexpensive products which are purchased frequently.

   1. Consumers purchase these products at a convenient location with minimal shopping effort.

   2. The marketing mix stresses intensive distribution (product availability at all available locations).

   3. Brand advertising and in-store placement are important marketing activities.

C. Shopping goods are products which involve more extensive decision-making and shopping effort to reduce the perceived risk associated with purchasing the product.

   1. Consumers make product comparisons of price, quality, style, and other auxiliary dimensions.

   2. Selective distribution is practiced by the marketer of shopping goods.

D. Specialty goods are those product brands for which consumers will not accept substitutes.

   1. Consumers are willing to expend considerable shopping effort to locate specialty goods.

   2. The marketing mix emphasizes a limited or exclusive distribution strategy.

   3. Strong brand loyalty exists.

IV. Industrial products

A. The demand for industrial products is derived from the demand for consumer products.

B. One classification of industrial products is given in Exhibit 9-1.

EXHIBIT 9-1

Classification of Industrial Products

Product	Description
Raw materials	Ingredients of the final product that must undergo processing.
Component parts and fabricated materials	Manufactured items incorporated into the final assembled product.
Process materials	Goods used in the production of a product but which do not become part of the finished product.
Installations	Primary production equipment and major capital items.
Accessory equipment	Accessory equipment that facilitates operations.
Operating supplies	Short-lived items that facilitate routine operations.
Services	Work provided by others.

V. The product line and the product mix

A. A group of closely related products comprise a firm's product line.

1. Bases of classification include product class, function performed, target market, channel outlets, price, and quality.

2. Organizational resources and marketer's goals are used to distinguish between product lines.

B. Product mix refers to all of the products offered by an organization.

VI. Branding

   A. Branding identifies and distinguishes an organization's products from competing products.

      1. A brand name is the verbal part of a brand.

      2. A brand mark is a unique identification symbol.

      3. A trademark is a legally protected brand name or brand mark.

   B. Generic brand names, which refer to a product class, cannot be registered.

   C. A good brand name is distinctive, yet easy to remember and easy to pronounce, and communicates product attributes.

   D. There are manufacturer (national) brands and distributor (private) brands.

   E. A generic product carries neither a distributor's brand name nor a manufacturer's brand name.

   F. Firms may use a strategy of brand extension.

      1. Family branding involves using the same brand name for all items in a product line.

      2. Licensing extends a brand name to products of another man- ufacturer.

      3. A strategy of individual brands (unique brand name for each item within a product line) is appropriate if products differ, more shelf space is desired, or more brands enhance target marketing.

   G. Brand image refers to the symbolic value associated with a brand.

   H. Environmental influences may necessitate changing a brand's name.

VII. Packaging

   A. Packaging is an extension of the product offered for sale.

B. Packaging performs the functions of protection, storage, convenience of use, identification, and promotion.

C. Labels carry the brand name and product information such as product content and instructions.

D. Packages must conform to legal requirements and guidelines.

VIII. Product warranties

A. A product warranty provides a written guarantee, in simple language, of a product's integrity and the manufacturer's responsibility for repairing or replacing defective parts.

B. Warranties suggest product quality.

IX. Legal concerns

A. Federal legislation impacts on product planning.

B. Exhibit 9-4, page 257, in the Zikmund and d'Amico textbook, highlights laws which require certain product quality, safety standards, and other product-related legislation.

SUMMARY

Learning Objective One: To discuss the topic "product" as that term is broadly defined.

Organizations offer products (goods, services, or ideas) to their target markets. Each product should be viewed as providing a bundle of satisfactions that includes tangible and intangible benefits to these target customers. Thus, a broad view of the product includes many intangible aspects that may be as important to the buyer as the physical product itself. These intangible aspects provide buyer satisfaction.

Learning Objective Two: To be familiar with the concept of the total product and its importance to effective marketing.

The many aspects and benefits of a product result in buyers receiving different bundles of satisfactions. Consequently, marketers refer to the total product as the totality of attributes (tangible and intangible benefits) connected with a product. This total product view enables effective marketers to segment markets according to benefits received and then provide buyers different benefits by adjusting the total product to fit their needs. More effective means of communicating and dealing with customers result.

<u>Learning Objective Three</u>: To be able to categorize various products as being convenience, shopping, or specialty goods.

Convenience goods are usually inexpensive products which are purchased at a convenient location with minimal shopping effort. These frequently purchased items involve little decision-making. In contrast to convenience goods, shopping goods involve more extensive consumer decision-making and shopping effort. Consumers make comparisons of price, quality, and other auxiliary dimensions prior to the purchase decision. Specialty goods are those items for which consumers will not accept substitutes. Consumers develop brand loyalty and will expend considerable shopping effort to obtain speciality goods.

<u>Learning Objective Four</u>: To show how many marketing activities help to build brand image.

As chapter 8 indicated, brand image results from one's perception of reality. All marketing activities contribute to the building of symbolic meanings associated with a product. For example, brand names can associate the product with an image or communicate product attributes (and associated symbolic meanings) better than other marketing activities. Auxiliary dimensions of a product may convey symbolic meanings. Promotional strategy contributes to building brand image while other symbolic meanings reflect price and distribution decisions.

<u>Learning Objective Five</u>: To discuss the development of effective brand names and the occasional need to change brand names.

An effective brand name communicates the product's attributes, is memorable, and easy to pronounce, yet distinctive and transferable to other cultures. The development of an effective brand name involves specifying criteria for the brand name, such as being distinctive and transferable to other markets. Given these criteria, brand name alternatives are generated and screened for criteria appropriateness. The alternatives which receive a favorable screening are then researched for market acceptability and trademark infringement. These consumer and legal research findings are used to select the brand name from the list of screened alternatives. The organization then communicates the brand name to target market(s).

The need to change a brand name exists when the effectiveness of a brand name decreases. Factors which may cause a brand name to be inappropriate include (1) market environment changes, (2) inadequate name selection initially, (3) pronunciation-related problems, (4) corporate mergers or diversification, (5) international market expansion, and (6) inadequate reflection of organizational purpose.

Learning Objective Six: To understand such terminology as brand, brand name, brand mark, and trademark.

A brand is a name, term, symbol, sign, or design that distinguishes one product from competitive products. A brand name is the verbal part of the brand whereas a brand mark refers to a brand's unique symbols. A trademark provides legal protection of a brand name and/or brand mark.

Learning Objective Seven: To discuss the importance of packaging in the development of an effective product.

Packaging is an extension of a product by performing protection, storage, identification, and promotion functions. Packaging should be consumer-oriented by providing conveniences that makes handling, storage, closure, and disposal easy. Such conveniences enhance the total product by providing consumer benefits. Beyond this, a competitive advantage may result from a package which makes a product unique. Furthermore, packages contribute to brand image by conveying symbolic meanings to consumers.

VOCABULARY BUILDING

Matching Exercise

Match the following by placing the letter of the concept or term on the blank preceding the phrase which best describes the concept or term. You should use a term or concept only once.

A. Product concept
B. Total product
C. Product strategy
D. Product class
E. Product category
F. Brand
G. Industrial goods
H. Raw materials
I. Component parts
J. Installations

K. Accessory equipment
L. Brand name
M. Brand mark
N. Logo
O. Manufacturer brands
P. Distributor brands
Q. Brand extension
R. Family branding
S. Label
T. Product warranty

_L_ 1. Verbal part of a brand.

_Q_ 2. The strategy of using an existing brand name for a new product.

_R_ 3. Strategy of naming all items in a product line with the same single brand name.

_C_ 4. Planning and developing the product attributes mix.

159

_I_ 5. Manufactured items incorporated into the final assembled product.

_N_ 6. Distinctive writing of a brand name or company name.

_S_ 7. Paper or plasticized sticker attached to a package or product.

_m_ 8. Identifies and distinguishes one marketer's product from competitive products.

_G_ 9. The name for an industrial product which is equipment that facilitates operations.

_T_ 10. Written guarantee of a product's integrity and the manufacturer's responsibility for repairing or replacing defective parts.

_A_ 11. Basic idea behind a product.

_B_ 12. Broad range of tangible and intangible benefits that a buyer might gain from a product.

_D_ 13. A phrase that is used to identify groups of items that may differ from each other while performing the same or similar task.

_P_ 14. A brand name owned by a wholesaler or retailer.

_H_ 15. Ingredients of the final product that must undergo processing.

VOCABULARY BUILDING

Programmed Learning Exercise

1. Products provide _____ and _____ benefits to consumers.
   [tangible, intangible]

2. The product _____ refers to the strategist's selecting and blending of a product's primary characteristics and auxiliary dimensions into a basic idea emphasizing a particular set of consumer benefits.
   [concept]

3. Marketers use product _____, product _____, and product _____ to help determine who is the competition.
   [class, category, brand]

4. Product _____ contain the major competitors because they reflect specific consumer wants, needs, and desires.
   [categories]

5. Consumer goods may be classified as _____, _____, and _____ goods.

[convenience, shopping, specialty]

6. _____ goods are relatively inexpensive and purchased on a regular and recurring bases.

[Convenience]

7. The distribution strategy for shopping goods is one of _____ distribution.

[selective]

8. Buildings, computer hardware, and assembly line equipment are examples of _____.

[installations]

9. The category of industrial goods closest to a convenience goods are _____ _____.

[operating supplies]

10. The firm's _____ _____ is a group of products that are closely related to one another in some way such as performing similar functions or being marketed through the same outlets.

[product line]

11. The _____ _____ encompasses all offerings of an organization.

[product mix]

12. Branding helps buyers determine which manufacturer's products to _____ and which to _____.

[seek, avoid]

13. The _____ Act declares that brand names cannot be confusingly similar nor used for the same purpose as registered trademarks.

[Lanham]

14. _____ _____ provide the same function for services that trademarks provide for products.

[Service marks]

15. Products that carry neither a manufacturer's brand nor a distributor's brand are referred to as _____ products or _____ brands.

[generic, generic]

16. The symbolic value associated with a brand is referred to as _____ _____.

[brand image]

17. _____ packaging requires no refrigeration.

[Aseptic]

18. The array of black bars readable by optical scanners on packages is referred to as a(n) _____ _____ _____.

[Universal Product Code]

19. The warranty communicates a message that suggests product _____.

[quality]

20. The _____ Act requires mandatory and accurate labeling of kitchen and bathroom products concerning content and weight.

[Fair Packaging and Labeling]

TRUE OR FALSE STATEMENTS

T F 1. A product is a bundle of satisfactions.

T F 2. Total product refers to the basic idea behind a product.

T F 3. Product classes are subsets of product types contained within a product category.

T F 4. Convenience goods are those goods purchased with minimal shopping effort at convenient locations.

T F 5. In store placement is more important for shopping goods than for convenience goods.

T F 6. Shopper conveniences such as location, retail sales assistance, and credit are used to classify goods as convenience goods.

T F 7. Buyers make comparisons of price and auxiliary dimensions for shopping products.

T F 8. For specialty products, a marketer can expect to encounter consumers with strong brand loyalty who will accept no substitutes.

T F 9. The demand for consumer products is derived from the demand for industrial products.

T F 10. Operating supplies are incorporated into the final product.

T F 11. Installations and accessory equipment are primary production equipment.

162

T F   12.   Toothpaste is a product line for Procter and Gamble.

T F   13.   Branding provides benefits to buyers and sellers.

T F   14.   A registered trademark protects brand names and brand marks.

T F   15.   Generic brands describe a product or item that is part of our standard vocabulary.

T F   16.   Since manufacturer brands are called national brands, distributor brands cannot have national distribution.

T F   17.   Distributor brands are intended to build loyalty for a retailer or wholesaler and thus provide a higher margin.

T F   18.   Brand names which are inappropriate for the market environment can be the cause of market failure of an otherwise acceptable product.

T F   19.   A label can be a package.

T F   20.   The Federal Food, Drugs, and Cosmetics Act (1938) gives the FTC additional authority over packaging, misbranding, and labeling.

MULTIPLE CHOICE QUESTIONS

1.   The total product concept refers to the
     a.   physical product plus auxiliary dimensions.
     b.   tangible benefits that a consumer derives from a product.
     c.   tangible and intangible benefits that a consumer derives from a product.
     d.   product concept.

2.   Which statement does not help distinguish between services and goods?
     a.   Goods are tangible while services are intangible.
     b.   Goods vary more in quality than services do.
     c.   Goods can be stored whereas services disappear quickly.
     d.   Goods are separable from their providers while services are not separable from providers.

3.   Which one is not an auxiliary dimension of a product?
     a.   Image.   c.   Brand name.
     b.   Warranty.   d.   Repair service.

163

4. A person wishing to purchase a book may select either a mystery, western, biography, or science fiction. This decision relates to product
   a. competition.
   b. class.
   c. category.
   d. brand.

5. Which statement is <u>incorrect</u> regarding Copeland's classification of goods scheme?
   a. Classifications are based on reasons for buying.
   b. Shopping effort affects the classification.
   c. Classifications are generalized.
   d. Copeland's system is used to classify both industrial goods and consumer goods.

6. A comparison of convenience, shopping, and specialty goods will reveal that
   a. convenience goods are purchased based on conveniences such as credit and delivery.
   b. high perceived risks are associated with shopping goods.
   c. price and quality comparisons are important for specialty products.
   d. convenience goods involve considerable shopping effort.

7. Which best illustrates a specialty product?
   a. <u>Journal of Marketing</u>.
   b. Sugar.
   c. Furniture.
   d. Sheets.

8. The concept that the demand for an industrial product depends on the demand for another product is
   a. generated demand.
   b. complementary demand.
   c. derived demand.
   d. double demand.

9. Which is <u>not</u> a classification of industrial goods?
   a. Installations.
   b. Operating supplies.
   c. Services.
   d. Specialty supplies.

10. Industrial goods that are consumed in the manufacturing process but are not part of the final product are
    a. raw materials.
    b. component parts.
    c. fabricated materials.
    d. process materials.

11. Sears' hammers, screwdrivers, and other tools comprise a product
    a. line.
    b. mix.
    c. brand.
    d. class.

12. Which is incorrect regarding an organization's product mix?
    a. Product mix encompasses all offerings of an organization.
    b. Larger organizations have more varied product mixes.
    c. An organization may have a varied, but unrelated, product mix.
    d. Product mix identifies an organization's entire group of products.

13. Product identification is provided by
    a. promotion.   c. branding.
    b. labeling.   d. packaging.

14. Which statement concerning a trademark is incorrect?
    a. A trademark is a legally protected brand name.
    b. A trademark cannot become a generic name.
    c. A trademark grants exclusive right to its use.
    d. Contrary to the question, all statements are correct.

15. A good brand name should have each attribute except
    a. be easy to pronounce.   c. have a mnemonic quality.
    b. be easy to remember.   d. be generic.

16. Brand names owned and advertised by retailers are
    a. individual brands.   c. family brands.
    b. national brands.   d. private brands.

17. An advantage of manufacturer brands compared to distributor brands is
    that manufacturer brands are intended to
    a. create loyalty toward manufacturer's product.
    b. support distributor brands.
    c. have higher margins.
    d. have consistently better quality.

18. Which is not a reason for an organization to use an individual brand
    name strategy?
    a. This strategy enables an organization to appeal to several target
       markets.
    b. This strategy is best for products that are similar.
    c. This strategy minimizes damages to a company's reputation if a prod-
       uct has poor quality.
    d. This strategy, at times, increases a company's share of shelf space.

19. Packaging does not perform the function of product
    a. price setting.   c. promotion.
    b. protection.   d. storage.

20. Each of these federal laws impacts on product planning except the
    a. Consumer Protection Act.   c. Fair Packaging and Labeling Act.
    b. Webb-Pomerene Act.   d. Consumer Credit Protection Act.

QUICK QUIZ

1Q.
Why do some marketers produce so many versions of the same product?

1A.
Because they are competing in many product categories. In the case of Lysol, the spray is a "different" product from the bottled liquid. It provides convenience in use and a portability that the other does not. It can, for example, more easily be taken on trips and used to disinfect a motel shower. Note that the differences between the products can also be psychological. Many users of bottled Lysol believe that there is just no substitute for getting out a mop and swabbing the bathroom floor with good old Lysol.

2Q.
Are there any words and names which cannot be trademarks?

2A.
Obscene or offensive names cannot be registered. Neither can seditious names like "Kill the Mayor Bullets." Generic terms may not be registered either, thus anticipating clever fellows who might seek to gain exclusive rights to words like "meat," "water," or "food."

3Q.
Are there brand names in use that seem to be "mistakes"?

3A.
Yes. For example, in Ohio there is a small chain of stores that sells merchandise obtained cheaply due to firms going out of business and similar difficulties. The shops are called "The Surplus Junk Stores." The problem is the goods sold are not junk, so

Prefers wine   _____   _____
Non-professional occupation   _____   _____
Likes inside activities   _____   _____
Sophisticated individual   _____   _____
Heavy smoker   _____   _____

Assignment

1. Check the cigarette brand (Marlboro or Virginia Slims) most appropriate for each buyer characteristic.

2. Explain what the above suggests about each brand.

   a. Marlboro: _____

   _____

   _____

   _____

   b. Virginia Slims: _____

   _____

   _____

   _____

3. Explain what this suggests about brands in general.

   _____

   _____

   _____

   _____

   _____

ANSWERS TO OBJECTIVE QUESTIONS

MATCHING

1. L	4. C	7. S	10. T	13. D
2. Q	5. I	8. F	11. A	14. P
3. R	6. N	9. K	12. B	15. H

TRUE OR FALSE

1. T	5. F	9. F	13. T	17. T
2. F	6. F	10. F	14. T	18. T
3. F	7. T	11. F	15. F	19. T
4. T	8. T	12. T	16. F	20. T

MULTIPLE CHOICE

1. c	5. d	9. d	13. c	17. a
2. b	6. b	10. d	14. b	18. b
3. a	7. a	11. a	15. d	19. a
4. c	8. c	12. b	16. d	20. b

CHAPTER 10

THE PRODUCT LIFE CYCLE AND RELATED STRATEGIES

OBJECTIVE

The product life cycle and the product portfolio are two important planning aids for effective marketing managers. The product life cycle presents general guidelines for the selection of an effective marketing strategy; whereas, the product portfolio concept reminds marketers of the need to consider cash flows and the interrelationships between different types of products within a product mix.

OUTLINE

I. The product life cycle

    A. The product life cycle (PLC) depicts graphically a product's sales volume from inception to market withdrawal.

        1. PLC is a planning tool for marketing management.

        2. PLC reflects the life of a product class or product category, but marketing managers also use PLC to evaluate product brands.

        3. Introduction, growth, maturity, and decline are the PLC stages.

    B. The PLC illustrates a general sales pattern.

        1. Sales start slowly during the introduction stage.

        2. The growth stage is a period of rapid growth.

        3. Sales are relatively level during the maturity stage.

        4. The decline stage is noted for decreasing sales and product withdrawal from the market.

171

C. Industry profits also follow a general pattern over the PLC.

    1. Losses are sustained prior to and during the introduction stage due to investments in product development and low market acceptance.

    2. Industry profits grow rapidly to a peak during the growth stage.

    3. Industry profits continue to fall during the maturity and decline stages.

D. All products follow a product life cycle, though the pattern may differ from the classical PLC pattern described above.

II. The product life cycle as a planning tool

A. Though useful as a planning tool, the PLC influences marketing strategy by emphasizing that environmental conditions change and marketers must understand these changes to adjust their product offerings effectively.

B. Strategies during the introductory stage are designed to get target market customers and channel organizations to accept the product.

C. Being cognizant of competitors entering the market, marketing managers develop strategies to increase market penetration and brand preferences.

D. Strategies to check competitive inroads and to defend a brand's position are implemented during the intensely competitive maturity stage of the PLC.

E. Marketing managers design strategies to milk the brand of all possible benefits before market withdrawal of the product brand.

F. Occasionally, changes in environmental conditions or marketing strategy may reverse the decline of a product.

G. The key to using the PLC concept is understanding the causes of the cycles, shifts, and fluctuations in marketing's environment, so that their implications can be considered for an organization's product.

H. Marketing strategy changes through the product life cycle.

1. Typical adjustments of marketing mix activities as a product moves through the life cycle stages are noted in Exhibit 10-4 in the Zikmund and d'Amico textbook.

2. Marketing strategy formulation should always consider the PLC.

3. Some products are developed intentionally to have a short life cycle.

III. Basic product/market strategies

A. The two major market-related strategies for existing products are market penetration and market development.

 1. Market penetration strategies are designed to increase usage among existing customers in existing markets.

 2. Strategies to attract new customers to existing products are called market development strategies.

B. Product development and product diversification are major market-related strategies for new products.

 1. Marketing innovative products to existing target markets is the market-related strategy of product development.

 2. Product diversification is the strategy of marketing new products to new target markets.

C. Product-related strategies are integrated with the four major market-related strategies.

 1. Product modification, including technological product improvements, is the foundation for the extension of the product life cycle strategy.

 2. A product differentiation strategy makes buyers aware of some tangible or intangible aspect of a product that distinguishes it from competitive products.

 3. An effective product-related strategy involves product quality adjustments which take into consideration the quality creep phenomenon and the "weakest link" concept.

IV. Matching products to markets: product line strategy

    A. Product line strategy involves matching an organization's resources assigned to each product to specific target market needs.

        1. Strategic options regarding depth of product line include a full-line, a limited-line, or a single product strategy.

        2. The advantages and disadvantages of full-line versus limited-line strategies are provided in Exhibit 10-6 in the Zikmund and d'Amico textbook.

    B. Product line extension can involve a strategy of flanker brands as well as result in cannibalized sales.

    C. Systematic product elimination efforts can increase profitability.

V. The product portfolio

    A. The product portfolio concept reminds marketing managers to consider cash flows and the interrelationships among different types of products within a product mix.

    B. The simplest product portfolio model classifies products according to relative market share (high or low) and market growth rate (high or low).

        1. Products which dominant (high market share) a low growth market are referred to as cash cows as these products generate positive cash flows to be utilized elsewhere.

        2. Products that dominant a high growth market are stars; whereas, a product with a low market share in a high growth market is classified as a problem child.

        3. Products with a low market share in a low growth market are known as dogs.

    B. The four types of products found in a product portfolio are interrelated through their generation and use of cash flows.

    C. The product portfolio concept has two major limitations.

        1. An unjustified feeling of security may result by classifying a product; however, no strategy is prescribed by the classification.

2. The portfolio concept addresses the marketing environment superficially.

D. The basic product portfolio model can be varied by the marketing manager to be more useful in the decision-making process.

SUMMARY

Learning Objective One: To be familiar with a powerful marketing tool, the product life cycle.

The product life cycle (PLC) portrays graphically a product's sales history from its market inception to its market withdrawal. Based on industry sales volume, the distinct PLC stages of introduction, growth, maturity, and decline can be identified. These stages reflect changes in marketing's environment which marketing managers must understand to adjust their product strategy effectively. In essence, the PLC provides a basis for developing effective marketing strategies.

Learning Objective Two: To understand the role of managing and lengthening the product life cycle.

Effective management of the product life cycle (PLC) necessitates that marketing managers understand that the PLC reflects changes occurring in the marketplace. Effective managing involves first developing strategies to introduce the product successfully into the market. After a successful product introduction, the next task is to achieve product brand recognition and/or preference while bringing the product to the maturity stage. At this time, a marketer's responsibility is to develop strategies to keep the product brand in the maturity stage. Product strategies such as product modifications and product line extensions are designed to lengthen the PLC. Product improvements and, at times, totally new products are developed to protect the demise of an organization's market offering. Effective management requires sufficient product research, acceptable price, proper communication with target markets, and appropriate distribution.

Learning Objective Three: To discuss characteristics of the various stages of the product life cycle and what they suggest to marketing managers.

Low sales volume, high marketing and production costs, and negligible profits characterize the introduction stage of the product life cycle (PLC). Basic strategy is designed to obtain target market and channel acceptance. The marketing mix tends to stress high prices, selective distribution, and heavy consumer and trade promotion. Consumer advertising and sales promotion efforts are designed to create product awareness and interest among early adopters while trade promotion efforts are intended to obtain channel acceptance and cooperation.

Industry sales volume grows rapidly while industry profits peak during the PLC's growth stage. Heavy consumer demand keeps prices high. The overall marketing mix strategy is designed to achieve market penetration by persuading target market members to prefer the product brand. A strategy of intensive distribution is pursued since demand is high and dealers desire to stock the product. Advertising is used to create awareness of the brand's benefits.

The PLC's maturity stage has level industry sales volume, decreasing industry profits, and intense competition among many competitors. Consequently, marketers design strategies to maintain or increase their brand's market position. These strategies evolve around competitive prices, intensive distribution, heavy trade allowances and consumer sales promotion, and product differentiation advertising. Some organizations produce private brands to increase their market share.

The decline in industry sales and profits make the market unattractive to many competitors. These conditions result in strategies designed to milk the brand of all benefits before its withdrawal from the marketplace. As a result, the product line is simplified and distribution channels are phased out. Advertising strategy emphasizes prices to decrease inventory levels. Minimal sales promotion activities are employed.

Learning Objective Four: To understand the purpose of the product portfolio.

The product portfolio suggests that marketing managers need to focus on the interrelationships among different types of products within a product mix. Managers should manage cash flows for the complete product mix rather than concentrating exclusively on strategies for isolated products. The type of product (cash cow, problem child, star, or dog) will influence the marketing strategy as well as the commitment of resources.

Learning Objective Five: To show how the interrelationships among products suggested by the product portfolio are useful to marketing management.

The interrelationships among products suggested by the product portfolio should enable managers to allocate resources more effectively. For example, cash generated by cash cows can be invested in the development of more stars--either new products or conversion of a problem child into a star. Dogs are maintained as long as benefits accrue to the organization. Dogs require less marketing support and consequently can be good cash generators. Stars need to be supported so that they can become future cash cows.

Finally, these product interrelationships remind managers of the need to develop a balanced product portfolio to enhance the organization's viability in the marketplace.

Learning Objective Six: To be able to describe product- and market-related strategies used by effective marketers to support their market offerings.

Four major market-related strategies are market penetration, market development, product development, and product diversification. These strategies are categorized on the basis of existing or new markets and existing or new products as noted in Exhibit 10-1 below.

EXHIBIT 10-1. Classification of Market-Related Strategies

MARKET	PRODUCT	
	EXISTING	NEW
Existing	Market Penetration	Market Development
New	Product Development	Product Diversification

Market penetration strategies are designed to increase the usage of existing products in existing markets. These strategies rely heavily on the marketing mix variables of promotion, price, and distribution to achieve this increase usage. A market development strategy consists of finding new customers for existing products. New markets can be readied through the expansion of channels or changes in promotion or in price strategies. A strategy of product development involves offering new products to existing customers with no major changes in the promotion, price, and distribution strategies. Product diversification involves marketing new products to new customers. These products may be developed internally or be acquired externally.

177

Basic product-related strategies are an extension of the product life cycle, product differention, and product quality strategies. The extension strategy involves modifying the basic product by incorporating technological improvements to satisfy the needs of target customers better. Product differentiation is a strategy of making buyers aware of tangible or intangible aspects of a product which provide a differential advantage relative to competitive products. Product quality is improved over a product's life through design changes and improvements in technology. Marketers should consider the quality creep phenomenon and the weakest link concept in the development of products.

Learning Objective Seven: To discuss the overall marketing problem of matching products to markets and to show how effective marketers weigh and counterweigh the economic realities of this problem.

Failure to match the product to the demands and needs of the buyer often results in the product not gaining market acceptance. An inadequate match exists if the product line is too narrow to satisfy the needs of the market or if the product line is so diverse the organization has insufficient resources to serve the different customers. In either case, marketers need to realign the product line and resources assigned to each product to meet the demands of selected target markets. Product line realignment and resource allocation involve decisions regarding product line extension and product elimination.

VOCABULARY BUILDING

Matching Exercise

Match the following by placing the letter of the concept or term on the blank preceding the phrase which best describes the concept or term. You should use a term or concept only once.

A.	Product life cycle	K.	Quality creep
B.	Introduction stage	L.	Weakest link concept
C.	Growth stage	M.	Product line
D.	Maturity stage	N.	Full-line strategy
E.	Decline stage	O.	Limited-line strategy
F.	Market penetration	P.	Single product strategy
G.	Market development	Q.	Flanker brands
H.	Product development	R.	Cannibalization
I.	Product diversification	S.	Product portfolio concept
J.	Product differentiation		

_____ 1. A marketing strategy which attempts to draw new customers to existing products.

_____ 2. A phenomenon that often occurs in the development of a product where improvements gradually remove the product from the desired target market.

_____ 3. The strategy of offering a large number of variations of a product.

_____ 4. Product life cycle stage with an overall strategy of market penetration and development of brand preference.

_____ 5. A marketing management tool that focuses on the interrelationships between differing types of products within a product mix.

_____ 6. The strategy of marketing new products to a new set of customers.

_____ 7. A term referring to the part of a product that will be the first to wear out.

_____ 8. A term referring to the introduction of a new product and the subsequent reduction in sales of other products in the product line.

_____ 9. A marketing management tool providing a graphical depiction of a product's sales history from inception to withdrawal from the market.

_____ 10. Product life cycle stage with an overall strategy of defending brand position.

_____ 11. The strategy of offering a smaller number of product variations.

_____ 12. The strategy of calling the attention of buyers to aspects of a product which sets it apart from its competitors.

_____ 13. Number of closely related product items.

_____ 14. A marketing strategy describing the growth of an established product by increasing the usage of existing customers in existing markets.

_____ 15. The marketing strategy referring to the introduction of innovative products to existing markets.

VOCABULARY BUILDING

Programmed Learning Exercise

1. Two major product planning tools are the _____ _____ _____ and the _____ _____.

   [product life cycle, product portfolio]

2. _____ _____ is the planning and developing of the mix of product attributes.

   [Product strategy]

3. Product life cycles are, in effect, _____ _____ curves.

   [sales volume]

4. The four stages in a product's life cycle are _____, _____, _____, and _____.

   [introduction, growth, maturity, decline]

5. Industry profits peak during the _____ stage.

   [growth]

6. When a product does not become popular, analysts find that the reasons parallel the hallmarks of _____ marketing.

   [ineffective]

7. The marketing mix to gain market acceptance during the introductory stage of the product life is focused on finding buyers and creating _____ _____ _____.

   [channels of distribution]

8. The _____ stage of the product life cycle is one of falling sales and profits on an industry-wide basis.

   [decline]

9. _____ _____ refers to marketing innovative products to existing markets.

   [Product development]

10. A product with a _____ _____ sets itself apart from competitive products.

    [differential advantage]

11. Marketers must _____ products to markets.

    [match]

180

12. A full product line matches product _____ with specific customer needs.

[attributes]

13. The _____ _____ strategy involves offering one product or one product with very few model options.

[single product]

14. _____ brands are products similar to existing items in a product line and are placed besides one another on grocery shelves.

[Flanker]

15. Marketers need to devote _____ attention to the elimination of no-longer-profitable products.

[systematic]

16. _____ are products with a high market share in a high growth industry.

[Stars]

17. A _____ _____ is a low market share product in a high growth market.

[problem child]

18. _____ _____ are products with a high market share in a low growth market.

[Cash cows]

19. Products with a low market share in a low growth market are called _____.

[dogs]

20. The product portfolio concepts suggests that managers should manage _____ _____ for complete mixes of products rather than concentrating exclusively on strategies for individual items.

[cash flows]

TRUE OR FALSE STATEMENTS

T F 1. Product life cycle and product portfolio are strategies.

T F 2. Product life cycle reflects the life of a product class or product category.

T F 3. Product life cycle cannot be used to evaluate a product brand.

T F 4. Sales increase at a decreasing rate during the growth stage.

T F 5. Marketing managers should be concerned with understanding changes in competitive conditions that occur at each stage of the product life cycle.

T F 6. Most products pass through product life cycle stages at the same speed.

T F 7. The only way an organization can increase market share during the growth stage of the product life cycle is to take market share away from competitors.

T F 8. Private brands are more apt to emerge during the mature stage of the product life cycle.

T F 9. Marketing efforts should cease once sales begin to drop during the decline stage.

T F 10. The various marketing mix elements remain more or less constant during a product's life cycle.

T F 11. Organizations offer new and improved versions of the product during the maturity stage of the product cycle.

T F 12. Market development is a market-related strategy for new products.

T F 13. An example of market development is a fast food chain opening an outlet in a different city.

T F 14. Increased usage may be a product life cycle extension strategy.

T F 15. Product differentiation may be accomplished by promoting one or more intangible attributes.

T F 16. Product elimination efforts should be directed toward all products comprising an organization's product mix.

T F 17. The product portfolio concept stresses profits for a complete mix of products.

T F 18. Products classified as dogs can be attractive to individual firms.

T F 19. One limitation of the product portfolio concept is that it only begins to address the reality of the marketplace.

T F 20. Proper use of the portfolio concept can replace managerial judgment.

MULTIPLE CHOICE QUESTIONS

1. The product life cycle is described in terms of
   a. sales volume and profits.
   b. sales volume and time.
   c. profits and time.
   d. sales volume and competition.

2. Industry sales of a product peak during the _____ stage of the product life cycle.
   a. introduction
   b. growth
   c. maturity
   d. decline

3. A reason for small profit margins as a product enters the growth stage is that
   a. economies of scale have not been achieved.
   b. sales volume and expenses are high.
   c. products are priced low to attract buyers.
   d. sales volume and sales revenue are low relative to expenses associated with developing the product and the marketing mix to introduce the product.

4. Which statement is incorrect regarding a product in the decline stage of the product life cycle?
   a. Industry sales and profits are declining.
   b. Firms compete within an ever-smaller market.
   c. Individual firms can enjoy high profits for products in the decline stage.
   d. Few firms withdraw from the market.

5. Marketing managers would agree with which statement regarding the product life cycle concept.
   a. The ultimate goal is to bring the product into the maturity stage and to keep it there as long as it makes an acceptable financial return.
   b. Product life cycle has little value as a planning aid.
   c. The product life cycle concept is inappropriate for most products.
   d. Major changes in the product have to be made during the introduction stage.

6. Which implication for marketing activities is <u>incorrect</u> for the growth stage of the product life cycle?
    a. Retail prices are generally high to take advantage of heavy consumer demand.
    b. Advertising strategy stresses brand benefits.
    c. The overall strategy is aimed at defending the brand's position.
    d. Small trade discounts are used.

7. Advertising becomes a vehicle for differentiation among otherwise similar brands during the
    a. introduction stage.   c. maturity stage.
    b. growth stage.   d. decline stage.

8. The overall strategy to persuade early adopters to try the product is advocated for the
    a. introduction stage.   c. maturity stage.
    b. growth stage.   d. decline stage.

9. Which is <u>not</u> a market-related strategy?
    a. Market penetration.   c. Product development.
    b. Market diversification.   d. Product diversification.

10. Which market-related strategy is a fast food operator using when the second sandwich is one-half off regular price?
    a. Market penetration.   c. Product development.
    b. Market diversification.   d. Product diversification.

11. The major emphasis of a product diversification strategy is to
    a. provide loyal customers with less expensive products.
    b. provide existing customers with newer uses of the same product.
    c. attract existing customers with new products.
    d. attract new customers with new products.

12. Which is <u>not</u> a product-related strategy?
    a. Product differentiation.   c. Product quality strategies.
    b. Product development.   d. Extension of product life cycle.

13. Which strategy is State University using when they add an Executive MBA Program to their product mix?
    a. Product differentiation.   c. Product quality strategy.
    b. Product development.   d. Product diversification.

14. Extension of a product's life cycle can be achieved by
    a. offering the product at prices lower than competition.
    b. changing the promotion variables of the marketing mix.
    c. altering the basic product.
    d. offering an innovative product.

15. Which statement regarding product quality strategies is true?
    a. Product design changes may improve product quality.
    b. Quality creep adds quality over time that customers want.
    c. Products should be built around the part which lasts the longest.
    d. Product quality cannot be the basis of a product differentiation strategy.

16. Matching products to markets involves decisions related to
    a. the product portfolio.
    b. product diversification.
    c. product line strategy.
    d. the product life cycle.

17. Which is <u>not</u> an advantage of a full-line strategy?
    a. Transportation costs are higher since more items are shipped from one source.
    b. There are more sales opportunities.
    c. Supplier's image may be enhanced.
    d. A full line may permit coordination of product offerings.

18. The primary contribution of the product portfolio concept is that it
    a. forces managers to treat the firm's various offerings as stocks within a portfolio.
    b. enables managers to classify the product mix into cows, dogs, stars, and problem children.
    c. replaces the product life cycle as a planning aid.
    d. focuses on interrelationships among differing types of products within a product mix.

19. For the Boston Consulting Group's portfolio model, products are classified on the basis of
    a. market share and market growth rate.
    b. market share and cash generated.
    c. market growth rate and market share dominance.
    d. cash generated and market share dominance.

20. The product portfolio concept suggests that managers should
    a. sell off problem-child products.
    b. manage cash flows for complete mixes of products.
    c. move cash cows to star status.
    d. keep only products in a high growth market.

QUICK QUIZ

1Q.
Could there be a product life cycle that has more than one peak?

1A.
Yes. Skate boards first came to great popularity in the early 1960s, then faded from the market. They became popular again in the late 1970s. Thus, skateboards have enjoyed two peak sales periods with sales during the intervening years being very low. However, it should be mentioned that when this phenomenon occurs, the "second" product often differs somewhat from the first. Improved plastic wheels found on skateboards today were not available in the 1960s. Then metal wheels were used. Some would argue, with considerable justification, that the two skateboards are in fact different products.

2Q.
Many products change over time. Today's commercial airline service is quite different from what commercial airline service was in 1953. Is there really a "life cycle" for a product which has had such radically different attributes over the years?

2A.
This problem has been addressed by some marketing scholars. A variation on the PLC, called the PEC for "Product Evolution Concept", has been proposed.* This scheme assumes the constant evolution of products in response to market forces, including government influence and management's creativity. While the evolution concept is perhaps more appealing than the PLC's more rigid stages, the product life cycle remains the better known and more widely employed theory.

*Gerald J. Tellis and C. Merle Crawford (1981), "An Evolutionary Approach to Product Growth

186

2. Identify the best basic product/market strategy for each organization and justify your selection.

ORGANIZATION	BEST BASIC STRATEGY	SELECTION JUSTIFICATION
Men's Clothing Store		
Hybrid Seed Corn Company		
Public City Library		

ANSWERS TO OBJECTIVE QUESTIONS

MATCHING

1.	G	4.	C	7.	L	10.	D	13.	M
2.	K	5.	S	8.	R	11.	O	14.	F
3.	N	6.	I	9.	A	12.	J	15.	H

TRUE OR FALSE

1.	F	5.	T	9.	F	13.	T	17.	F
2.	T	6.	F	10.	F	14.	T	18.	T
3.	F	7.	F	11.	T	15.	T	19.	T
4.	F	8.	T	12.	F	16.	F	20.	F

MULTIPLE CHOICE

1.	b	5.	a	9.	b	13.	b	17.	a
2.	c	6.	c	10.	a	14.	c	18.	d
3.	d	7.	c	11.	d	15.	a	19.	c
4.	d	8.	a	12.	b	16.	c	20.	b

CHAPTER 11

MARKETING NEW PRODUCTS

OBJECTIVE:

The development and introduction of new products to the marketplace require careful planning. Characteristics associated with successful new products are reviewed. An understanding of these characteristics and the new product development process will increase a new product's chances for success. Marketing managers need to consider the diffusion process and the adoption process in the introduction of new products.

OUTLINE

   I.   What is a new product?

        A.   A new product may be a major technological innovation, an addition to a product line, a "me, too" product, or a product that offers new benefits.

        B.   New product is a relative term which is influenced by one's perceptions.

   II. Management's perspective of new products

        A.   Based on the dimensions of newness to market and newness to company, new products may be classified as (1) new-to-the-world products, (2) new product lines, (3) additions to existing product lines, (4) improvements in/revisions to existing products, (5) repositionings, and (6) cost reductions.

        B.   From a company perspective, managers must consider technology, investment, and markets in making new product decisions.

        C.   New product risk to the buyer and to the marketer is a function of perceived newness and similarity to existing products.

D. Three types of innovations exist from a consumer's perspective.

    1. Discontinuous innovations require new consumption patterns as the products are so new that no previous product performed an equivalent function.

    2. A dynamically continuous innovation refers to a product which differs from previous products but does not require major changes in buying and usage patterns.

    3. A continuous innovation is a new product differing by minor changes from previous products.

E. Slim chances of market success exist for any new product idea.

III. The characteristics of success

A. New products that offer buyers a relative advantage over existing, competing products are more likely to be successful.

B. Market acceptance is faster for new products that have compatibility with existing consumption patterns by requiring no major lifestyle changes.

C. A new product's trialability enhances its market acceptance by providing future buyers the opportunity for testing with little risk or effort to them.

D. The observability of a new product's relative advantage influences the product's chances for success in the marketplace.

E. New product complexity decreases the product's chances for success.

IV. New product development

A. Most innovations are the result of research and development efforts of organizations.

B. The length of the new product development process varies.

C. The five general stages in the new product development process are exploration, screening, business analysis, development, and commercialization.

D. The exploration stage involves a continuing search for product ideas that are consistent with target market needs and organizational objectives.

E. The analysis of new product ideas to determine their appropriateness and reasonableness relative to organizational goals is the focus of the screening stage of the new product development process.

F. During the business analysis stage, the new product idea is evaluated in terms of detailed quantitative analysis of sales and market forecasts, costs, and buyer studies.

G. Products are developed during the development stage.

H. Commercialization involves the decision to produce and to market a new product, usually with a major commitment of resources and managerial effort.

I. Reasons for product failure include poor market research, technical problems, poor timing, underestimating competition and the diffusion rate, inadequate knowledge of costs and top management involvement, departing from company's expertise, and assigning inadequate resources to market development.

J. Marketing managers can reduce failures by utilizing their experiences and experiences of others regarding new product introductions.

V. The diffusion process

A. The adoption process refers to the psychological stages (awareness, interest, evaluation, trial, and adoption) that individuals go through in adopting a product.

B. The diffusion process refers to the spread of a new product through society as the product is adopted by various groups of buyers (innovators, early adopters, early majority, late majority, and laggards).

C. The small venturesome group of customers who try the product first is referred to as innovators.

D. Early adopters help to determine the market acceptance of new products through their roles as opinion leaders.

E. The mass market is comprised of the group of customers who are referred to as early and late majorities.

1. Members in the early majority group are of average socio--economic status but slightly more educated and better-off financially than those in the late majority group.

2. Late majority group members tend to be older and more conservative and traditional than those in the early majority.

F. Laggards are the last group to adopt a product.

G. Those individuals who never buy the new product are termed non-adopters.

H. Marketing managers can use the adopter categories to aid market segmentation efforts and the development of marketing plans.

VI. Organization for new product development

A. New product development is enhanced by an appropriate organizational structure.

B. Organization structures include the product manager system, new product manager, the venture team, new products department, new products committee, and the task force.

C. A product manager system has the responsibility for planning and implementing the marketing of a single product, including, at times, developing new products.

D. The new product manager form is more appropriate for companies confronting a market in which marketing issues predominate.

E. The venture team is a group of specialists in various functional areas of an organization who attempt to develop a new business in an entrepreneurial environment.

F. New products departments are headed by a high-ranking organizational official who is assigned the responsibility of developing new products.

G. High-ranking executives comprise a new products committee.

H. The responsibility of a task force form of organization is to ensure that the various departments of an organization provide adequate support and resources to the new project.

VII. Putting it altogether: the development of Kodak's disc camera

   A. Each stage of the product development process was employed in the development of Kodak's disc camera.

   B. A total systems approach was implemented to solve a photographic problem uncovered by marketing research.

SUMMARY

Learning Objective One: To discuss the idea that there are degrees of newness suggested by the term "new product" and to differentiate between these levels of newness.

   The term "new product" is a relative term whether viewed from the perspective of a consumer or of a marketing manager. From a consumer's perspective, newness refers to the changes required in consumers' consumption and usage patterns. New consumption and usage patterns are necessary for discontinuous innovations since no previous product performed an equivalent function. Dynamically continuous innovations are new products which differ from previous products but do not require major buying and usage pattern changes. A continuous innovation is a new product differing by minor alterations from previous products. The degree of newness varies from a breakthrough to a major change to an on-going alteration.

   From management's perspective, product newness can be portrayed in terms of consumer perception of newness and the similarity/dissimilarity to existing products. The relative newness of a product increases as consumer perception of newness increases and the similarity to existing products decreases. As noted in Figure 11-2 in the Zikmund and d'Amico textbook, newness can range from products resulting from a brand proliferation strategy to totally new-to-the world products. Risk increases to consumers and marketing managers as a product's newness increases.

Learning Objective Two: To comment on the chances of success and failure faced by new products in the marketplace, and to explain why these are likely to vary considerably from industry to industry.

   The chances of commercial success for any new product is relatively low. One study indicated that 90 percent of all new products ideas are failures. Booz, Allen, and Hamilton indicated that one new product is generated from 40 new product ideas--a rather low success rate. The success rate increases to 67 percent for new product introductions. Ineffective marketing practices contribute to a high failure rate.

The success rate is lower for the consumer package goods market than the industrial (producer) market. This higher failure rate is attributable, in part, to the dynamic nature of the consumer marketplace and consumers' inability to articulate to marketers exactly what new products will satisfy them. On the other hand, industrial buyers can provide detailed information to manufacturers and suppliers on their needs. However, the organizational marketplace is more limited.

Learning Objective Three: To know and be able to define the general product characteristics associated with successful new products.

The general product characteristics associated with successful new products are relative advantage, compatibility, trialability, observability, and complexity. The characteristic of relative advantage refers to new products that offer buyers clear-cut advantages over existing products. The harmonious match of a new product to existing consumption and lifestyle patterns concerns the compatibility characteristic. Trialability refers to the opportunity for buyers to test the new product with little effort and risk. Observability is the chance for buyers to see the relative advantage, or newness, of the new product while complexity refers to a product's complicacy. A new product's chances for success increase if the product offers an observable relative advantage and provides trialability, compatibility, and minimal complexity.

Learning Objective Four: To explain the stages of new product development and to describe the steps likely to be associated with each.

The new product development process has the general stages of exploration, screening, business analysis, development, and commercialization. The exploration stage involves the continuing search for product ideas that are consistent with the organization's goals. Procedures need to be developed to ensure a steady flow of product ideas from various sources such as employees, customers, and research departments. The screening stage evaluates these product ideas in terms of target market needs, organizational resources, market and sales potential, and profit expectations. New product ideas that survive the screening process are subjected to more detailed quantitative analysis during the business analysis stage. The business analysis stage uses buyer research studies, sales and market forecasts, break-even analysis, and other research efforts to provide a listing of product features, information on resources needed, and a marketing plan. The product concept is developed into a concrete product during the development stage. During this stage, the product is used in test markets, by selected industrial customers, or tested in other ways to determine its market acceptance. Products which pass the development stage successfully enter the commercialization stage. Commercialization refers to an organization's decision to produce and market the new product. Chapter 10 discusses the steps involved in marketing a product.

<u>Learning Objective Five</u>: To be familiar with the new product adoption process and the several groups of adopters to which marketing managers may ultimately have to appeal.

The new product adoption process refers to the psychological stages an individual goes through to be an adopter of the new product. These mental stages are awareness, interest, evaluation, trial, and adoption. Since individuals go through these stages at differing speeds, groups of buyers can be identified. These adopter categories are innovators, early adopters, early and late majorities, and laggards. These groups differ in their initial willingness to try the new product. Those in the earlier adopter groups are more venturesome while those in the later adopter groups are more conservative and traditional. The socio-economic and lifestyle characteristics of the members of the various adopter categories are important in developing marketing plans and market segmentation efforts.

<u>Learning Objective Six</u>: To describe six organizational forms associated with the successful development and introduction of new products and the advantages associated with each.

The product manager system assigns the planning and implementing responsibilities for marketing a single product or brand to one individual. Because product managers are extremely knowledgeable about their markets, product managers are, at times, given the additional responsibility of developing new products for their markets. Their market expertise should enable them to detect market opportunities, to identify product line additions, and to evaluate the success chances of a new product offering.

The new product manager form of organization for product development separates the marketing of an existing product and the developing of a new product. Since a new product manager knows both new product possibilities and the market to be targeted, this organizational structure is appropriate for consumer goods companies confronting a market in which marketing issues predominate.

Specialists from various functional areas within an organization form a venture team. These specialists operate in an entrepreneurial environment to develop a new business. The success of this organizational form in developing successful new products is attributable to its independent role.

A new products department is a permanent department headed by a high-ranking official. Thus, this individual can expedite matters related to product development more easily.

Members of a new products committee are administrators of the organization's functional departments under the chairmanship of the chief executive officer. This organizational form for product development provides support of high-ranking executives behind new products as well as be used in connection with other new product organizational structures.

A task force is a group of individuals in an organization given the responsibility to ensure that the various departments provide adequate support and resources to the new project. Advantages of the task force approach relate to its group composition and its responsibility to provide continued attention until the new project is either dropped or marketed.

VOCABULARY BUILDING

Matching Exercise

Match the following by placing the letter of the concept or term on the blank preceding the phrase which best describes the concept or term. You should use a term or concept only once.

A. New product
B. Continuous innovation
C. Dynamically continuous innovation
D. Discontinuous innovations
E. Relative advantage
F. Trial sampling
G. Divisibility
H. Exploration stage
I. Screening stage
J. Business analysis stage
K. Commercialization

L. Diffusion process
M. Innovators
N. Early adopter
O. Early majority
P. Late majority
Q. Laggards
R. Non-adopters
S. Product manager
T. Venture team
U. New products committee
V. Task force

_C_ 1. A new product that is a great improvement over existing products but does not greatly alter buying and usage patterns.

_H_ 2. New product development stage involving a continuing search for product ideas which are consistent with the organization's objectives.

_M_ 3. The group of consumers who are the first to buy a new product.

_J_ 4. The stage in the development of a new product where detailed quantitative analysis of the product occurs.

15. _____ _____ are conceived of as opinion leaders in the diffusion process of a new product.

[Early adopters]

16. The _____ _____ is a person in an organization responsible for planning and implementing the marketing of a single product.

[product manager]

17. The _____ _____ system of organizing for new product development results in more truly new products than do other systems.

[venture team]

18. The form of organizing for new product development which involves the establishment of a permanent group within an organization headed by a director or vice-president is called _____ _____ _____ .

[new products department]

19. Advantages identified by marketing research need to be translated into _____ the consumer would quickly recognize.

[benefits]

20. _____ _____ are the lifeblood of most organizations.

[New products]

TRUE OR FALSE STATEMENTS

T F 1. From a consumer's perspective, if the bundle of benefits offered by a product differs from the bundle already available, then the product can be said to be new.

T F 2. The Booz, Allen, and Hamilton study indicated that the highest risk products (new product lines and new-to-the-world products) accounted for 30 percent of all introductions and 60 percent of the "most successful" new products.

T F 3. New products that are dynamically continuous innovations are old products with minor changes.

T F 4. Marketers constantly seek to improve products because minor improvements can provide a competitive advantage.

T F 5. The success rate for introduction of new products is higher in the consumer package goods market than in the industrial goods market.

203

T F 6. If a new product lacks one of the characteristics that influence a new product's chances for success in the marketplace, then it is impossible for the product to become a success.

T F 7. A relative advantage can be based on performing the same functions less expensively or faster than existing products.

T F 8. Test marketing is the activity of giving free samples of a new product to potential customers.

T F 9. Advertising testimonials by expert users of a new product can provide product observability.

T F 10. Most new products are a result of accident or luck rather than careful planning.

T F 11. The screening stage is the first stage in the product development process where effort at sorting alternative ideas is undertaken.

T F 12. The business analysis stage of the product development process emphasizes qualitative evaluations rather than quantitative analysis.

T F 13. The basic marketing plan is developed during the initial phase of the commercialization stage.

T F 14. Marketing managers can reduce failures by paying attention to their experiences and the experiences of others.

T F 15. The five stages in the adoption process are awareness, interest, trial, adoption, and post-purchase dissonance.

T F 16. The diffusion process refers to the mental stages an individual goes through in adopting the new product.

T F 17. Innovators are not extremely important in the adoption process as they constitute only $2\frac{1}{2}$ percent of the whole population.

T F 18. Organizations should use only one of the organizational forms for new product development.

T F 19. The brand manager system works better for existing products than new products.

T F 20. The new product manager form of organization for development of products is most likely found in a consumer goods company confronting a market in which marketing issues predominate.

MULTIPLE CHOICE QUESTIONS

1. One way of defining "newness" in a product is to say that a product is new if it offers a benefit to consumers that existing products do not offer. Which statement is correct?
   a. A "new improved" shampoo with "extra brighteners" is not really new.
   b. This definition is consistent with the look-to-the-consumer attitude that is the basis of the marketing concept.
   c. The benefit must be something real, not something psychological.
   d. The benefit must be in the product itself, not derived from the price charged for the product.

2. According to the Booz, Allen, and Hamilton study, different kinds of new products include all <u>except</u>
   a. product elimination.   c. new product lines.
   b. repositionings.   d. improvements in existing products.

3. In making new product decisions, marketing managers must consider the three variables of
   a. technology, engineering, and markets.
   b. investment, technology, and engineering.
   c. markets, investment, and technology.
   d. engineering, markets, and investment.

4. Which statement about new products is true?
   a. New products are always resisted by the marketplace.
   b. New products are based on extensive research and development work.
   c. New products vary from one another with respect to their degrees of newness.
   d. New products take several years to gain popularity once they are introduced to the marketplace.

5. Which definition best explains "continuous innovation?"
   a. A pioneering product so new that no previous product performed an equivalent function.
   b. A product that is a minor improvement over existing products.
   c. A product that requires major changes in consumption patterns.
   d. A product that is a great improvement over existing products but requires only minor changes in consumption patterns.

6. According to a recent study conducted by Booz, Allen and Hamilton, which statement is correct regarding the number of new product ideas that leads to a new product success.
   a. One out of three new product ideas is a success.
   b. One out of forty new product ideas is a success.
   c. One out of fifty new product ideas is a success.
   d. The study made no statement regarding the number of new product ideas necessary to achieve a successful new product.

7. Which statement indicates that the marketer is taking a proper approach to introducing new products?
   a. A retailer says, "These things are the cutest things I've ever seen. They'll sell like crazy. Give me ten cases."
   b. A wholesaler says, "The manufacturer of these things assures me that they will sell, and he's always a good guesser. That's why I loaded up on these items."
   c. An international marketing manager says, "This thing sold like mad in areas of Peru. You can bet the same thing is going to happen when we ship them to New Guinea."
   d. An international marketer says, "These foot-operated pumper sewing machines sold great in the U.S. before there was widespread availability of electricity. Let's do some research to see if they will sell today in rural South America."

8. Which is not a product characteristic that influences a new product's chance for success?
   a. Product differentiation.   c. Complexity.
   b. Observability.   d. Trialability.

9. New industrial products which provide cost reductions over current competing products
   a. are repositioned products.
   b. are cash cows.
   c. have a relative advantage over competing products.
   d. have easy access to the general market.

10. New products which are incompatible with existing consumption and usage patterns are
    a. easily repositioned to be compatible with these patterns.
    b. less likely to be accepted by the market.
    c. adopted readily since traditional consumption and behavior patterns do not need to be changed.
    d. usually flanker brands.

11. When Richardson-Vicks, Inc. introduced Saxon^{tm} lotion for men, small bottles of the lotion were delivered to selected households. This promotional effort was designed to increase the product's
    a. relative advantage.
    c. differentiation.
    b. observability.
    d. trialability.

12. The new product development process includes all stages except
    a. exploration.
    c. commercialization.
    b. market acceptance.
    d. development.

13. Which statement regarding the new product development process is correct?
    a. New products may pass through these stages at varying speeds.
    b. The new product development process takes a long time.
    c. There are six general stages in the process.
    d. The development stage prededes the business analysis stage.

14. The first stage in the new product development process is the
    a. ideation stage.
    c. screening stage.
    b. business analysis.
    d. exploration stage.

15. Which research tool is least likely to be used during the screening stage?
    a. Concept testing.
    b. Discussions with salespersons.
    c. Discussion with knowledgeable consumers.
    d. Detailed market study.

16. Which stage of the new product development process is likely to use sales forecasts, break-even analysis, and buyer research studies?
    a. Exploration.
    c. Business analysis.
    b. Screening.
    d. Development.

17. Which statement is incorrect regarding the "innovators" and "early adopters" groups of consumers in the adoption of new products?
    a. Both groups are more adventurous than other groups.
    b. Both groups comprise the mass market for the product.
    c. Members of both groups have a relatively higher income than members of other groups.
    d. Both groups have many similar characteristics.

18. The group of consumers who influence their friends, neighbors, and co-workers in the adoption of new products are referred to as
    a. innovators.
    c. early majority.
    b. early adopters.
    d. risk takers.

19. Which is <u>not</u> a major form of organization to aid in the development and introduction of new products?
   a. Functional managers.
   b. Product manager system.
   c. New products committee.
   d. Venture team.

20. A major drawback of the task force approach to new product development is that the task force
   a. cuts across organizational boundaries, thus creating political problems within the organization.
   b. lacks team effort and cooperation in developing the new product.
   c. is so diverse that its members have major communication problems.
   d. has difficulty in finding proper members to constitute the group.

QUICK QUIZ

1Q.
Why is it important to know how many new product ideas never reach the marketplace?

1A.
Because marketing managers are thereby taught to generate a sufficient flow of new product ideas to support their growth objectives.

2Q.
Are the members of the innovator, early adopter, and other adopter groups the same for each new product offered to the market?

2A.
The categories are product-specific. That is, the innovator or early adopter of a new form of squash racquet may be a late majority adopter of a new type of automobile tire. However, when they speak of discontinuous innovations, they are often similar, if not exactly the same, in terms of their demographic characteristics. Also, they may include some of the very same individuals who are, for example, early adopters of many different products.

Assignment

1. Estimate the market potential for this product idea (skin tone enhancement for women) using the appendix to Chapter 2 in the Zikmund and d'Amico textbook.

2. Indicate an appropriate marketing strategy to introduce this new product successfully. As noted in Chapter 3 of the Zikmund and d'Amico textbook, a marketing strategy involves selecting a target market and planning a marketing mix strategy.

   Target market(s) selected: _____

   _____

   _____

   _____

   Marketing mix strategy

   a. Objective(s): _____

   _____

   _____

   _____

   _____

b. Product strategy: _____

_____

_____

_____

_____

c. Channel strategy: _____

_____

_____

_____

_____

d. Price strategy: _____

_____

_____

_____

_____

e. Promotion strategy: _____

_____

_____

_____

_____

ANSWERS TO OBJECTIVE QUESTIONS

MATCHING

1.	C	4.	J	7.	B	10.	Q	13.	R
2.	H	5.	T	8.	F	11.	K	14.	U
3.	M	6.	L	9.	V	12.	P	15.	O

TRUE OR FALSE

1.	T	5.	F	9.	T	13.	F	17.	F
2.	T	6.	F	10.	F	14.	T	18.	F
3.	F	7.	T	11.	T	15.	F	19.	T
4.	T	8.	F	12.	F	16.	F	20.	T

MULTIPLE CHOICE

1.	b	5.	b	9.	c	13.	a	17.	b
2.	a	6.	b	10.	b	14.	d	18.	b
3.	c	7.	d	11.	d	15.	d	19.	a
4.	c	8.	a	12.	b	16.	c	20.	d

CHAPTER 12

THE NATURE OF DISTRIBUTION

OBJECTIVE

A channel of distribution bridges the distance between the producer and consumer by providing a means to transfer the product and its title. Channel members share the responsibility for performing marketing functions. Distribution strategy requires determining the structure of the channel and the intensity of distribution.

OUTLINE

I. Distribution delivers a standard of living to society

   A. Distribution involves the related activities of delivering products at a reasonable cost to buyers in the right place at the right time.

   B. Time and place utilities are created by distribution.

   C. Distribution spans the gap between the producer and the final user(s) of a product.

II. Distribution in the marketing mix: a key to success

   A. Distribution is increasingly more important to organizations because of changing environmental conditions.

   B. Distribution may be the basis for an organization's differential advantage over competitors.

   C. Not-for-profit organizations and providers of services also need to make their products available to users at the right place at the right time.

III. Distribution: a cause of failure

    A. Marketing failures can attest to the importance of distribution in effective marketing.

    B. A firm's distribution strategy should be based on target market needs, marketing intermediary considerations, and environmental conditions.

IV. Channel of distribution defined

    A. A channel of distribution consists of a group of interdependent organizations, including producer and consumer, that are aligned to facilitate the flow of the product and the title to the product from producer to consumer.

    B. A different channel of distribution emerges when the form utility of the product changes.

    C. Marketing intermediaries or middlemen are involved in all channels of distribution except the direct channel of manufacturer-to-consumer.

        1. Merchant intermediaries take title to the product.

        2. Agent intermediaries do not take title to the product.

        3. Channel members form a coalition to exploit joint opportunities in the marketplace.

            a. Loosely aligned, relatively autonomous marketing organizations comprise the conventional channel of distribution.

            b. A vertical marketing system is a formally organized system that is owned or administered by a channel member or based on a contractual relationship.

        4. Facilitators, such as transportation companies or financial institutions who assist the flow of product, are not members of the channel of distribution.

V. Marketing functions performed by intermediaries

    A. Who should perform the marketing functions?

        1. Marketing functions can be shifted forward or backward to other intermediaries in the channel of distribution, but these functions cannot be eliminated.

2. Marketing managers should determine channels of distribution according to which intermediaries can perform the marketing functions efficiently and effectively.

B. Physical distribution is a major function performed by a channel of distribution.

   1. Intermediaries or middlemen perform a breaking-bulk or sorting function when they allocate smaller quantities of a homogeneous product to other channel members or to buyers of the product.

   2. An assembler is an intermediary who accumulates quantities of a homogeneous product from small producers and performs the accumulating bulk function.

   3. Intermediaries perform the assorting function when they accumulate assortments of heterogeneous products and make these assortments available to customers.

   4. Middlemen reduce the number of transactions necessary to facilitate and expedite exchanges.

   5. Intermediaries perform transportation and storage functions.

C. The communication function involves exchanging information (promotion and research) and title.

   1. Middlemen provide a selling function for producers.

   2. Intermediaries provide a buying function for other channel members and final users.

D. Intermediaries provide facilitating functions.

   1. Middlemen perform a service function including management services, post-sale repair services, and honoring manufacturers' guarantees.

   2. When channel intermediaries offer some form of credit service, they are performing a credit function.

   3. Middlemen perform a risk-taking function (credit risk, legal risk, and economic risk).

VI. Channels of distribution: a system of interdependency

A. Member interdependency exists within any channel of distribution.

B. Channel interdependency affects channel efficiency and channel success.

VII. Alternative channels of distribution

A. The direct channel from producer to user is more common in the marketing of industrial products than the marketing of consumer products.

B. The manufacturer-retailer-consumer channel emerges when large retailers prefer to deal directly with manufacturers to achieve their goals more efficiently and effectively.

C. The manufacturer-wholesaler-industrial user channel typically involves an industrial distributor wholesaler who functions much like a retailer.

D. The manufacturer-wholesaler-retailer-consumer channel is the most common channel structure for consumer goods.

E. The manufacturer-wholesaler-wholesaler-retailer-consumer channel can involve agents, either on a permanent basis, such as manufacturers' agents or selling agents, or on a temporary basis, such as brokers.

F. Most channels of distribution are variations of the major channels of distribution.

VIII. Are channels of distribution what textbooks say they are?

A. Marketing behavior of channel institutions complicates the determination of a channel.

B. Multiple channel strategy increases channels of distribution complexity.

IX. Vertical marketing systems

A. In a vertical marketing system (VMS), the channel institutions are managed as a centrally administered distribution system to achieve technological, managerial, and promotional economies of scale.

B. A corporate vertical marketing system is based on ownership of adjacent stages (forward and/or backward integration) of the channel of distribution by a channel member--producer or middleman.

C. An administered vertical marketing system requires a dominant channel member to coordinate marketing activities of all channel members to enhance their mutual benefits.

D. The three subtypes of contractual vertical marketing systems are retail cooperative organizations (retailer-sponsored), voluntary chains (wholesaler-sponsored), and franchises.

X. Managing the channel of distribution

A. Determining the structure of the channel of distribution is the first major strategic distribution decision.

1. The marketing mix strategy (product characteristics, pricing strategy, and promotion strategy) influences the length of the channel of distribution.

2. Organizational-related resources which influence the length of the channel include financial resources, existing channels, size of product mix, and intensity of distribution.

3. Two external environmental criteria which influence channel length are consumer preferences and market behavior and the nature and availability of middlemen.

B. The intensity or extent of distribution at each channel level is the second major distribution strategy decision.

1. An intensive distribution strategy seeks to obtain maximum product exposure at the retail level.

2. A strategy of selective distribution restricts the product to a limited number of outlets in a geographical area.

3. When a producer grants a middleman an exclusive area in which to market the product, a strategy of exclusive distribution is being implemented.

XI. Issues concerning the interdependency among channel members

A. Channel conflict exists when the marketing objectives and strategies of vertical channel members are not harmonious, that is, channel cooperation does not exist.

B. A channel leader or channel captain refers to the channel organization which is able to exert its power over other members of the channel.

XII. Reverse distribution

    A. Recycling involves a backward channel of distribution or reverse distribution.

    B. The consumer is the first stage (producer) in a backward channel.

XIII. Political and legal forces in distribution management

    A. Exclusive dealing refers to a restrictive distribution arrangement prohibiting a middleman from selling the products of two competing suppliers and this arrangement is illegal if less competition results due to this agreement.

    B. Exclusive territories are permissible if competition is not restricted and the territorial restrictions and allocations serve a legitimate business purpose.

    C. Tying contracts require a channel intermediary to purchase supplementary product lines to obtain the product desired and are violations of the Clayton Act unless the tying contract can be justified on the basis of an attempt to (1) maintain standards of quality, (2) enter a new market or industry, or (3) preserve market identity.

    D. International marketing increases the legality problems associated with distribution.

SUMMARY

Learning Objective One: To discuss the general purpose of distribution in the marketing mix.

The general purpose of distribution in the marketing system is to provide products in the right place at the right time. Distribution bridges the gap or distance that exists between the producer and the final user(s) of a product through the creation of time and place utilities. Effective distribution, in essence, delivers a standard of living to society.

Learning Objective Two: To understand how distribution contributes to an effective marketing mix.

An effective marketing mix is characterized by the four marketing variables of product, distribution, price, and promotion working together to accomplish the organization's goals. Thus, distribution complements the other marketing mix variables by making the product available at the right time and at the right place. Distribution strategy involves determining the structure of the channel of distribution and the intensity of distribution. The length of the channel structure must complement the product characteristics. For example, perishable products, technical products, or large, bulky, heavy products require a short channel (no or few marketing intermediaries). Or, selection of middlemen (high volume outlets or high margin outlets) must be consistent with an organization's pricing strategy. Finally, channel structure influences the size and type of sales force, advertising, and sales promotion efforts.

Learning Objective Three: To know that all marketers engage in some distribution activities.

Manufacturers, not-for-profit organizations, and providers of services engage in distribution activities to some extent. Manufacturers develop a distribution strategy to bridge the distance between their manufacturing facilities and the final users of their products. This strategy involves decisions regarding channel structure, intensity of distribution, and physical distribution activities. Not-for-profit organizations and providers of services, including accountants, lawyers, and doctors, make decisions regarding location, intensity of distribution or number of outlets, and a traditional or nontraditional distribution strategy.

Learning Objective Four: To describe the major channels of distribution used by consumer goods and industrial goods marketers.

The major channels of distribution in the marketing of consumer products are (1) the direct channel of producer to consumer, (2) the manufacturer-retailer-consumer channel, (3) the manufacturer-wholesaler-retailer-consumer channel, and (4) the manufacturer-wholesaler-wholesaler-retailer-consumer channel. For industrial goods, the major channels include (1) the direct channel of producer or manufacturer to industrial user, (2) the manufacturer-wholesaler- industrial user, and (3) the manufacturer-wholesaler-wholesaler-industrial user. The direct channel is the most common channel in the marketing of industrial products; whereas, the manufacturer-wholesaler-retailer-consumer channel is the most common channel of distribution used by consumer goods marketers. Examples of these channels of distribution are provided in Exhibit 12-4 in the Zikmund and d'Amico textbook. In reviewing these major channels of distribution, two aspects need to be highlighted. First, there are many variations of these major channels of distribution. Second, the retailer is a marketing intermediary unique to the marketing of consumer products.

Learning Objective Five: To be able to name and discuss the functions performed by channel intermediaries.

Channel intermediaries perform physical distribution, communication, and facilitating functions. The physical distribution functions include breaking-bulk, accumulating bulk, creating assortments, reducing transactions,

221

transportation, and storage. The breaking-bulk or sorting function of inter-mediaries involves the allocation of smaller quantities of a homogeneous product to other channel members or buyers of the product. The accumulating bulk function requires an intermediary, called an assembler, to accumulate quan-tities of a homogeneous product from small producers in order to offer larger quantities to buyers who prefer large purchases. The creation of assortments (assorting function) necessitates that an intermediary accumulates an assort-ment of heterogeneous products desired by its customers. Compared to direct channels of distribution, channels utilizing intermediaries reduce the number of transactions necessary to achieve a certain level of exchanges. Transportation involves physically moving the product from its point of production to its point of consumption; whereas, storage refers to holding the product along its route from producer to consumer or final user until the product is consumed.

The communication function within a channel of distribution involves exchanging information and title. Intermediaries perform a selling function for suppliers and a buying function for customers. In the performance of these functions, information is gathered from customers through marketing research or a marketing intelligence system and disseminated to customers through promotion efforts and the title is transferred to buyers.

The facilitating functions of intermediaries are service, credit, and risk-taking. The service function includes post-sale repair services, honoring manufacturers' guarantees, and offering management services such as store layout planning, inventory planning, site selection, computerized accounting services, and management training programs. Intermediaries perform a credit function when some kind of credit service is made available to facilitate purchases. The risk-taking function involves credit risk, legal risk, and economic risk.

Learning Objective Six: To know the major legal concerns associated with channel construction and management.

The three main legal restrictions that affect channel construction and management are exclusive dealing arrangements, exclusive territorial arrange-ments, and tying contracts. An exclusive dealing arrangement exists when an intermediary carries the product of one manufacturer and is restricted from carrying products of competing suppliers. Exclusive dealing arrangements are illegal if the arrangement lessens competition. An exclusive territorial arrangement exists when a manufacturer grants to a wholesaler or retailer a geographical area with the condition that no other wholesalers or retailers will be assigned to that territory. Exclusive territories are permissible if competi-tion is not restricted and the territorial restriction serves a legitimate purpose. Tying contracts require a channel intermediary to purchase product lines which the seller sees as supplementary to the products the buyer actually wants to buy. These contracts are illegal unless the tying contract can be justified when attempting to (1) maintain standards of quality, (2) enter a new market or industry, or (3) preserve market identity.

Learning Objective Seven: To name the major vertical marketing systems and tell how they are organized.

The major vertical marketing systems (VMS) are corporate VMS, administered VMS, and contractual VMS. A corporate VMS is organized on the basis of ownership of adjacent stages in the channel of distribution by the producer or an intermediary. An administered VMS is based on the leadership of a dominant channel member exerting channel power to coordinate marketing activities of all channel members for their mutual benefit. In a contractual VMS, channel leadership is assigned by a contractual agreement. The three subtypes of contractual VMS are retail cooperative organizations (retailer-sponsored), voluntary chains (wholesaler-sponsored), and franchises.

VOCABULARY BUILDING

Matching Exercise

Match the following by placing the letter of the concept or term on the blank preceding the phrase which best describes the concept or term. You should use a term or concept only once.

A. Channel of distribution
B. Merchant intermediaries
C. Agent intermediaries
D. Facilitators
E. Bulk-breaking function
F. Accumulating bulk
G. Assorting function
H. Transportation
I. Storage
J. Vertical marketing systems
K. Corporate vertical marketing systems
L. Administered vertical marketing systems
M. Contractual vertical marketing systems
N. Cooperative organization
O. Voluntary chain
P. Intensive distribution
Q. Selective distribution
R. Exclusive distribution
S. Channel cooperation
T. Channel conflict
U. Channel leader
V. Exclusive dealing
W. Exclusive territories
X. Tying contracts

_____ 1. A channel member who performs activities between the producer and final user and does not take title to the product.

_____ 2. The physical moving of products from the point of production to the point of consumption.

_____ 3. A situation where a marketing intermediary carries only one manufacturer's products and not those of other manufacturers.

223

_____ 4. Wholesaler-sponsored organization which combines services to a group of independent retailers.

_____ 5. Functional specialists who sell a service that helps the flow of products but are not included in the channel of distribution.

_____ 6. A strategy that attempts to obtain maximum exposure at the retail level.

_____ 7. A channel member who performs activities between the producer and final user and takes title to the product.

_____ 8. A channel of distribution that is a formally organized system that is either owned by a manufacturer or distributor, linked by strong contracts, or coordinated as an integrated system.

_____ 9. Channel organization that is able to exert its power and influence over other channel members.

_____ 10. The sorting activity of buying in relatively large quantities and selling in smaller quantities.

_____ 11. A strategy that restricts the sale of a product to a limited number of outlets.

_____ 12. A situation where the desires of channel members are not sufficiently integrated.

_____ 13. Retailer-sponsored organization in which a group of independent retailers combine their financial resources and expertise in order to control more effectively their wholesaling needs.

_____ 14. The creation of assortments of merchandise that would be otherwise unavailable.

_____ 15. Geographic area granted by a manufacturer to a wholesaler or retailer with the condition that no other wholesalers or retailers will be assigned to that territory.

_____ 16. Channel of distribution integrated on basis of ownership.

_____ 17. A situation where the marketing objectives and strategies of two or more channel members are harmonious.

_____ 18. A channel of distribution based on coordination of marketing activities achieved through planning and management of a mutually beneficial program to all parties.

_____ 19. Channel function of holding the product at various spots between point of production and point of consumption, inclusively.

_____ 20. Comprised of organizations that are aligned to provide a vehicle that makes the passage of title or possession of product from producer to consumer possible.

VOCABULARY BUILDING

Programmed Learning Exercise

1. Distribution is estimated to account for about _____ percent of the price of consumer goods.

[25]

2. Distribution creates _____ and _____ utilities.

[time, place]

3. The marketing function of _____ spans the gap between the producer of a product and the final user of that product.

[distribution]

4. The _____ _____ is characterized by loosely aligned, relatively autonomous marketing organizations that have developed a system to carry out a trade relationship.

[conventional channel]

5. Marketing functions performed by marketing intermediaries can be _____ but not _____.

[shifted, eliminated]

6. A marketing intermediary who performs the function of accumulating bulk is called an _____.

[assembler]

7. In exchanging the title to products, middlemen perform the _____ and _____ functions.

[buying, selling]

8. _____ functions are referred to as intermediaries' "hidden" tasks.

[Facilitating]

9. The three major categories of facilitating functions are _____, _____, and _____.

[service, credit, risk-taking]

225

10. Any channel of distribution is a system of _____ among its members.

[interdependency]

11. The number of channel intermediaries determine the _____ of the channel.

[length]

12. _____ are marketing intermediaries unique to consumer goods channels.

[Retailers]

13. A wholesale intermediary in an industrial channel of distribution who performs a function much like that of a retailer is referred to as an _____ _____ or a _____ .

[industrial distributor, jobber]

14. Many manufacturers use _____ channels in distributing their product(s) in different ways to satisfy the desires of particular customers.

[multiple]

15. _____ _____ occurs when a product is sold in many different types of retail stores.

[Scrambled merchandising]

16. The three types of vertical marketing systems are _____ , _____ , and _____ .

[corporate, administered, contractual]

17. Distribution strategy requires making the major decisions of determining the _____ of the channel and the _____ of distribution.

[structure, intensity or extent]

18. Channel length is influenced by the marketing mix strategy, _____ resources, and _____ _____ criteria.

[organizational, external environmental]

19. The three levels of intensity of distribution are _____ , _____ , and _____ .

[intensive, selective, exclusive]

20. The strategy of intensive distribution is most appropriate for products classified as _____ goods.

[convenience]

21. Channel conflict is a term used to discuss _____ conflicts among members of the same channel of distribution.

[vertical]

22. Multiple channel strategy can result in _____ conflict between two similar intermediaries at the same level in the channel.

[horizontal]

23. When one organization in a channel of distribution is able to exert its influence over other channel members, this organization has _____

_____.

[channel power]

24. The consumer becomes the first link in a _____ channel of distribution.

[backward or reverse]

25. _____ _____ require a channel intermediary or a buyer to purchase lines of merchandise which the seller sees as supplementary to the merchandise a purchaser actually wants to sell.

[Tying contracts]

TRUE OR FALSE STATEMENTS

T F 1. The overall goal of marketing intermediaries and of those who develop methods of physical distribution and channel management is efficiency of operation consistent with the desires of customers.

T F 2. Distribution creates time and form utilities.

T F 3. Distribution is of little or no concern for managers of not-for-profit organizations.

T F 4. Marketing intermediaries are organizations specializing in distribution which are external to the producing organization.

T F 5. Both the transfer of the title to the product and the physical movement of these goods to their ultimate destination follow the same path in a channel of distribution.

T F 6. Agent middlemen take title to the product.

T F 7. Though there are many kinds of channels of distribution, there are no channels of distribution for services.

T F 8. Facilitators are not marketing intermediaries.

T F 9. You do not eliminate the middleman's functions when you eliminate the middleman.

T F 10. An assembler in the distribution channel buys in large quantities and performs the breaking-bulk function for the convenience of its customers.

T F 11. The creation of a product mix by marketing intermediaries is referred to as the assorting function.

T F 12. A reduction in the number of transactions is a type of communication function.

T F 13. A key function that wholesalers and retailers perform is the communication of important information between consumers and the manufacturer.

T F 14. Manufacturers force marketing intermediaries to perform facilitating functions such as repair service.

T F 15. Channel intermediaries perform the risk-taking function for suppliers rather than customers.

T F 16. A channel of distribution is a system of interdependency among all of its members.

T F 17. The importance of large retailers has made the manufacturer-retailer-consumer channel the most common channel for consumer products.

T F 18. Other than for the direct channel of distribution, most industrial channels include retailers.

T F 19. Selling agents are used on a permanent basis while brokers are used on a temporary basis.

T F 20. Channels of distribution are like those described and discussed in textbooks.

T F 21. In an administered form of a vertical marketing system, channel coordination is achieved through the leadership and channel power of one channel member.

T F 22. A major selection criterion in determining the structure of a channel of distribution is consumer preferences and market behavior.

T F 23. Intensive distribution is more commonly used for convenience products.

T F 24. Different marketing functions are performed in a backward channel than in a forward channel.

T F 25. In a tying contract, a manufacturer selects a dealer and assigns this dealer exclusive territorial rights in which to market the product(s).

MULTIPLE CHOICE QUESTIONS

1. In terms of society's needs, the major purpose of marketing is
    a. to create ownership utility.
    b. to satisfy human needs by delivering products to buyers when and where they want them at a reasonable price.
    c. to produce and distribute products at a reasonable price.
    d. to generate profits to create more employment opportunities.

2. Which is not a major reason for the increased importance of the marketing function of distribution in the economy?
    a. Increasing levels of unemployment.
    b. Consumer concerns with efficiencies in marketing.
    c. Cost-consciousness.
    d. Increasing levels of domestic and foreign competition.

3. Which statement is incorrect regarding channels of distribution?
    a. A channel of distribution may consist of a manufacturer, wholesaler, and retailer.
    b. Wholesalers and retailers are marketing intermediaries.
    c. Marketing channels always include producers and consumers or final users.
    d. Channels of distribution usually lead to consumers paying more for the products they purchase.

4. Marketing intermediaries who take title to the product are called
    a. wholesalers.   c. agent intermediaries.
    b. merchant intermediaries.   d. middlemen.

5. Which is a major reason for the distribution segment being the most maligned segment of the economy?
    a. Intermediaries are slow in delivering the product to consumers.
    b. Retailers are perceived as highly efficient organizations, but wholesalers are perceived as inefficient and unnecessary organizations.
    c. Many consumers perceive that marketing intermediaries do not perform any major service and thus cause prices to increase.
    d. Low standards of living are caused by distribution inadequacies.

6. If a manufacturer decided to stop using a wholesaler in a given channel of distribution, choosing instead to perform the wholesaler functions itself, the manufacturer has
   a. eliminated the wholesaler functions.
   b. shifted the wholesaler function forward onto the retailers.
   c. shifted the wholesaler function backward onto itself.
   d. shifted the wholesaler function forward onto itself.

7. Which is not a physical distribution function?
   a. Assorting.   c. Transportation.
   b. Title movement.   d. Breaking-bulk.

8. A supermarket which accumulates several kinds of spices and makes these spices available for customers to buy is performing the _____ function.
   a. accumulating bulk   c. sorting
   b. breaking bulk   d. assorting

9. If there are five producers of goods and five buyers of goods, and all producers traded with all buyers, the addition of a single middleman dealing with all parties would reduce the number of transactions _____ percent.
   a. 0   c. 60
   b. 40   d. 150

10. Which function is not performed by channel intermediaries?
    a. Manufacturing products.   c. Selling.
    b. Risk taking.   d. Management services.

11. Which is not a facilitating function that intermediaries may perform?
    a. Offering credit to sellers and buyers.
    b. Gathering market information.
    c. Providing management services and assistance.
    d. Honoring manufacturers' guarantees.

12. Which statement is correct regarding the length of a channel of distribution?
    a. The greater the time a product takes to reach its destination, the longer a channel is.
    b. The channel is short if the manufacturer has control over the actions taken by channel intermediaries.
    c. The length of the channel is determined by the distance the product travels from producer to consumer.
    d. The more intermediaries in the channel, the longer the channel is.

230

13. The direct channel from manufacturer to consumer or user is most commonly found in the case of
    a. industrial products.
    b. consumer products.
    c. government products.
    d. consumer cooperative stores.

14. An industrial distributor is most likely to handle
    a. component parts.
    b. raw materials.
    c. installations.
    d. all of the above.

15. The most commonly used channel structure for consumer goods is the
    a. direct channel.
    b. manufacturer-retailer channel.
    c. manufacturer-wholesaler-retailer channel.
    d. manufacturer-agent-wholesaler-retailer channel.

16. Which channel intermediary can be used by a manufacturer on a temporary basis best?
    a. Jobber.
    b. Selling agent.
    c. Manufacturers' agent.
    d. Broker.

17. Which statement is incorrect regarding channels of distribution?
    a. Channels of distribution are not what textbooks say because many manufacturers use multiple channels.
    b. Channels of distribution are not what textbooks say because of the marketing phenomenon called scrambled merchandising.
    c. Channels of distribution are relatively uncomplicated as the textbooks portray channels.
    d. Unavailability of channel intermediaries in an area may result in channels not being as portrayed by textbooks.

18. The corporate vertical marketing system is characterized by a channel member
    a. being assigned a leadership role by virtue of a contract.
    b. having considerable channel power.
    c. assuming a channel captain role.
    d. owning one or more adjacent levels in the channel.

19. An example of an administered vertical marketing system would be
    a. Midas.
    b. Kraft Cheese.
    c. Holiday Inn.
    d. McDonalds.

20. All are types of corporate vertical marketing systems except a
    a. franchise.
    b. retail voluntary organization.
    c. cooperative organization.
    d. voluntary chain.

21. Company A is financially sound and has large available financial resources. Company B is like Company A in every way except that it does not have large available financial resources. Given this information, how would their channels of distribution differ?
    a. A would be more likely than B to use a longer channel of distribution.
    b. A would eliminate distribution from its marketing mix, B would not.
    c. A would be more likely than B to have its own sales force, while B would be more likely to utilize intermediaries to reach customers.
    d. B would be more likely than A to have its own sales force since it has less financial strength.

22. Which would a marketer be least likely to consider in determining the structure of the channel of distribution?
    a. Extent of distribution.   c. Product characteristics.
    b. Availability of middlemen.   d. Customer preferences.

23. Marketers of shopping products are more likely to use a(n) _____ distribution strategy.
    a. intensive   c. exclusive
    b. selective   d. inclusive

24. Vertical channel conflict results when channel members have
    a. no clearly identified focus of formal channel power.
    b. harmonious channel objectives and strategies.
    c. an established channel captain.
    d. economic competition between two intermediaries at the same level.

25. A manufacturer of energy efficient windows establishes a network of dealerships in which each dealer was given an exclusive territory. Which defense is least likely to hold up in court?
    a. This exclusivity is necessary to recruit dealers because of large investment necessary to start the dealership.
    b. This exclusivity is necessary to protect the quality image of the product.
    c. This exclusivity is essential to protect the luxury or exclusive image of the product.
    d. Since each dealer is an independent business, the manufacturer can establish exclusive territories to enable these dealers to succeed.

232

1Q.
If channel intermediaries are doing so much to increase the efficiency of our distribution system, why do we still hear the call to "Eliminate the middleman and save money."?

1A.
For some advertisers, this motto is used as an advertising approach even though these marketers should know that eliminating the middleman does not necessarily lower prices. A more important answer to the question is that most people do not realize the contributions made by intermediaries until these contributions are pointed out to them. Some of the arguments made in this chapter defending intermediaries may seen "obvious" to you, especially after you read them. Many citizens simply do not realize the many "obvious" tasks that intermediaries perform in our economy.

2Q.
It seems that constructing the channel of distribution is the task of the manufacturer of a product. Is this the case?

2A.
Our discussion has created that impression, in part for the sake of convenience in discussing a complex topic, in part because manufacturers have such a strong stake in moving their products. However, all channel members have an interest in "constructing" channels. Retailers, wholesalers, and other intermediaries should give careful attention to this matter. Like the manufacturer, their livelihood depends on good channel operation. Intermediaries frequently lead the way in developing channels. The task is not always the manufacturer's.

3Q.
Are all products traded internationally likely to encounter legal
problems as they "cross borders?"

3A.
Almost certainly. Obviously proprietary drugs, nuclear products, and arms are controlled as carefully as possible, but, for example, Canada restricts the "shipment" of U.S. television transmissions and commercials into Canada via cable systems. A U.S. product Japan abhors to accept is not guns or cars, but oranges.

EXPERIENTIAL ACTIVITIES

12-A. Understanding Marketing Intermediaries

The chief executive officer (CEO) of the local Association of Commerce and Industry commented recently that college students, particularly non-business students, are unaware of the important role that marketing intermediaries perform in our economy. This statement upsets you so much that you made an appointment with the CEO to discuss her remark. During your conversation with the CEO, agreement was reached on several issues.

1. College students do not understand the general purpose of marketing intermediaries or middlemen.

2. College students do not understand the marketing functions performed by marketing intermediaries.

3. College students do not perceive marketing intermediaries and middlemen to be the same.

4. College students confuse facilitators or facilitating agents with marketing intermediaries or middlemen.

5. College students believe marketing costs can be reduced, if marketing intermediaries or middlemen are eliminated from distribution.

6. College students equate wholesalers as middlemen, but not retailers.

The CEO asks you to conduct a survey to determine how college students perceive marketing intermediaries. You agreed to conduct the study.

234

1. State the study's research objective and the study's research hypothesis.

    Research objective: _____

    _____

    Research hypothesis: _____

    _____

2. Develop a short, but simple questionnaire to obtain the information needed to determine college students' perceptions toward marketing intermediaries.

3. Ask five <u>non-business students</u> at your college or university who have not taken any marketing or introduction to business courses the questions contained in your questionnaire above.

Question 1 responses:

Student 1: _____

_____

Student 2: _____

_____

Student 3: _____

_____

Student 4: _____

_____

Student 5: _____

_____

Question 2 responses:

Student 1: _____

_____

Student 2: _____

_____

Student 3: _____

_____

Student 4: _____

_____

Student 5: _____

_____

Question 3 responses:

Student 1: _____

_____

Student 2: _____

_____

Student 3: _____

_____

Student 4: _____

_____

Student 5: _____

_____

Question 4 responses:

Student 1: _____

_____

Student 2: _____

_____

Student 3: _____

_____

Student 4: _____

_____

Student 5: _____

_____

Question 5 responses:

Student 1: _____

_____

Student 2: _____

_____

Student 3: _____

_____

Student 4: _____

_____

Student 5: _____

_____

Question 6 responses:

Student 1: _____

Student 2: _____

Student 3: _____

Student 4: _____

Student 5: _____

Question 7 responses:

Student 1: _____

Student 2: _____

Student 3: _____

Student 4: _____

Student 5: _____

Question 8 responses:

Student 1: _____

Student 2: _____

Student 3: _____

CHAPTER 13

DISTRIBUTION INSTITUTIONS

OBJECTIVE

Wholesaling and retailing intermediaries are the major distribution institutions that make our marketing system work. Different types of wholesaling and retailing institutions have evolved to perform more efficiently and more effectively the different functions demanded by their customers.

OUTLINE

I. Retailing

    A. Retailing consists of all activities involved with the sale of products to final consumers.

    B. Retailing is important in the United States.

        1. There are about 2 million retail institutions with sales approaching $1 trillion.

        2. Approximately 13 percent of those employed in the United States are in retailing.

    C. Retail institutions are dynamic organizations which evolve as the external environment changes.

    D. Retailers can be differentiated on the basis of the variety of their product assortment.

        1. General merchandise retailers carry a wide variety of products and product lines, usually offering a shallow selection of products.

        2. Limited-line retailers carry a general line of goods within particular product classes.

3. Specialty stores specialize within a particular product line usually offering a deep selection of products.

E. On the basis of ownership, retailers can be classified as independent retailers, chain stores, and ownership groups.

F. Specific types of retail institutions respond to particular marketing opportunities.

   1. Supermarkets are large departmentalized retail establishments primarily selling food items.

      a. Supermarkets practice scrambled merchandising.

      b. Convenience food stores are small supermarkets.

   2. Department stores are typically chain store members with a wide selection of items (for example, furniture, clothing, home appliances, etc.) and a full range of services.

   3. Discount stores are large self-service establishments that offer a variety of products at low prices.

   4. The various types of discounters include general merchandise discount retailers and specialty store discount retailers.

      a. In food retailing, one type of discounter is the box store supermarket.

      b. Many types of discounters have adopted the concept of supermarket retailing.

      c. Warehouse retailers combine wholesaling and retailing functions.

      d. A catalog showroom is a self-service retail store which publishes a large catalog to identify its products for sale.

G. Types of non-store retailing are direct mail and direct-response retailing, vending machines, door-to-door retailing, and in-home retailing.

II. Patterns of retail development

A. The wheel of retailing theory postulates that new retailing institutions enter the marketplace as low-status, low-price operations, and then move toward higher status and price positions.

244

B. The dialectic view of retail development posits that new retailing institutions (synthesis) evolve due to competition and opposition of a newer type of institution (antithesis) to an older established form of retailing (thesis).

C. Another explanation of retail development is the general [stores]--specific [specialty stores]--general [stores] theory.

D. These theories of retail development have low predictive value, but they raise questions which marketing planners must consider.

III. Retail management strategies

A. The retail marketing mix involves strategic decisions related to merchandise assortment, location, and store layout which impact on a store's image.

B. Retailers perform an assorting function when they develop their product or merchandise assortment.

1. This product assortment provides a competitive or differential advantage for one organization over other organizations.

2. Retailers must match the merchandise assortment to the target market's needs.

C. Store location is strongly influenced by preferences of target customers and type of business.

D. The layout and interior design of a store create its ambiance.

IV. Wholesaling

A. A wholesaler is a marketing intermediary that sells the finished product to retailers or other institutions that use or resell the product.

1. Of the approximately 383,000 wholesale trade establishments, 307,000 are merchant wholesalers, 40,500 are manufacturers' sales branches and offices, and 35,000 are agents and brokers.

2. Wholesalers, like retailers, perform buying and selling functions, create time and place utilities, and create a customer-oriented product assortment.

B. Two major types of wholesalers are merchant wholesalers and agent wholesalers.

C. Merchant wholesalers take title to the products that they market and may be classified on the basis of the services performed.

   1. Full-service merchant wholesalers offer a complete array of services to their customers.

      a. Full-service wholesalers are also called full-function wholesalers.

      b. General merchandise wholesalers, general line wholesalers, and specialty wholesalers are types of full-service wholesalers.

   2. Limited-service or limited-function wholesalers have developed to serve customers who do not want the complete array of services offered by full-service merchant wholesalers.

      a. Cash-and-carry wholesalers eliminate the delivery and credit functions.

      b. Truck wholesalers or truck jobbers usually sell a limited line of perishable items to small buyers.

      c. Mail-order wholesalers operate similar to mail-order retailers.

      d. Drop shippers do not take possession nor handle the products that they sell.

      e. Rack jobbers contract with retailers to stock and display certain products within the retail store.

D. Agents bring buyers and sellers together but they do not take title to the products they sell.

   1. Brokers are agent middlemen whose primary role is to put sellers in touch with buyers and to assist with contractual negotiations.

   2. Commission merchants have more negotiating powers, such as establishing price, than brokers do.

   3. Auction companies bring buyers and sellers together in a central location.

   4. Manufacturers' agents or manufacturers' representatives represent one or more non-competing manufacturers in a limited geographic territory.

5. Selling agents have greater responsibilities than manufacturers' agents and are not restricted to a limited geographic territory.

E. Manufacturers may elect to perform the wholesaling function utilizing sales offices (no inventory) and/or sales branches (carry inventory).

F. Wholesalers will continue to adapt to the dynamic marketing environment.

SUMMARY

Learning Objective One: To describe the purposes of wholesaling and retailing in the distribution system and the activities performed by each.

Retailing and wholesaling refer to exchanges within channels of distribution. Retailing involves dealing with ultimate consumers who acquire products for their personal use; whereas, wholesaling focuses on similar activities directed toward producers, marketing intermediaries, and other institutions that acquire products for resale or to produce other products. Retailers and wholesalers perform the marketing activities which were discussed in Chapter 12. For example, both act as buying agents for their customers and as selling agents for their suppliers. They also perform physical distribution and facilitating services functions in performing their activities while creating time and place utilities. The specific activities performed vary by type of wholesaler or retailer.

Learning Objective Two: To understand the impact of retailing and wholesaling on our economy.

A comparison of the number of wholesale and retail institutions in America reveals that there are over five times as many retail institutions (about 2 million) as wholesale institutions (382,800). However, annual wholesale sales are more than double annual retail sales ($2.3 trillion versus $1.0 trillion). The average dollar sales per retail institution are about $500,000; whereas, the corresponding wholesaling figure exceeds $6,000,000. Retail sales account for approximately 97 percent of the personal income component of the GNP. Finally, more than one out of ten (13%) American workers are employed in retailing.

Learning Objective Three: To be aware of the various kinds of retailers and the several variables that can be used to classify them.

Retailers can be classified according to product variety, ownership, and prominent operational activity or style. The three types of retailers, according to product variety, are general merchandise retailers, limited-line retailers, and specialty store retailers. Independent retailers, chain stores, and ownership groups are types of retail ownership. Retailers can also be classified according to whether the prominent style of operation is in-store or non-store. Supermarkets, department stores, and discount stores are major retail institutions in terms of the in-store classification. Mail-order, direct-response retailing, vending machines, door-to-door selling, and in-home retailing are the means of non-store retailing.

Learning Objective Four: To describe the operations of supermarkets, discounters, closed-door houses, and non-store retailers.

Supermarkets are large departmentalized self-service operations offering a wide variety of products. Supermarkets practice scrambled merchandising as they offer many non-food items as well as the traditional food products. Discount stores are large self-service retail institutions which sell a wide variety of high-turnover products at low prices. Discount stores offer fewer customer services than supermarkets do. One type of discounter is the closed-door house in which customers must be members of the store in order to enter the store and to purchase products. Convenience is the primary patronage motive for non-store retailing. Other patronage motives that are associated with at-home shopping include safety and [usually] liberal return policies. Low operating costs, computerized mailing lists, and specialty-type products are associated with mail-order retailing. Vending machines typically offer low-priced convenience products. Door-to-door selling is expensive (high labor costs) and has local legality problems (Green River Ordinances).

Learning Objective Five: To discuss the historical patterns found in American retailing and several theories that have been constructed to explain them.

Retailing institutions are dynamic and continually evolving as they respond to environmental changes. Three theories that have been constructed to explain this evolutionary institutional development are the wheel of retailing, the dialectic view, and a general-special-general explanation. The wheel of retailing theory postulates that new retailing institutions enter the marketplace as low-status, low-price, low-margin operations and evolve toward higher status, higher price, and higher margin positions. As these institutions trade-up, new retailing institutions emerge to fill the low-status, low-price, low-margin retailing institutional void. The dialectic view of retail development hypothesizes that new retailing institutions (synthesis) emerge when a newer form of retailing (antithesis) competes and opposes an older established type of retailing institution (thesis). For example, the convenience store (synthesis) emerged from the competition and opposition of the supermarket (antithesis) to the neighborhood grocery store (thesis). The general-specific-general explanation posits that shopping malls (new type of general store) combines smaller specialty-type stores (specific) which replaced the general stores prominent in early American retailing.

Learning Objective Six: To name the elements of the retail marketing mix and to discuss their significance in successful retailing.

In developing a retail marketing mix, retailers must make decisions regarding the four basic mix variables of product, place, price, and promotion. Product elements of the marketing mix include merchandise for sale, depth of selection, variety of merchandise, services to offer, and psychological variables such as image. Place variables include store location, branch locations, and layout. Price decisions revolve around the general price level of merchandise, credit plans, credit cards accepted, and assistance with bank loans. Promotion concerns the activities of advertising, personal sales, sales promotion, and publicity. Three decision areas of special importance to retailers are merchandise assortment, location, and store layout. In selecting the merchandise assortment, the retailer must match the product assortment to the target market's needs. Otherwise, these targeted customers are unlikely to patronize the retailer's store. The right location varies by type of business and the target customer. Layout affects the ambiance of the store. These marketing mix variables enable retail marketers to attract and to satisfy target markets. A competitive or differential advantage should emerge from a retailer's marketing mix.

Learning Objective Seven: To understand the difference between merchant wholesalers and agents and to describe how these organizations contribute to marketing goals.

Wholesalers can be distinguished on the basis of whether they take title to the products they sell. Merchant wholesalers take title to products they sell while agent middlemen do not take title to the products with which they facilitate title transfers. As discussed in Chapter 12 of the Zikmund and d'Amico textbook, wholesalers perform the functions of physical distribution, communication, and facilitating services. Wholesalers facilitate the transportation and/or the title transfer of products. In performing their functions, wholesalers become selling agents for their suppliers and buying agents for their customers.

Learning Objective Eight: To show how full-service wholesalers and the many forms of limited-service wholesalers fit into the marketing system.

Full-service and limited-service wholesalers are merchant middlemen. Full-service wholesalers provide a complete array of services--delivery, credit, managerial assistance, marketing information, and product assortment--to their customers who are willing to pay for these services. Limited-service wholesalers serve those buyers who do not want, or are not willing to pay for, selected services. Types of limited-service wholesalers include cash-and-carry wholesalers, truck wholesalers, mail-order wholesalers, drop shippers, and rack jobbers. Cash-and-carry wholesalers provide no credit or delivery functions while truck wholesalers offer delivery of a limited line of products, usually perishable, to small buyers. Mail-order wholesalers obtain mail or phone orders from buyers and use the mail to deliver the ordered products. Drop shippers do not handle the products they sell, but ship the product directly from the producer to the buyer. Rack jobbers offer a wide variety of small products of which they are responsible to stock within retail stores.

Learning Objective Nine: To discuss the contributions to marketing of such agent intermediaries as brokers, auction companies, and selling agents.

Agent wholesalers offer expert market-knowledge as they facilitate exchanges by putting sellers in touch with buyers. Brokers, commission merchants, auction companies, manufacturers' agents, and selling agents are types of agent intermediaries. Brokers assist in contractual negotiations with the buyers and sellers they bring together on a temporary basis. Commission merchants perform a seller's pricing function and often take possession of the product. Auction companies offer such conveniences as product inspection and anonymity to buyers and sellers in bringing buyers and sellers together. Manufacturers' agents represent a seller in a geographic area with responsibil- ities similar to a sales person; whereas, a selling agent functions like a mar- keting department in marketing all of the products produced by a manufacturer.

VOCABULARY BUILDING

Matching Exercise

Match the following by placing the letter of the concept or term on the blank preceding the phrase which best describes the concept or term. You should use a term or concept only once.

A.	Retailing	M.	Wholesaling
B.	General merchandise retailers	N.	Full-service merchant wholesalers
		O.	Specialty wholesalers
C.	Limited-line retailers	P.	Cash-and-carry wholesaler
D.	Specialty stores	Q.	Truck wholesaler (truck jobber)
E.	Chain store	R.	Drop shipper
F.	Ownership group	S.	Rack jobber
G.	Supermarket	T.	Agent
H.	Department store	U.	Broker
I.	Discount store	V.	Commission merchant
J.	Wheel of retailing	W.	Manufacturers' agent (manufacturers' representative)
K.	Dialectic theory		
L.	General-specific-general	X.	Selling agent

_W_ 1. An agent intermediary who represents one or more non-competing manufacturers within a geographically <u>limited</u> area.

250

_S_ 2. A type of limited-function wholesaler contracted to stock certain products and prepare displays in a retail store. Rack jobber S

_I_ 3. A large, self-service retail store selling a variety of high-turnover products at low prices. Discount Store

_A_ 4. All activities involved with the sale of products to ultimate consumers. Retailing

_N_ 5. Wholesalers which typically maintain a sales force, carry inventory, deliver goods, extend credit, and provide information and assistance. Full-Service Merchant Wholesaler

_P_ 6. A limited-function wholesaler that does not provide credit and delivery services. Cash-a-Carry Wholesaler

_E_ 7. Two or more stores of a similar type, centrally owned and operated. Chain Store

_X_ 8. ✓ A type of agent intermediary given more extensive powers, such as the pricing of products, by the sellers that use them.

_G_ 9. Retailers which carry a wide line of merchandise cutting across generic lines of goods. General Merchandise

_W_ 10. ✓ An agent intermediary representing one or more producers and often responsible for product pricing and advertising. Selling Agent

_M_ 11. All activities concerned with the sale of products to buyers who are not the ultimate users of the product. Wholesalers

_U_ 12. Agent intermediary whose role is largely one of putting sellers in touch with buyers and assisting with contractual negotiations. Broker

_H_ 13. A large, departmentalized retail store selling a variety of products and generally providing a full range of customer services. department store

_F_ 14. Various stores with a separate name, identity, and image but with a central owner. Ownership group

_R_ 15. Merchant wholesaler that takes title to products but do not take possession of the products or handle them in any way. drop shipper

_C_ 16. D Retailers specializing within a particular product line, selling only those items deemed appropriate to a narrow market segment. Specialty Wholesale

251

___J___ 17. A theory positing that new retailers enter the marketplace as low-status, low-price operations and then gradually move toward higher status and price positions. *Wheel of retailers*

___Q___ 18. A limited-function wholesaler typically selling a limited line of perishable items to small buyers. *Truck jobber*

___B___ 19. Retail establishments which carry a wide assortment of one product line or a small number of product lines. *Limited-line*

___V___ 20. An intermediary which may take possession of products but does not take title to them. *Agent*

VOCABULARY BUILDING

Programmed Learning Exercise

1. An intermediary is counted as a retailer in government business statistics if this intermediary has at least ___50___ percent of sales to ultimate consumers.

   [50]

2. There are about _____ retailers in the United States.

   [2 million]

3. Most retailers are _independent_ retailers operating as single-unit entities.

   [independent]

4. A corporation operating a variety of retailing concerns often with some degree of centralized management is referred to as a _____.

   [conglomerchant]

5. _Supermarkets_ are large, departmentalized retail stores selling a variety of products, but mostly food items.

   [Supermarkets]

6. A retail store that stocks non-traditional items is practicing _scrambled merchandising_

   [scrambled merchandising]

7. Profits earned by supermarkets are about ___1___ or ___2___ percent of sales.

   [one, two]

8. Managers of various departments within a department store who have considerable independence in buying and selling their departments' products are referred to as _____ .

[buyers]

9. _____ _____ has been used to describe many discount stores that have adopted the supermarket concept of large inventories displayed on a self-service basis.

[Supermarket retailing]

10. Retailers, such as Levitz, which combine wholesaling and retailing functions are referred to as _____ retailers.

[warehouse]

11. A self-service retail store which publishes a large catalog identifying its products for sale is called a _Catalog Showroom_ .

[catalog showroom]

12. The _____ _____ _____ is a type of catalog store which requires customers to be members of the store.

[closed door house]

13. The _____ is a kind of discount superstore with at least 50,000 square feet selling a wide variety of products.

[hypermarket]

14. The factor that most attracts consumers to mail-order retailing is _____ . _Convenience_

[convenience]

15. Retailers who market their product by advertising on television and who urge viewers to order immediately over the phone are called _____ - _____ retailers.

[direct-response]

16. Vending machines have been used most successfully in the sale of _Convenience_ products.

[convenience]

17. Local ordinances which make door-to-door selling difficult are referred to as _Green River_ Ordinances.

[Green River]

18. According to the _Dialectic_ Theory of retail development, the evolution of institutions follows a pattern of thesis, antithesis, and synthesis.

[Dialectic]

19. Three problem areas of special importance to retail marketers are
_____ _____, _____, and _____ _____.
[merchandise assortment, location, store layout]

20. Retailers perform the _____ function when they build desired assortments of products.

[assorting]

21. A _wholesaler_ is a middleman who neither produces nor consumes a product, and does not sell the product to an ultimate consumer.

[wholesaler]

22. There are approximately _____ U.S. wholesale establishments.
[382,800]

23. _Merchant_ wholesalers take title to the product while _agent_ wholesalers do not take the product's title.

[Merchant, agent]

24. An _____ _____ is an agent intermediary providing the convenience of gathering buyers and sellers of products in a central location.
[auction company]

25. A manufacturer's wholesaling establishment which carries inventory is
referred to as a manufacturer's sales _Branch_ while a manufacturer's
sales _office_ does not carry inventory.

[branch, office]

TRUE OR FALSE STATEMENTS

T F 1. Each marketing intermediary type represents marketing's response
to developments within the marketplace.

T F 2. Retailing involves all exchanges within a consumer channel of distribution.

T F 3. Retailers need to implement consumer-oriented marketing plans just
as producers do.

T F 4. The largest retailing company in the United States, as measured
by dollar sales in the United States, is K-Mart.

T F 5. Few or no retailers carry inventories that fit the description of
wide variety and deep selection.

254

T F 6. Limited-line retailers succeed because they develop considerable expertise in their particular product lines.

T F 7. Most retailers in the United States operate two or more independent stores.

T F 8. Convenience food stores are a synthesis of neighborhood grocery stores (thesis) and supermarkets (antithesis).

T F 9. Discount retail operations are limited to general merchandise and limited-line retailers only.

T F 10. A closed door house is a form of non-store retailing.

T F 11. Vending machines illustrate the "wheel of retailing" hypothesis.

T F 12. The recent popularity of boutique retailing institutions is caused by the low markup of these specialty retailers.

T F 13. The "wheel of retailing" theory considers both producers' and buyers' costs.

T F 14. The usefulness of various explanations of retail institutional development to retail planners is their ability to raise questions.

T F 15. Retailers consider store hours as a product-related variable.

T F 16. Retailers perform an assorting function.

T F 17. A store's ambiance is created largely by interior design and layout.

T F 18. There are more agent wholesalers than merchant wholesalers.

T F 19. Average sales per wholesaling establishment exceed average sales per retailing establishment.

T F 20. Specialty wholesalers are classified as limited-service wholesalers.

T F 21. Desk jobbers are likely to handle large, bulky items.

T F 22. Brokers are more likely than agents to represent buyers or sellers on a permanent basis.

T F 23. Commission merchants are merchant wholesalers.

T F 24. Manufacturers' representatives function similar to marketing departments.

T F 25. Manufacturer's sales offices do not carry inventory.

MULTIPLE CHOICE QUESTIONS

1. Which statement does <u>not</u> describe retailing?
   a. Retailing provides the final link in the process that brings goods from manufacturers to ultimate consumers.
   b. Retailing involves dealing with customers who are acquiring products for their personal use.
   c. Retailing involves dealing with consuming units such as households and organizational buyers.
   d. Retailing includes selling, renting, and leasing to ultimate consumers.

2. Which statement regarding the importance of retailing is <u>incorrect</u>?
   a. Retail sales exceed wholesale sales.
   b. The number of retailing institutions exceed the number of wholesaling institutions.
   c. Retail sales are approximately one trillion dollars.
   d. Retailing employs roughly 13 percent of American workers.

3. Retailers are classified in the Zikmund and d'Amico textbook according to
   a. product variety, ownership, and investment costs.
   b. ownership, investment costs, and prominent operational activity.
   c. investment costs, prominent operational activity, and product variety.
   d. prominent operational activity, product variety, and ownership.

4. An example of a general merchandise retailer is
   a. Toys-R-Us.   c. K-Mart.
   b. Radio Shack.   d. McDonalds.

5. Big retailers like Sears, Wards, and others are called
   a. conglomerchants.   c. specialty stores.
   b. mass merchandisers.   d. combination houses.

6. The success of modern specialty stores may be attributed to
   a. the narrow line of merchandise they offer.
   b. effective market segmentation and target marketing.
   c. their high turnover of inventory.
   d. their high profit margin on the products carried.

256

7. Chain store systems like Kroger and Safeway have been very successful
    for many reasons, but one of the most important reasons is that they
    a. have been able to attract experienced managers and bright trainees.
    b. have lower personnel costs.
    c. are able to obtain better locations than other retailing types.
    d. have been able to take advantage of economies of scale in buying
        and selling.

8. A big difference between a chain store system and an ownership group
    is that
    a. stores in an ownership group operate under different names and
        keep their own images, while chain members do not.
    b. managers of ownership group member stores do not report to execu-
        tives "above" them on the organization chart.
    c. chain store managers are little more than clerks since they have no
        authority to make local decisions.
    d. chain store systems are made up of limited-line stores and ownership
        groups are made up of general merchandise stores.

9. Convenience stores offer the conveniences of
    a. store location and credit.
    b. product assortment and in-store promotion.
    c. the days and hours that the store is open and trained personnel.
    d. store location and time.

10. One would not expect a department store to offer
    a. higher prices than discount stores.
    b. a wide product assortment.
    c. a deep product assortment.
    d. a full-range of services.

11. _____ are major competitors of department stores.
    a. Catalog stores   c. Warehouse retailers
    b. Supermarkets   d. Discount stores

12. The major reason for lower prices in discount stores is that they
    a. offer limited services.
    b. buy distress merchandise.
    c. advertise less and use salespersons who receive a commission.
    d. are open shorter hours than other types of retailers.

13. Various types of retailing discounters include all except
    a. warehouse retailers.   c. catalog showrooms.
    b. supermarkets.   d. factory outlets.

14. Which is not a type of non-store retailing?
    a. Mail-order retailing.   c. Drop shipping.
    b. Vending machines.   d. Direct-response retailing.

15. Which statement regarding mail-order retailing is incorrect?
    a. Mail-order retailing is more important for general merchandise retailers than specialty retailers.
    b. Mail-order retailing offers safety to the consumer.
    c. Mail-order retailing offers many opportunities to reduce costs.
    d. Mail-order retailing grows annually in the United States.

16. Which type of goods lends itself best to in-home or door-to-door retailing?
    a. Shopping goods.
    b. Goods that are not mechanical or otherwise difficult to use and understand.
    c. Goods that particularly benefit from demonstration.
    d. Goods that are expensive.

17. The "wheel of retailing" concept
    a. suggests why many stores do not have to change or adapt.
    b. implies that retailers themselves create situations which lead to the decline of retailing institutions.
    c. suggests that retailing institutions do not have a life cycle.
    d. predicts which new forms of retailing institutions will emerge.

18. The advantage of the dialectic view of retail development over the "wheel of retailing" hypothesis is that the dialectic view incorporates
    a. competition.   c. price.
    b. store location.   d. management.

19. Which source or influence should be most influential in helping a retailer determine what product assortment to carry?
    a. Trade magazines.
    b. Information of what competitors are doing.
    c. Suggestions from manufacturers and wholesalers.
    d. The target market's needs and wants.

20. Which wholesaler does not take title to the product?
    a. Rack jobber.   c. Broker.
    b. Drop shipper.   d. Full service.

21. Which wholesaler would one expect to have the lowest operating costs?
    a. Rack jobbers.   c. Truck jobbers.
    b. Drop shippers.   d. Sales branches.

258

22. Which is not an agent wholesaler?
    a. Commission merchant.   c. Broker.
    b. Rack jobber.   d. Auction company.

23. A major difference between the "manufacturers' agent" and the "selling agent" is that manufacturers' agents
    a. are limited to a geographic area unlike selling agents.
    b. offer more market expertise than selling agents do.
    c. are paid a salary while selling agents receive a commission.
    d. take possession of the product whereas selling agents do not take possession of the product.

24. Many manufacturers perform the wholesaling functions themselves through the use of sales offices and sales branches in order to control _____ more effectively.
    a. price   c. channel intensity
    b. warehouse location   d. information

25. In regards to wholesaling in the future, one would expect wholesalers to
    a. decline substantially in number.
    b. adapt to the environment effectively.
    c. become more generalized in services and products offered.
    d. become of lesser importance as channel intermediaries.

QUICK QUIZ

1Q.
Why would an ownership group buy independent stores and continue to operate them under the original names? Why not operate all under one name as does Woolworth, Sears, and The Gap?

1A.
Managers of ownership groups feel that locally popular stores should keep their original names and images for as long as those are attractive to customers who continue to shop at the "local" store, a store in fact owned by a corporation headquartered in some far-off city. Too, some ownership groups operate two, three, or more "different" stores in the same city to better appeal to various market segments and to achieve high shares of markets in those cities.

2Q.
What effect has the two-career family had on door-to-door retailing?

2A.
This development in the environment of marketing would appear to cut two ways. On one hand, the "working wife" would seem to have reduced the door-to-door merchant's effectiveness simply by being away from the home through most of the day. On the other hand, the "working wife" might be expected to want to save shopping time by shopping at home. Unfortunately for in-home sellers, the pressures of a job leave the evening hours even more crowded, making consumers less willing to deal with "peddlers." This may account for the increased popularity of the "party" system of in-home selling. In this situation, at least the buyer can plan in advance to attend a "party," and not be taken by surprise by a door-to-door salesperson just dropping by.

3Q.
Agents never take title to goods, but do merchant wholesalers and retailers ever sell products for which they did not take title.

3A.
Yes, though when they do, they technically step out of their role as merchants. Some manufacturers or other suppliers of goods may decide to sell to buyers on consignment. In this case, the retailer or other merchant intermediary takes possession of the goods and attempts to sell them, but legally the title never passes to the merchant. Thus the merchant can never get stuck with an unsold item and therefore carries no obvious risk. Such plans are used by producers of new, untried products for which

260

demand is uncertain and may be the only way dealers can be enticed to sell the product. The big danger to the producer is that intermediaries, facing no risk, will order large quantities of goods and then return them at a later date.

EXPERIENTIAL ACTIVITIES

13-A. Retail Location Study

You were retained by a developer of regional shopping centers to survey residents of a PSA (Primary Statistical Area) regarding their preferences for additional retail shopping facilities. Personal interviews were conducted with 400 residents of the PSA. Selected results are presented below.

Table 1. Least Driving Time to Selected PSA Locations

Location	Percent of Respondents
Downtown	40%
Veteran and East Main	40%
West College at I-75	20%

Table 2. Most Shopping at Selected PSA Locations

Location	Percent of Respondents
Veteran and East Main	50%
Downtown	30%
West College and I-75	10%
Other	10%

Table 3.   Shopper's First Store Preference for Non-grocery Items

Store	Percent of Respondents
Mason's	25%
Penney's	15%
J.L. Hudson	15%
Jacob's	10%
Sears	10%
Wards	5%
Carson's	5%
K-Mart	5%
Others	10%

Table 4.   Stores Unfamiliar to Shoppers

Store	Percent of Respondents
Carson's	60%
Herpolsheimer's	50%
J.L. Hudson	30%
Jacob's	7%
Mason's	2%
Sears	2%
Wards	2%
Penney's	1%

Table 5.   Preferred Location of Additional Non-grocery Stores

Location	Percent of Respondents
East of Veteran Avenue	15%
Between Veteran Avenue and I-75	25%
West of I-75	20%
Other locations	10%
No preferences, too many stores	30%

CHAPTER 14

PHYSICAL DISTRIBUTION MANAGEMENT

OBJECTIVE

Physical distribution involves those activities related to the efficient movement of finished products to consumers. A total cost approach should be implemented in striving to achieve the overall physical distribution objective to minimize total distribution cost while maximizing customer services.

OUTLINE

I. Definitions

    A. Physical distribution describes the activities related to the physical aspects of the efficient movement of finished products from producers to industrial users or consumers.

    B. Physical distribution management concerns the design and administration of systems to control the flow of products.

    C. Material management involves activities which bring raw materials and supplies to the point of production.

    D. Logistics incorporates both physical distribution and materials management activities.

II. The objectives of physical distribution

    A. The overall objective of physical distribution is to minimize cost while maximizing customer service.

    B. In order to achieve this objective with conflicting components, marketing managers must evaluate cost in terms of customer wants and needs and competitor's physical distribution policies.

267

III. The components of a physical distribution system

  A. The components of physical distribution include inventory management, order processing, warehousing and storage, materials handling, protective packaging and containerization, and transportation.

  B. These components operate as a system as they interact toward achieving maximum customer service at minimal cost.

IV. The total cost concept

  A. In physical distribution, total cost refers to all distribution-related costs associated with a particular system of distribution.

  B. Managers who practice the total cost concept direct their efforts at reducing total system cost rather than the individual component cost, while maintaining the level of customer service.

V. The "last frontier" of marketing

  A. Physical distribution has been referred to as the "last frontier" of marketing for two reasons.

    1. Computerization, automation, and modern quantitative techniques have been profitably adapted to physical distribution activities.

    2. Physical distribution activities are performed behind the scenes.

  B. An organization's differential advantage can be based on its physical distribution system.

  C. Opportunities to reduce costs can result from adjustments to the physical distribution system.

VI. Management of the components of physical distribution

  A. Six major areas of managerial responsibility in physical distribution are transportation, warehousing, inventory control, materials handling, order processing, and packaging.

  B. Management of the transportation component involves selecting the specific mode(s)--motor carrier, air freight, railroads, water transportation, and pipelines--to move the products.

    1. Accessibility and flexibility are two advantages of motor carriers.

2. Air freight has the advantages of speed, distance capabilities, and reliable delivery.

3. Railroads are appropriate to move heavy, bulky products long distances where slow delivery is appropriate.

4. Water transportation is an inexpensive way to move bulky, nonperishable products which frequently have a low unit value.

5. Pipelines provide reliable delivery for a limited number of products, primarily natural gas and crude petroleum.

6. In descending rank order of ton miles in domestic intercity traffic, the various modes of transportation are railroads, pipelines, motor vehicles, inland waterways, and airways.

C. Storage and breaking bulk are the primary activities of the warehousing function.

1. Storage involves holding and housing goods in inventory to balance discrepancies between production and consumption cycles.

2. Breaking bulk involves allocating inventory to buyers as needed.

3. Major warehousing decisions which confront managers focus on the number, location, and types of warehouses and the inventory levels to be stocked.

D. Inventory control requires that managers balance inventory levels and stock-outs.

1. Factors which influence inventory control are sales forecasts, past sales, turnover rates, inventory investment, and carrying costs.

2. The major costs associated with holding inventory are acquisition costs, holding costs, and out-of-stock losses.

E. Materials handling involves the physical handling and moving of inventory.

F. Order processing needs to be expedient and reliable to minimize total distribution cost.

G. Protection is the primary function of packaging in physical distribution.

269

VII. Materials management

    A. Materials management involves getting production materials to the plant and transporting semi-finished goods within the manufacturing facility.

    B. One aspect of materials management requires managers to evaluate sources of suppliers and to acquire production materials to avoid uninterrupted production.

VIII. Logistical coordination

    A. Logistics involves coordinating physical distribution and materials management activities.

    B. Logistical planning must be market-oriented.

IX. Trends in physical distribution

    A. New computer-related technology, energy costs, and interorganizational cooperation are environmental conditions which have influenced trends in physical distribution.

    B. These environment conditions have had both positive and negative impact on trends in physical distribution.

SUMMARY

Learning Objective One: To be familiar with the important role played by physical distribution in the marketing mix.

Effective marketing necessitates that products be available consistent with targeted customers preferences--when and where customers want the products. The marketing activities which are related to the efficient movement of finished products from producers to industrial users or consumers are referred to as physical distribution. These physical distribution activities create time and place utilities and are elements of all exchange situations. Management of these activities involves designing and administering systems to control the flow of products.

Learning Objective Two: To discuss the major objective of physical distribution--satisfying buyers while reducing costs--and to explain what managers of distribution can do to bring about this partially self-contradictory goal.

The major objective of physical distribution is to minimize total distribution cost while maximizing the level of service demanded by target customers. The paradox is that increasing the level of customer service increases distribution costs, or conversely, reducing cost usually requires decreasing the level of services. Physical distribution managers can resolve this paradox by implementing the marketing concept. These managers should design consumer-satisfying systems to fit target customers' needs consistent with prices that they are willing to pay. Finally, competitive physical distribution policies should be considered in designing the distribution system. Each part of the distribution system needs to be considered in attempting to satisfy customer service demands at a reasonable cost.

Learning Objective Three: To explain the total cost approach to physical distribution.

The total cost approach to physical distribution refers to a systems-philosophy of distribution management. Managers who practice this systems-philosophy direct their efforts at reducing total distribution system cost consistent with level of service specified by a target group of customers. The implementation of this approach may necessitate a higher cost of some component of the distribution system to effect a greater cost reduction in another system component. Customer satisfaction is always a concern of managers who adhere to the total cost concept of distribution.

Learning Objective Four: To be familiar with the various modes of transportation of products available to shippers and their comparative advantages and disadvantages.

The modes of transportation available to shippers include motor carriers, air freight, railroads, water transportation, and pipelines. In general, motor carriers offer shippers transportation which is very accessible and flexible, but relatively expensive compared to other modes of transportation. Air freight has the advantages of speed, distance capabilities, and reliable deliveries; its disadvantages include high costs and specialized facilities. Railroads have the ability to move heavy, bulky items long distances at low cost. Railroads offer specialized services such as piggyback service and diversion-in-transit privileges. In addition to slower delivery, railroads have a reputation for damaged goods and unreliable delivery. Water transportation is an inexpensive, but slow, way to transport goods. Like railroads, water transportation has a reputation for unreliable delivery and damaged goods. Pipelines provide reliable delivery of undamaged goods. Specialized facilities and the ability to carry only limited products (natural gas and crude petroleum) are disadvantages of pipelines. A general comparison of the attributes of these five transportation modes is provided by Exhibit 14-4 in the Zikmund and d'Amico textbook.

271

Learning Objective Five: To understand the purposes of such distribution-related activities as warehousing, order processing, materials handling, and inventory control.

Warehousing involves the marketing activities of storage (holding and housing of inventory to match production and consumption cycles) and breaking bulk (allocation of inventory to buyers). Decisions regarding number, location, and types of warehouses and levels of inventory must be made. Inventory control involves determining what level of inventories will provide customer service without overstocking nor excessive stockouts. The distribution-related activity of materials handling involves the physical handling and moving of inventory. The purpose of order processing is to expedite orders quickly and accurately to minimize total distribution costs.

Learning Objective Six: To distinguish among the terms physical distribution, logistics, and materials management as these terms are technically defined.

Physical distribution and materials management comprise logistics. Materials management encompasses those activities associated with getting raw materials to the manufacturing facilities and movement of goods-in-process within the factory. Physical distribution involves those activities dealing with the efficient movement of finished products between production and consumption.

VOCABULARY BUILDING

Matching Exercise

Match the following by placing the letter of the concept or term on the blank preceding the phrase which best describes the concept or term. You should use a term or concept only once.

A. Physical distribution
B. Physical distribution management
C. Materials management
D. Logistics
E. Total cost concept
F. Transportation
G. Piggyback service

H. Diversion-in-transit
I. Warehousing
J. Storage
K. Breaking bulk
L. Inventory control
M. Materials handling
N. Order processing

_____ 1. The use of muscle power, machinery, or other methods to identify, check, load, and unload raw materials and other goods.

_____ 2. The broad range of activities concerned with the design and administration of systems to control the efficient movement of finished products.

272

_____ 3. The privilege of directing a rail shipment to a specific destination that was not specified at the start of the trip.

_____ 4. The marketing activity of holding and housing goods before shipment to buyers.

_____ 5. The distribution process that entails getting production materials to points of production.

_____ 6. The physical movement of products through a channel of distribution.

_____ 7. The area of marketing concerned with physically, but efficiently, moving products from the point of production to the place of consumption or other use.

_____ 8. The physical distribution function of holding and housing goods in inventory.

_____ 9. The activities involved in deciding questions of inventory size, placement, and delivery.

_____ 10. A systematic procedure followed to fill customer orders after these have been received by the sales office.

VOCABULARY BUILDING

Programmed Learning Exercise

1. The overall objective of physical distribution is to minimize _____ _____ while maximizing _____ _____.

   [total cost, customer service]

2. In developing reasonable physical distribution objectives, marketing management should start with the marketing _____.

   [concept]

3. From a physical distribution perspective, the _____ _____ concept entails consideration of associated costs that occur when a particular method of distribution is used.

   [total cost]

4. The area of _____ _____ has been referred to as the "last frontier" of marketing.

   [physical distribution]

5. The major alternative modes of transportation include _____ _____, _____ _____, _____, _____ _____, and _____.

   [motor carrier, air freight, railroads, water transportation, pipelines]

6. Railroads have a comparative advantage over other transportation modes when the freight to be hauled consists of _____ and _____ items.

   [heavy, bulky]

7. _____ is the slowest mode of transportation.

   [Water]

8. _____ are used to transport natural gas and crude petroleum.

   [Pipelines]

9. The two key functions of warehousing are _____ and _____.

   [storage and breaking bulk]

10. High-capacity _____ warehouses are located near manufacturing points.

    [storage]

11. _____ costs are the expenses incurred in obtaining inventory.

    [Acquisition]

12. _____ costs are costs incurred as a result of keeping inventory housed.

    [Holding]

13. Losses that occur when customers demand goods that the marketer cannot provide are referred to as _____ losses.

    [out-of-stock]

14. The goal to get products out of storage and into the hands of buyers is better reflected through the concept of a _____ _____ rather than the concept of a warehouse.

    [distribution center]

15. Materials management is concerned with materials that are _____ to the point of production; whereas, physical distribution management focuses on _____ products.

    [inbound, outbound]

16. _____ involves activities concerned with achieving a smoothly controlled flow of goods through an organization and its channels of distribution.

[Logistics]

17. _____ encompasses materials management and physical distribution functions.

[Logistics]

18. Logistical planning should be _____-oriented.

[market]

19. _____ warehouses are operated by organizations for their own use.

[Private]

20. _____ warehouses are open to use by any organization willing to rent space in them.

[Public]

TRUE OR FALSE STATEMENTS

T F 1. Some aspect of physical distribution can be found in every exchange situation.

T F 2. Physical distribution connotes the design and administration of systems to control the flow of products.

T F 3. A realistic objective of physical distribution is to minimize each distribution component cost while maintaining customer service.

T F 4. The systems concept focuses on the idea that physical distribution elements are interrelated and interact toward achieving one goal.

T F 5. One potential payoff of increasing some system costs may come in the form of greater buyer satisfaction.

T F 6. Cost considerations in designing a physical distribution system should be evaluated on the basis of what customers want.

T F 7. Physical distribution cannot be used by a marketer to establish a differential advantage over rivals which produce homogeneous products.

T F 8. In selecting a specific mode of transportation, the physical distribution manager should consider total distribution costs first.

T F 9. Motor vehicles have a larger percentage of total ton miles in domestic intercity traffic than pipelines do.

T F 10. Trucks are less likely to have damages in transit than when rail freight is used.

T F 11. Air freight enables buyers to reduce inventory and associated warehousing costs.

T F 12. The transportation method known as "piggyback services" combines the economy of rail transportation with the speed and on-time record of air transportation.

T F 13. Pipelines are the slowest mode of transportation.

T F 14. The term "warehousing" is synonymous with the term "storage."

T F 15. Distribution warehouses are located near the manufacturer.

T F 16. Mistakes in order processing can carry through the whole process of getting products to customers.

T F 17. Packaging's primary purpose, as a physical distribution component, is protection against breakage, spoilage, and dirt.

T F 18. Materials management involves decisions related to inventories of raw materials and goods-in-process.

T F 19. Logistical management is a cost-oriented process.

T F 20. Physical distribution operates within a dynamic environment.

MULTIPLE CHOICE QUESTIONS

1. Physical distribution focuses on
    a. the movement of supplies to a manufacturing plant.
    b. all flows within a channel of distribution.
    c. the physical aspects of the flow of products through channels of distribution.
    d. the movement and control of raw materials, goods-in-process, and finished goods inventories.

2. The basic goal of physical distribution is to
    a. minimize cost of each distribution component.
    b. minimize total distribution costs.

c. maximize customer service while minimizing cost of each distribution component.
d. maximize customer service while minimizing total distribution cost.

3. Which is not a component of physical distribution?
   a. Containerization.
   b. Materials management.
   c. Order processing.
   d. Storage.

4. A letter arrives at Maid of Scandinavia, a mail-order retailer in Minneapolis, requesting a set of "ironware" cooking pots. The woman who opens the letter arranges for the merchandise to be shipped and charges the cost of the pots to the customer's MasterCard number. This activity is
   a. inventory management.
   b. transportation.
   c. order processing.
   d. packaging.

5. Which is not a reason physical distribution is described as the "last frontier" of marketing?
   a. Channels complexity hinders physical distribution activities.
   b. The physical distribution function is performed behind the scenes.
   c. Computerization and automation can be used extensively, but profitably, in physical distribution.
   d. Contrary to the question, all (a, b, c) are reasons why physical distribution is the "last frontier" of marketing.

6. Which is not a potential area for a differential advantage based on physical distribution?
   a. Delivering undamaged goods.
   b. Reliable delivery.
   c. Avoiding order processing errors.
   d. Price differentials.

7. Which is not an activity of managerial responsibility associated with the physical distribution function of movement of products?
   a. Handling of finished products.
   b. Procuring supplies and raw materials.
   c. Transporting of finished products.
   d. Warehousing of finished products.

8. Which is not an advantage that trucks have over railroads when it comes to carrying freight?
   a. Trucks have a worse record than trains in terms of freight becoming damaged.
   b. Trucks are more flexible in their operations than are trains.
   c. Trucks are more accessible to shippers of merchandise.
   d. Trucks are more efficient in moving comparatively small shipments.

277

9. The primary advantages of air freight over other modes of transportation are
   a. cost and speed.
   b. distance capabilities and cost.
   c. speed and distance capabilities.
   d. reliable delivery and cost.

10. Which is not a disadvantage of railroads?
    a. Delivery is relatively slow.
    b. Railroads have a reputation for damaging goods-in-transit
    c. Railroads have an unreliable delivery record.
    d. Railroads cannot haul large, bulky items.

11. The mode of transportation which carries the largest percentage of ton miles in intercity domestic traffic is
    a. airplanes.   c. railroads.
    b. motor carriers.   d. pipelines.

12. Given the choice of having a small group of large high-capacity warehouses, or a large group of smaller warehouses located near customers, an effective marketer would choose
    a. the option of having a larger group of smaller warehouses located near customers since this is more consistent with the marketing concept.
    b. having a smaller group of larger warehouses since this is more consistent with the marketing concept.
    c. whichever option is least expensive.
    d. whichever option would best satisfy customers' desires for good delivery at a price they are willing to bear.

13. Which terms describe which areas of activity in the diagram below?

    SOURCE OF MATERIALS $\xrightarrow{\text{"A"}}$ POINT OF PRODUCTION $\xrightarrow{\text{"B"}}$ CUSTOMERS
    └─────────────────────────────── "C" ───────────────────────────────┘

    a. "A" is materials management, "B" is physical distribution, "C" is logistics.
    b. "A" is physical distribution, "B" is materials management, "C" is logistics.
    c. "A" is materials handling, "B" is physical distribution, "C" is logistics.
    d. "A" is logistics, "B" is materials management, "C" is physical distribution.

278

14. The three major costs associated with holding inventory are
    a. acquisition costs, holding costs, and out-of-stock costs.
    b. holding costs, out-of-stock costs, and handling costs.
    c. out-of-stock costs, handling costs, and acquisition costs.
    d. handling costs, acquisition costs, and holding costs.

15. Which is not a procurement activity?
    a. Materials specifications.
    b. Materials handling.
    c. Value analysis.
    d. Buying transportation inbound.

QUICK QUIZ

1Q.
What if a marketing organization discovers it cannot find a proper balance between the goals of maximum service and minimum costs?

1A.
Careful planning should permit an effective marketer to reach some balance acceptable to the target customer. However, it can happen that the maintenance of high service increases costs to an unacceptable level, or that holding costs down diminishes service to a too-low level. The marketing concept does not say an organization has to go broke trying to please its customers. Our system is such, however, that failures do occur when, for whatever reason, proper marketing mixes cannot be constructed.

2Q.
Materials management sounds a bit like purchasing. What is the difference?

2A.
Purchasing is a part of materials management. Materials management aims to integrate and manage all activities dealing with raw materials and supplies right up to the point of production. Obviously, purchasing is part of this process, but as Exhibit 14-7 in Zikmund and d'Amico shows, many more activities are included in materials management. One could

279

draw a parallel between purchasing and materials management and selling and marketing. Marketing includes selling and draws an entire process of buyer satisfaction together into one major business activity. Materials management does much the same thing with purchasing.

EXPERIENTIAL ACTIVITIES

14-A. Establishment of a Realistic Physical Distribution Objective

You are the new physical distribution manager for Tire Specialties Companies, a wholesaler of motor vehicle parts and equipment to garages, service stations, and car dealers located in five eastern states. During your evaluation of Tire Specialties' physical distribution system, you found no policy regarding level of customer service even though the company services 40 percent of its customers within one week and another 50 percent within two weeks. For the last eight months, major competitors have been servicing 70 percent of their customers within one week. During this time period, Tire Specialties' sales have decreased 30 percent--customers are placing smaller orders. Your responsibility as physical distribution manager has been to minimize total physical distribution costs without consideration of level of customer service. You feel your responsibility should be to minimize total costs given a customer service level policy. Based on various levels of customer service, you have compiled these cost data.

Customer Service Level (Percent of Customers Serviced Within One Week)	Transportation Costs (000)	Warehousing and Inventory Costs (000)
10%	$525	$ 75
20	425	100
30	350	125
40	275	175
50	200	225
60	150	250
70	125	300
80	200	350
90	250	450
100	325	575

CHAPTER 15

INTRODUCTION TO PRICING CONCEPTS

OBJECTIVE

This chapter explains the concept of price as a statement of value. Pricing objectives must be consistent with marketing and company objectives related to income, sales, competition, and/or social concerns.

OUTLINE

I.   What is price?

    A. Price is a statement of value, usually expressed in dollars.

    B. Value is the power of one product to attract another product.

II. Price in the economy

    A. The major purpose of price is to help allocate products within our economy.

    B. The importance of the price variable increases during inflationary periods.

III. Pricing in marketing strategy

    A. Sales revenue equals price times unit sales volume.

    B. Price influences unit sales volume and can add symbolic value to a product.

    C. Pricing strategies support an organization's other marketing strategies with which they must be coordinated.

IV. Considerations in determining pricing strategies

   A. Marketers need to consider the importance of price to their target market, competitors' prices and actions, costs, demand, and legal ramifications when evaluating pricing alternatives.

   B. Price competition is more prevalent in industries where competing products are not distinctive than in industries where a differential advantage can be based on other marketing variables (non-price competition).

   C. The ability of an organization to maintain prices and unit volume under competitive conditions indicates an effective marketing plan.

   D. Target market considerations are significant factors in determining pricing strategies.

V. Pricing objectives

   A. Pricing objectives establish what is to be accomplished with price.

   B. Pricing objectives must be consistent with marketing and company objectives.

   C. Pricing objectives may be classified according to orientation: income, sales, competition, or social concern.

   D. Return on investment (ROI) is the ratio of profits to assets (or net worth) and serves as a standard when evaluating alternative pricing standards.

      1. ROI is influenced by turnover rate (sales divided by tangible assets).

      2. Though the ROI formula is a frequently used income-oriented pricing objective, marketing managers use judgment in determining the ROI standard.

   E. Other income-related pricing objectives are those related to cash flow, maximizing profits, and keeping a going-concern.

   F. Sales-oriented pricing objectives are designed to improve or maintain share of market (company sales as percentage of industry sales) and survival.

   G. Competition-oriented objectives are those which attempt to meet, avoid, or undercut competition.

1. Competition influences pricing objectives.

2. Price stabilization (match competitors' prices) is a common pricing objective.

3. Organizations should maximize long-term profits by charging prices consistent with target market and government perceptions.

4. Price leadership exists when some regular relationship exists between the leader's price and other firms within the industry.

H. Two social-oriented pricing objectives relate to maintaining employment and having ethical behavior.

SUMMARY

Learning Objective One: To define price and discuss its place in our society.

Price is a statement of value--the power of one product to attract another product in an exchange. Price facilitates exchange, especially when expressed in terms of a monetary value such as dollars in the United States economy, by enabling buyers and sellers to determine the relative value of the products.

Learning Objective Two: To show that price is both an economic and marketing tool.

Price helps allocate products within our economy to those members who demand and have the ability and willingness to pay for those items. Thus, price helps to achieve equilibrium between supply and demand. As a marketing tool, price can be increased if demand exceeds supply or if people attach symbolic value to more expensive products. Conversely, price can be adjusted downward through rebates, coupons, or special sales to make the value of the product more attractive to customers, especially in inflationary times. Marketers use price to achieve financial and market-share objectives since price is one of the major determinants of sales revenues as well as influencing unit sales volume. Marketing managers can adjust price quickly to respond to environmental changes.

Learning Objective Three: To know how price interacts with the rest of the marketing mix.

The four major marketing variables--product, place, price, and promotion--must blend into an effective marketing strategy to stimulate demand. Each variable's strategies must support and, in turn, be supported by strategies of the other major mix variables. Premium prices, which sustain sales volume, provide additional funds for product development, more efficient distribution, and more effective promotion to communicate the product's value to potential buyers. A premium pricing strategy may reflect quality products or high customer service levels. Non-price competition, rather than price competition, tends to lead to an effective long-term differential advantage. In summary, properly priced products facilitate exchanges, enhance the effectiveness of the other variables, and are indicative of a sound marketing plan.

Learning Objective Four: To discuss how inflation affects the consumer's view of price and the marketer's view of price.

Inflation reduces the buying power of consumers while increasing their sensitivity to price changes as they search for better values and lower prices. Thus, marketers place greater emphasis on the price variable during these inflationary periods. In order to offer lower-priced products, marketers modify products or reduce distribution-related costs. Promotion stresses lower prices and better values.

Learning Objective Five: To explain how price is related to the organization's objectives.

Pricing objectives must be consistent with marketing and company objectives from which they are derived. Since marketing is the revenue-generating function of an organization, pricing objectives must enable an organization to achieve its financial, sales, and competitive objectives. Exhibit 15-1 in the Zikmund and d'Amico textbook highlights the role that pricing can play in attaining selected types of organizational goals.

VOCABULARY BUILDING

Matching Exercise

Match the following by placing the letter of the concept or term on the blank preceding the phrase which best describes the concept or term. You should use a term or concept only once.

A.	Value	F.	Pricing objective
B.	Barter	G.	Return on investment (ROI)
C.	Price	H.	Turnover
D.	Price competition	I.	Share of market
E.	Non-price competition	J.	Price stabilization

_I_ 1. Percentage of total product sales accounted for by a particular brand.

_A_ 2. The power of one product to attract another product in exchange.

288

_G_ 3. The ratio of profits to assets or net worth for an organizational segment.

_C_ 4. A statement of value which can be used to relate the relative value of products.

_F_ 5. Desired result associated with a particular pricing strategy.

_J_ 6. A pricing strategy of matching the competitor's price.

_B_ 7. Exchange of products without the use of money.

_E_ 8. Competition among firms where marketing variables other than price are emphasized to gain a strategic advantage.

_H_ 9. Sales divided by tangible assets.

_D_ 10. Competition among firms with homogeneous products where price is emphasized to gain a strategic advantage.

VOCABULARY BUILDING

Programmed Learning Exercise

1. Price serves to _allocate_ products within relatively free market economies.

   [allocate]

2. Price multiplied by unit sales volume equals _Sales Revenue_.

   [sales revenue]

3. The most flexible element of the marketing mix is _Price_.

   [price]

4. Pricing strategies support the firm's other marketing strategies which, in turn, support the pricing strategies as all four variables of the _marketing mix_ must fit together to stimulate demand.

   [marketing mix]

5. When competing products are not distinctive, _Price_ becomes the key marketing mix variable.

   [price]

6. IBM obtains a price substantially above many of its competitors. By emphasizing other marketing mix elements, IBM is employing _____ competition.

[non-price]

7. Pricing of products is still an _____.

[art]

8. Pricing objectives can relate to _____, _____, _____, and social concern.

[income, sales, competition]

9. Prices are set to bring about a _____.

[result]

10. Pricing objectives must be coordinated with the firm's other marketing objectives which flow from the company's overall objectives.

[marketing]

11. Return on investment serves as a comparison _____ when evaluating alternative prices.

[standard]

12. ROI is called the Profit target.

[profit]

13. A marketer can stabilize prices by matching competitors' prices.

[stabilize]

14. It is good marketing to maximize profits over the long -term by charging prices that satisfy the public.

[long]

15. An "all the traffic will bear" approach to pricing violates a major premise of the _____ _____.

[marketing concept]

TRUE OR FALSE STATEMENTS

(T) F   1. Barter is the power of one product to attract another product in exchange without the use of money.

(T) F   2. Marketers are more concerned with price in periods of higher inflation rates.

290

T (F) 3. If a price is increased and unit volume and costs remain the same, only sales revenue will be increased.

(T) F 4. Other marketing strategies must support an organization's pricing strategies.

(T) F 5. Managerial judgment is important in determining pricing strategies.

(T) F 6. Promotion helps to show that the price charged is justified.

(T) F 7. Price competition is more prevalent in industries with relatively homogeneous products.

T (F) 8. Pricing is seldom indicative of overall marketing effectiveness.

T (F) 9. Customers always want the lowest price for any product.

(T) F 10. Pricing objectives help facilitate the determination of price.

T (F) 11. Marketing managers set prices about equal to those of competitors to avoid competition.

(T) F 12. Maintaining employment is a social concern objective.

(T) F 13. Marketers adjust prices and discounts to encourage purchases and rapid payment with an objective to increase cash flow.

T (F) 14. A manufacturer of effective prescription drugs should use a profit maximization pricing objective only.

(T) F 15. A high return on investment can be achieved through a low profit margin and a high turnover.

T (F) 16. ROI pricing involves little or no judgment by the marketing manager.

(T) F 17. Market leaders would be most likely to use a pricing objective of maintaining market share.

T (F) 18. A price stabilization strategy is likely to be followed by a company which has introduced a new, unique product.

(T) F 19. An "all the market will bear" objective may result in threats and boycotts.

(T) F 20. A typical pricing strategy is matching the competition or offering competitive prices.

MULTIPLE CHOICE QUESTIONS

1. Which does not fit under the definition of price?
    a. Interest paid to a bank for money it loans.
    b. Tuition paid for a correspondence course.
    c. Toll paid to use a turnpike.
    d. Value added to a product by distribution.

2. In relatively free economies most items of value are distributed to those who demand those items and
    a. have the means to pay for those items.
    b. are willing to pay for those items.
    c. have a need for those products.
    d. have both the means and the willingness to pay for those items.

3. During periods of inflation, marketers may try all but which one to appeal to price-conscious shoppers?
    a. Adjust products to bring out lower priced goods.
    b. Stress value more in promotional messages.
    c. Decrease all promotional efforts.
    d. Cut back services to hold prices down.

4. Which statement regarding price is incorrect?
    a. Price influences unit sales volume.
    b. Price cannot add symbolic value to a product.
    c. Price can be justified by promotion.
    d. Price supports other marketing mix variables.

5. Which factor would be least important to know when evaluating pricing alternatives?
    a. Competitive capacity.   c. Legal influences.
    b. Costs.   d. Pricing objectives.

6. Which major marketing mix variable is least effective as a long-term basis for a differential advantage?
    a. Product.   c. Price.
    b. Place.   d. Promotion.

7. When a company can charge a high price for its products and still sell a reasonably large quantity of products, this indicates
    a. the rest of the company's marketing must be excellent.
    b. the customers are obviously not making good, rational decisions.
    c. competition is very severe in this market.
    d. customers in this industry think price is unimportant.

292

8. The most significant factor that affects a marketing manager's pricing decisions is
    a. the product's production and marketing costs.
    b. the target market's demand for the product.
    c. competitors' prices.
    d. other elements of the marketing mix.

9. Which is not an income-based pricing objective?
    a. Achieve a target ROI.
    b. Maximize profits.
    c. Increase cash flow.
    d. Encourage sales growth.

10. When a marketer adjusts price and discounts to encourage more purchases by existing customers and to attract new customers, this marketer has a pricing objective to
    a. avoid competition.
    b. encourage sales growth.
    c. increase cash flow.
    d. achieve a target ROI.

11. Pricing objectives do not reflect
    a. legal barriers.
    b. social concern.
    c. competition.
    d. sales.

12. Which pricing objective can be used to evaluate alternative marketing strategies?
    a. Sales growth.
    b. Cash flow.
    c. ROI.
    d. Profit maximization.

13. How does turnover affect the company's return on investment?
    a. The lower the turnover, the higher the ROI.
    b. For companies with low profit margins, high turnover means higher ROI.
    c. As one increases, the other decreases.
    d. Turnover has no relationship to ROI.

14. In which situation would competition be least likely to be a major influence on pricing objectives?
    a. Avoid competition.
    b. Maximize long-term profits.
    c. Stabilize prices.
    d. Sales growth.

15. Successful price leaders tend to have all of these characteristics except
    a. large advertising budgets.
    b. large share of the industry's production capacity.
    c. large market share.
    d. strong distribution system.

QUICK QUIZ

1Q.
At a fast food franchise, how are product and price related?

1A.
The higher priced items are either bigger, better, or served in special ways so that the product "supports" the price.

2Q.
For what kinds of product categories are buyers likely to want higher prices rather than lower prices?

2A.
Buyers often judge quality by price, thus, for almost any product category, some buyers will prefer a higher price. Examples are theatre tickets, champagne, specialty food items, restaurants, and hotel rooms.

3Q.
Can you be a member of more than one target market, that is, use price as a basis for segmentation?

3A.
Yes. You might buy a J.C. Penney sports shirt for yourself, but a Lacoste sports shirt as a present.

EXPERIENTIAL ACTIVITIES

15-A. Pricing in Marketing Strategy

You need to obtain the prices of five food products from six stores located near your university or college. These prices should be recorded on the form on page 295. The mix of six stores should include, if available, two supermarkets and/or warehouse stores, two neighborhood grocery stores and/or convenience food stores, and two nonconventional food outlets. If a product is not available at a store, your statistics and interpretation should reflect its unavailability.

Assignment

1.   Complete the form on page 295.

	Supermarket or Warehouse		Convenience or Neighborhood		Unconventional	
	Store 1	Store 2	Store 3	Store 4	Store 5	Store 6
Store Name						
Store Address						
Date Visited						
Time Visited						
Product	Price	Price	Price	Price	Price	Price
1 large tube (8.2 oz.) of AquaFresh toothpaste						
1 Dozen Eggs (Grade A medium)						
1 quart of whole milk (lowest price)						
1 6-pack of 12 oz. cans of Like						
1 twin pack of potato chips						
TOTAL PRICE						

2. Explain how price supports the marketing mix for each type of store you surveyed in your local area.

Supermarkets: _____

_____

_____

_____

Warehouse stores: _____

_____

_____

_____

Neighborhood grocery stores: _____

_____

_____

_____

Convenience stores: _____

_____

_____

_____

Nonconventional food stores: _____

_____

_____

_____

3. Explain the importance of price as a component in the marketing mix for each type of store surveyed.

Supermarkets: _____

_____

_____

_____

Warehouse stores: _____

_____

_____

_____

Neighborhood grocery stores: _____

_____

_____

_____

ANSWERS TO OBJECTIVE QUESTIONS

MATCHING

1.	I	3.	G	5.	F	7.	B	9.	H
2.	A	4.	C	6.	J	8.	E	10.	D

TRUE OR FALSE

1.	T	5.	T	9.	F	13.	T	17.	T
2.	T	6.	T	10.	T	14.	F	18.	F
3.	F	7.	T	11.	F	15.	T	19.	T
4.	T	8.	F	12.	T	16.	F	20.	T

MULTIPLE CHOICE

1.	d	4.	b	7.	a	10.	b	13.	b
2.	d	5.	a	8.	b	11.	a	14.	d
3.	c	6.	c	9.	d	12.	c	15.	a

CHAPTER 16

COSTS AND DEMAND: HOW THEY INFLUENCE PRICING DECISIONS

OBJECTIVE

Pricing methods should consider costs and demand. Cost-oriented methods of pricing include markup, cost-plus, average-cost, target return pricing, and full-line pricing. Break-even analysis and marginal analysis are two demand-oriented pricing methods.

OUTLINE

I. Determining price levels

    A. Marketing managers should follow a logical pricing procedure when determining a product's price.

    B. Costs and demand are two major pricing considerations.

II. Cost-oriented pricing methods

    A. Many marketing intermediaries use the mark-up on selling price method to set prices.

        1. Mark-up on selling price and mark-up on costs differ in terms of the percentage of mark-up.

        2. Marketers must know the product's cost and the mark-up percent on selling price or its equivalent mark-up percent on costs to determine price.

        3. The mark-up margin needs to provide funds to cover all selling and administrative expenses and profit.

    B. Manufacturers often use a cost-plus method to establish price.

C. The average-cost method necessitates that marketers divide required profits plus total costs at a given level of output by the number of units produced at this level to obtain the average cost of a single unit.

D. Under target return pricing, marketing managers first calculate per unit fixed costs and per unit target return and then add variable costs per unit to obtain price.

E. Full-line pricing recognizes that pricing an item in a product line should consider the prices of the other product line items.

F. Cost-oriented methods do not consider units demanded by the market at the established price.

III. Demand-oriented pricing

A. Marketers can estimate demand schedules using such techniques as surveys of buyers' intentions, analysis of past sales data, or surveys of knowledgeable executives or salespersons.

B. The demand curve is a graphical representation between price and the amount of a product demanded at particular prices.

   1. The "standard" demand curve depicts that more quantity of a product is demanded as price decreases.

   2. Marketers seldom have an exact demand schedule.

C. Price elasticity of demand measures the ratio of the change in the quantity demanded to the change in a product's price.

   1. Price inelasticity of demand exists when there is little variation in the quantity demanded as price changes.

      a. Total revenue increases when price increases.

      b. Total revenue decreases when price decreases.

   2. Price elasticity exists when there is much variation in the quantity demanded as price changes.

      a. Total revenue decreases when price increases.

      b. Total revenue increases when price decreases.

D. Cross-elasticity of demand measures the relationship between the price elasticity of one product and the price elasticity of a substitute or complementary product.

E. Total revenue equals total cost at the break-even point--neither profit nor loss exists.

F. Price has an impact on when the break-even point is achieved.

G. Break-even analysis considers demand as well as costs.

   1. Marketers need to determine the effect of a price change on demand to use break-even analysis effectively.

   2. Break-even analysis can be used to eliminate extreme pricing situations and to evaluate alternative marketing strategies.

H. Marketing managers can determine profitable prices by overlapping the estimated demand curve and a series of break-even points.

IV. Marginal analysis

A. Marginal analysis deals with determining the cost and revenue associated with the production and the sale of each <u>additional</u> unit of a product.

B. An organization maximizes profits where marginal revenue equals marginal costs.

SUMMARY

Learning Objective One: To know how to use several tools employed in determining what a particular product's price will be.

   This chapter discusses five cost-oriented and two demand-oriented methods to determine price. The cost-oriented methods are mark-up on selling price or mark-up on costs, cost-plus, average-cost, target return pricing, and full-line pricing. These five methods recognize that costs establish the floor for prices. Break-even analysis and marginal analysis incorporate demand considerations into the pricing strategy. Since four of these pricing methods are addressed by other learning objectives, only three cost-oriented methods will be discussed here.

   In order to use the mark-up on selling price method, the marketer must know (a) the product's cost, (b) its mark-up percent on selling price, and (c) its equivalent mark-up percent on costs to determine price. One converts the

303

mark-up percent on selling price to mark-up percent on costs using this formula: mark-up percent on selling price divided by the quantity of 100 percent less the mark-up percent on selling price. For example, if the mark-up percent on selling price is 20 percent, the equivalent mark-up percent on costs is 25 percent [20%/(100%-20%)]. If a retailer purchased a shirt for $10 and used a 20 percent mark-up on selling price, the price of the shirt would be $12.50 ($10 plus 25% of $10). To convert mark-up percent on costs to its equivalent percent on selling price, one would use this formula: mark-up percent on costs divided by the quantity of 100 percent plus the mark-up percent on costs. Thus, a 25 percent mark-up on costs is the same as a 20 percent mark-up on selling price [25%/(100% + 25%)].

The cost-plus method requires that marketing managers determine the costs of producing and marketing the product and adding to these costs a profit figure or a percent of the costs to arrive at price. If a product costs $100 to manufacture and distribute and the firm adds 20 percent of costs to the product, the product's price is $120.

The average-cost method necessitates that one identifies all costs (fixed and variable) associated with a given level of production or forecasted sales and a profit margin in order to arrive at an average cost. For example, if total costs are $150,000 at an anticipated sales level of 100,000 units and the desired profit margin is $50,000, the product's price would be $2.00 ($150,000/100,000 + $50,000/100,000 = $1.50 + $0.50).

Learning Objective Two: To understand target return and full-line pricing.

In using target return pricing, the suggested price equals variable costs per unit plus fixed costs per unit and target return per unit. The fixed costs per unit and target return per unit are based on the number of units expected to be sold. One can illustrate target return pricing by assuming that (a) total fixed costs equal $100,000, (b) target return is 10 percent of a $250,000 investment or $25,000, (c) variable costs are $2.50 per unit, and (d) expected sales volume is 10,000 units. The suggested price would be $15.00 [($100,000 + $25,000) /10,000 + $2.50]. If the actual number of units sold differs from the forecasted level, the target return will vary directly with the difference between the units sold and units forecasted. For example, if actual sales were 12,000 units, the return would be $50,000 or $25,000 over the target return [2,000 units times $12.50--the difference between selling price and variable costs per unit]. If, however, sales were 7,500 units, the organization would sustain an actual loss of $6,250. This is $31,250 (2,500 units times $12.50) below the target revenue necessary to achieve the $25,000 target return. At 7,500 units the actual price should be $19.17, not $15.00.

Full-line pricing is appropriate for organizations which market many products with common fixed costs. Since equitable allocation of these shared fixed costs to many products is difficult, marketers often use variable costs as a pricing floor. Any price above variable costs contributes to fixed costs and profits. These prices, however, must be consistent with consumers' perceptions toward the prices established for the full line of products.

Learning Objective Three: To understand that demand changes as prices change.

For most products, an inverse relationship exists between the quantity demanded and price. More of a product will be demanded as price decreases. And, as price increases, the quantity demanded decreases. Marketers need to estimate the demand schedule for their products to set prices effectively.

Learning Objective Four: To understand the price elasticity of demand.

Price elasticity of demand measures the change in the quantity demanded compared to the change in price. Price inelasticity of demand exists when the relative change in quantity is less than the relative change in price. If a product has relative price inelasticity of demand, a marketer can increase total revenue by increasing price. In this situation a decrease in price will decrease total revenue. Price elasticity of demand exists when the relative change in quantity exceeds the corresponding change in price. For products with relative price elasticity of demand, marketers can increase total revenue by lowering price. However, if price is raised, total revenue decreases.

Learning Objective Five: To understand break-even analysis and marginal analysis.

Break-even analysis enables marketers to determine the quantity (break-even point) at which total revenue equals total costs. An organization sustains a loss below the break-even quantity; whereas, above this point, a profit is realized. A lower break-even quantity can be attained by reducing costs (fixed or variable) or increasing price--provided price inelasticity of demand exists. Marketing managers must recognize that customers may not respond to the higher price. One can illustrate break-even analysis by assuming that (a) total fixed costs equal $120,000, (b) variable costs are $4 per unit, and (c) price per unit is $10. The break-even quantity (BEQ) is 20,000 units where BEQ = TFC/(P-VC) = $120,000/($10-$4). If price is increased to $12, the BEQ would be 15,000 units [$120,000/($12-$4)], assuming the market would buy at least 15,000 units at the price of $12 each. By overlapping demand analysis and break-even analysis, marketing managers can identify a range of profitable prices.

Marginal analysis focuses on the costs and revenue associated with each additional unit of a product. Profits continue to increase as long as marginal revenue exceeds marginal cost. In fact, profits are maximized when marginal revenue equals marginal cost or MR=MC. If marginal cost exceeds marginal revenue, the organization has sustained a loss on that additional unit and can increase profits by reducing operations until MR=MC.

Learning Objective Six: To show how managerial judgment is used to finally establish a product's market price.

Costs and demand are major influences on the pricing decision. Neither factor can be determined with certainty. Full-line pricing acknowledges the difficulty of allocating costs. Thus, allocating costs of various items in a product line or product mix involves judgment.

VOCABULARY BUILDING

Matching Exercise

Match the following by placing the letter of the concept or term on the blank preceding the phrase which best describes the concept or term. You should use a term or concept only once.

A. Mark-up on selling price	G. Cross-elasticity
B. Mark-up on cost	H. Break-even point
C. Full-line pricing	I. Marginal analysis
D. Target return pricing	J. Marginal costs
E. Demand curve	K. Marginal revenue
F. Elasticity of demand	

_____ 1. A pricing method that determines a price intended to yield a particular level of profit to the organization.

_____ 2. The revenue associated with selling one additional unit of a product.

_____ 3. The amount added to the cost of a product divided by its selling price.

_____ 4. A measure of the degree in which a change in price affects demand.

_____ 5. The quantity at which revenues and costs are equal.

_____ 6. The expenses associated with producing and marketing one additional unit of a product.

_____ 7. The approach to pricing that recognizes that items in a product line should not be priced independently of other items in the product line.

306

_____ 8. The relationship between the price elasticity of one product and that of substitutable or complementary products.

_____ 9. The method concerned with determining the costs and revenue associated with the sale of each additional unit of a product.

_____10. Graphically depicts the relationship between various prices and the amount of product desired at those prices.

VOCABULARY BUILDING

Programmed Learning Exercise

1. The two major considerations in pricing decisions are _____ and _____.

    [costs, demand]

2. _____ provide the floor on which to build most pricing strategies.

    [Costs]

3. Marketers who price by adding a given amount to costs use a _____-_____ approach to set price.

    [cost-plus]

4. _____ costs fluctuate with the level of sales volume.

    [Variable]

5. _____ costs expire with passage of time regardless of volume.

    [Fixed]

6. In _____ _____ pricing, the manager includes fixed costs, variable costs, and a desired profit level.

    [target return]

7. In _____-_____ pricing, variable costs, which are attributable to a product, are used as a pricing floor in the expectation that revenues above this amount will contribute to fixed costs and profits.

    [full-line]

8. The relationship between price and demand is expressed by the _____ _____.

    [demand schedule]

9. As price increases, the quantity demanded _____ for the "standard" demand curve.

    [decreases]

307

10. Price elasticity of demand measures the sensitivity of the market to _____ in price.

[changes]

11. If prices are increased when demand is price inelastic, total revenue will _____.

[increase]

12. If a demand curve is perpendicular to the price axis, the demand curve will show complete price _____.

[elasticity]

13. Cross-elasticity of demand measures the relationship between two _____ or _____ products.

[complementary, substitutable]

14. The break-even point is _____ when variable costs are reduced.

[decreased]

15. _____ are maximized where MR = MC.

[Profits]

TRUE OR FALSE STATEMENTS

T   F   1. Marketing managers should follow a logical pricing procedure when setting price.

T   F   2. For a $30 profit margin, the mark-up on costs is larger than the mark-up on selling price.

T   F   3. Mark-up on costs is commonly used by marketing intermediaries since most records are based on costs.

T   F   4. In the average-cost method there is little risk that the quantity demanded will not equal the sales forecast.

T   F   5. A target return is usually represented as a percentage of investment.

T   F   6. Fixed costs vary with the level of production.

T   F   7. Marketing managers are concerned with the pricing of various items within a product line with full-line pricing.

T   F   8. The dominant problem with all cost-oriented pricing methods is that they do not consider demand.

308

T F   9.   Break-even analysis is a cost-oriented pricing approach.

T F   10. Demand is a major factor in determining price.

T F   11. Cost-oriented pricing methods make greater use of judgment than demand-oriented approaches.

T F   12. All marketers face demand schedules even though they cannot draw the demand curve.

T F   13. For the "standard" demand curve, demand moves in the opposite direction of the price change.

T F   14. If a demand curve is perpendicular to the quantity axis, the demand curve would show complete price elasticity.

T F   15. Published trade association information can be used to determine the nature of a product's demand curve.

T F   16. Perfect inelasticity of demand exists when the prices and demand for one product affect those of another product.

T F   17. The break-even point is the quantity at which costs and revenues meet.

T F   18. Demand has little impact on what the break-even quantity will be.

T F   19. The experience curve refers to the phenomenon that every doubling of production volume in manufacturing decreases the cost per unit a constant percent.

T F   20. It is at the lowest average cost where the average cost and marginal cost curves are equal.

MULTIPLE CHOICE QUESTIONS

1.   Which of the following is the best description of cost-oriented pricing methods from the marketer's point of view?
   a. Costs should be used to determine selling price by simply adding a profit margin to the cost of the product.
   b. Costs are matters for the accounting department to worry about.
   c. Marketers never price products offered for sale below the costs incurred in obtaining and selling those products.
   d. Costs should be considered as one of many variables important in the determination of price.

2. All are cost-oriented pricing methods except
   a. target return pricing.   c. break-even analysis.
   b. mark-up on selling price.   d. full-line pricing.

3. If a product costs $4.50 and the retailer marks it up 33 1/3% on the selling price, the selling price for this product would be
   a. $6.00.   c. $7.25.
   b. $6.75.   d. $9.00.

4. If a product costs $12 and the retailer used a 33 1/3% mark-up on costs, the selling price would be
   a. $16.00.   c. $20.00.
   b. $18.00.   d. $24.00.

5. If a product sells for $10 and the retailer used a 33 1/3% mark-up on costs, the mark-up on selling price would be
   a. 25%.   c. 66 2/3%.
   b. 50%.   d. indeterminant.

6. Using the average cost method of pricing, the selling price would be _____ if all costs are $150,000, the profit margin is $30,000, and the number of units produced and expected to be sold is 3,000.
   a. $10.00   c. $60.00
   b. $50.00   d. indeterminant

7. Using the target return pricing method, the selling price would be _____ if fixed costs equal $97,000, variable costs are $3.76 per unit, target return is $123,000, and 7,275 units are expected to be sold.
   a. $13.33   c. $30.24
   b. $17.09   d. $34.00

8. If the company in question 7 only sold 3,275 units, the company should price their product at
   a. $67.18.   c. $74.70.
   b. $70.94.   d. $78.46.

9. Which statement is incorrect according to the "standard" demand schedule?
   a. Quantity demanded increases as the price decreases.
   b. Quantity demanded increases as the price increases.
   c. Quantity demanded decreases as the price increases.
   d. Demand changes as price changes.

310

10. If there is price elasticity of demand,
    a. a change in price results in a significant change in quantity demanded.
    b. a change in price has no effect on quantity demanded.
    c. demand is flexible when price is changed.
    d. demand is not very flexible when price is changed.

11. Which person would demonstrate the most inelastic demand?
    a. A person buying a bar of soap.
    b. A person interested in a new stereo.
    c. A person who needs insulin and buys it from a pharmacist.
    d. A person who has low brand loyal toward toothpaste.

REFER TO THE FOLLOWING GRAPH FOR QUESTIONS 12 AND 13.

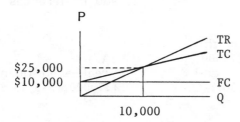

12. The $10,000 in the graph shows
    a. total variable costs.   c. the break-even amount.
    b. total fixed costs.   d. total revenue.

13. At 10,000 units, one finds that
    a. demand is perfectly inelastic.
    b. the firm is making a profit.
    c. MR = MC.
    d. the firm is breaking even.

14. If for some reason either variable or fixed costs increase, what would happen to the break-even quantity?
    a. Nothing.
    b. It would shift to the left.
    c. It would remain where it is, but at a different dollar amount.
    d. It would shift to the right.

15. Marginal analysis attempts to determine the cost and revenue associated with
    a. reaching the break-even point.
    b. cross-elasticity of demand.
    c. producing and marketing each additional unit of a product.
    d. producing and marketing more units of a product.

QUICK QUIZ

1Q.
What is the mark-up on selling price if an item costs $75 and sells for $125?

1A.
The mark-up on selling price is 40% or $50/$125.

2Q.
Are cost figures and profit goals all the marketer needs to price the product? That is, do fixed costs plus profit goals plus variable costs equal price?

2A.
No. Marketers must consider the market, that is, the demand for the product and consumer wants and preferences.

3Q.
What is the break-even quantity if total fixed costs are $7,000, selling price is $15.98, and variable cost per unit is $3.36?

3A.
Break-even quantity is 555 units [$7,000/($15,98-$3.36)].

4Q.
What price would a marketer recommend if total fixed costs, including profits, are $112,500, variable cost per unit is $2.75, and the break-even quantity is 50,000 units?

4A.
The suggested price would be $5.00. The price can be determined by using the formula P = (TFC/BEQ) + AVC, giving ($112,500/50,000) + $2.75.

5Q.
Can you explain why profits are maximized where marginal costs equal marginal revenue?

5A.
The logic is explained in the Box entitled "The Logic of Marginal Analysis" on page 456 in the Zikmund and d'Amico textbook.

EXPERIENTIAL ACTIVITIES

16-A. Break-even Analysis

A product manager of Electronics, Inc. needs to determine the price for a new miniaturized hand-held electronic wrestling game. She knows that fixed costs are $722,294 and that per unit variable costs will be minimized at 472,321 units (forecasted sales). At this level of forecasted sales, variable costs per unit will be $3.361.

Assignment

1. What price should the product manager recommend to break-even given these data and assuming there is sufficient demand?

   Price: _____

2. What price should be recommended if the firm expects a 16 percent return on their investment of $16,375,000?

   Price: _____

3. What is the break-even point if management sets the price at $9.95, variable costs remain $3.361 per unit, and fixed costs, including target return, are $3,250,000?

   Break-even point: _____

4. What is the break-even point if variable costs are reduced to $3.025 per unit, selling price and fixed costs, including target return, are $9.95 and $3,250,000 respectively.

   Break-even point: _____

313

5. What is the break-even point if fixed costs, including return, are reduced to $2,925,000, selling price and variable costs per unit are $9.95 and $3.361 respectively?

Break-even point: _____

16-B. Profit Maximization

As a research analyst, you have been asked by a product manager to compile cost-revenue-profit data regarding a battery cell container. A review of company records revealed the data provided in the table below. Other data indicate that:

a. average total cost (ATC) decreases by $30 when the quantity increases to three units from two units,

b. total variable costs (TVC) for four units is $21 more than for three units, and

c. average variable costs (AVC) is the same for five and seven units and AVC is $7 less for five units than for four units.

Quantity	Price	TR	MR	TFC	AFC	AVC	ATC	TVC	TC	MC	Profit
0	---	---	---		---	---	---	---		---	
1	100								180		
2	96										
3	90									66	
4	83										
5	76										
6	70						58				
7	64										
8	59								480		
9	54								580		
10	50				10				700		

314

TR:	Total revenue	ATC:	Average total costs
MR:	Marginal revenue	TVC:	Total variable costs
TFC:	Total fixed costs	TC:	Total costs
AFC:	Average fixed costs	MC:	Marginal cost
AVC:	Average variable costs		

Assignment

1. Complete the cost-revenue-profit table above.

2. The price which maximizes profit is $ _____

3. This price maximizes profit because _____

    _____

    _____

4. Draw the MR and MC curves on the graph below.

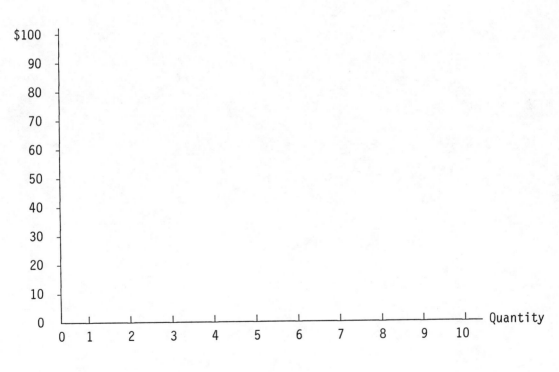

ANSWERS TO OBJECTIVE QUESTIONS

MATCHING

1.	D	3.	A	5.	H	7.	C	9.	I
2.	K	4.	F	6.	J	8.	G	10.	E

TRUE OR FALSE

1.	T	5.	T	9.	F	13.	T	17.	T
2.	T	6.	F	10.	T	14.	F	18.	F
3.	F	7.	T	11.	F	15.	T	19.	T
4.	F	8.	T	12.	T	16.	F	20.	F

MULTIPLE CHOICE

1.	d	4.	a	7.	d	10.	a	13.	d
2.	c	5.	a	8.	b	11.	c	14.	d
3.	b	6.	c	9.	b	12.	b	15.	c

CHAPTER 17

PRICING STRATEGIES AND TACTICS

OBJECTIVE

Marketing managers must use judgment in determining prices, pricing strategies, and discount policies that reflect market realities related to target market selection, geographic factors, and legal considerations.

OUTLINE

I. Pricing strategies

A. Marketing managers must decide whether to adhere to a one-price policy or a variable-price policy.

1. The one-price policy offers the simplicity of administration as all buyers are offered the same price.

2. The variable-price policy enables different buyers to obtain different prices either by using negotiation or by being perceived as different types of buyers.

B. Marketers select between a skimming (high price) or penetration (low price) pricing strategy when introducing a new product.

1. A skimming strategy is effective when the firm faces relatively inelastic demand and/or the firm segments the market on the basis of price.

2. An effective penetration strategy results when at least one of these four conditions exist--elastic demand, economies of scale, strong competitive threat, and mass market acceptance.

C. An individual product may be priced low in order to increase total profit on several complementary and/or related items (total profit pricing rather than item profit pricing).

D. Leader pricing is another strategy which sacrifices item profits.

   1. Loss leaders are frequently-purchased products priced at a loss to attract customers; whereas, a cost leader or a low-profit leader is priced at cost or at a small profit.

   2. Bait pricing is a strategy to attract buyers by advertising low-priced models with the expectation to trade the customer up to a higher margin item.

   3. Bait and switch exists when the seller does not intend to sell the bait item but only the higher margin item.

E. Marketers face kinked demand curves for products sold at traditional or customary prices.

F. A price lining strategy involves the determination of price points and subsequently adjusting prices to these points.

G. An odd price is a few cents below the nearest round dollar price (even price) and it is intended to lower the price psychologically.

H. Other types of pricing strategies include prestige pricing (status products priced high to convey a quality image), gentleman's pricing (fees charged for performing professional services), ethical pricing (lower prices attributable to social concern), special pricing (prices related to special marketing situations such as in-store announcements or second product at one-half price), and purchase-guarantee pricing (prices which protect buyers against price declines or price increases).

II. Distribution-based price policies

A. A F.O.B. price indicates the point at which the buyer assumes responsibility for shipping costs and where title transfers.

B. A delivered pricing or freight allowed pricing strategy builds delivery costs into the product's price.

   1. Uniform delivered pricing (postage stamp pricing) charges the same price at all locations.

   2. Zone pricing involves the determination of geographical zones and the establishment of a uniform delivered price within each zone.

C. A basing point pricing system determines the product's price by adding published freight charges between the basing point closest to the buyer and the product's cost at the point of production.

   1. The basing point does not have to be the same location from which the merchandise originated.

   2. Phantom freight exists if the billed transportation costs exceed the actual transportation costs.

   3. Industry-wide pricing systems involving phantom freight are illegal in the United States.

III. List prices

   A. List prices are basic price quotes without any price adjustments.

   B. Examples of price adjustments are seasonal discounts, rebates, and price discounts.

IV. Discount policies

   A. Cash discounts are designed to encourage prompt payment of the amount due.

   B. Trade or functional discounts are given to marketing intermediaries for the performance of certain marketing functions.

   C. Quantity discounts can be non-cumulative (based on an individual order to encourage large orders) or cumulative (based on orders over a period of time to encourage patronage).

   D. Seasonal discounts are designed to encourage buyers to purchase and take delivery of merchandise during the off-season.

   E. Chain discounts indicate how the price that a buyer pays is determined.

   F. Promotional allowances in the form of cash or merchandise are designed to reimburse marketing intermediaries for their promotional assistance.

V. Pricing and the law

   A. Fair trade or resale price maintenance statutes prohibit marketing intermediaries from reducing price below the price set by manufacturers.

319

B. Unfair sales practice acts are state statutes which specify that certain products must be sold at prices no lower than the minimum prescribed mark-ups.

C. The Robinson-Patman Act of 1936 is a federal law that makes it illegal to give, induce, or receive discriminatory prices.

   1. A discriminatory price exists when two similar non-household customers receive different prices that results in a competitive advantage to one buyer.

   2. Brokerage allowances are discounts to wholesalers (brokers) for sales volume generated and are illegal if the broker (wholesaler) and the buyer are the same entity or if the buyer controls the broker.

   3. The Robinson-Patman Act permits price discrimination if the competitive situation demands that different prices be charged to similar buyers or if there is an a priori cost justification.

D. Many state and local laws influence pricing practices.

E. Government can influence pricing practices through threat of legislation, support programs, and other actions designed to raise or lower prices.

SUMMARY

Learning Objective One: To show how price must be related to the intended target market.

As mentioned in Chapter 15, marketing managers must answer the question, "Who are our customers and what do they want the price to be?". Customers may prefer higher prices because of the associated status and quality image (prestige pricing), additional product features, or expected benefits of other marketing mix elements. In fact, successful marketers offer reasonably-priced products that are popular to target markets.

Target market demand is a major force in the determination of an appropriate price level. A product's demand schedule influences the firm's adoption of pricing strategies related to customary pricing, price lining, odd prices, and special prices. And, marketers can use price elasticity of demand to select between a skimming (inelastic demand) or a penetration (elastic demand) pricing strategy for the introduction of new products. One-price, variable-price, total profit pricing, item profit pricing, and loss leaders are other pricing strategies which reflect intended target market considerations. In summary, marketing managers determine prices, pricing strategies, and discount policies consistent with market realities.

Learning Objective Two: To understand how the marketing manager determines actual prices to be charged using judgment as well as cost and return-on-investment decisions.

In arriving at an actual price to be charged, the marketing manager should follow a logical pricing procedure that considers costs and demand. This procedure should recognize that (1) costs become the floor on which to build a pricing strategy, (2) expected profit (return-on-investment) must be achieved, and (3) the actual price reflects demand considerations. Quantitative methods can be employed to determine pricing guidelines or prices that incorporate costs, expected profits, and demand. Then, managerial judgment becomes important in determining which pricing strategies and discount policies appeal to the intended target market in establishing the actual price.

Learning Objective Three: To describe the many price options available to marketing managers.

Marketing managers may select from a wide range of pricing strategies and discount policies. Managers must decide whether to use a one-price policy (fixed price to all buyers) or a variable-price policy (price varies from buyer to buyer), item profit pricing or total profit pricing over several related items, leader pricing (prices slightly above, equal to, or below costs) or bait pricing (advertise low-priced models in order to trade customers up to higher margin items), odd prices (slightly below a dollar figure) or even prices, and skimming (price high given relatively inelastic demand) or penetration (price low given relatively elastic demand) pricing strategies. Other pricing strategies include traditional pricing (price at customary level), price lining (price at established price points), and prestige pricing (price status products high to convey quality image).

Discount policies relate to adjustments to the list price. Cash and anticipation discounts are designed to encourage payment. Trade discounts are given to marketing intermediaries to perform marketing functions. The promotional allowance is used to encourage marketing intermediaries to promote the product to local customers. Quantity discounts are designed to encourage large individual orders (non-cumulative quantity discount) or patronage (cumulative quantity discount). Seasonal discounts encourage buyers to purchase products during the off-season. Other price options concern geographic-related price policies (see Learning Objective Four).

<u>Learning Objective Four</u>: To explain how geography influences pricing decisions.

Price policies may be based on the geographic distance separating the buyer from the point of production or point of sale. Geographic pricing options include F.O.B. pricing, delivered pricing, and basing point pricing. These policies indicate when the buyer assumes the responsibilities regarding shipping costs. A F.O.B. policy indicates the place at which the buyer assumes the responsibility of shipping and ownership. The seller is responsible for shipping costs prior to the stated F.O.B. place. A delivered pricing policy builds transportation costs into the product's price. This freight-allowed pricing policy can set zone prices (list price within a geographic zone is identical to all buyers) or uniform delivered price (same price at all locations). The basing point pricing system adds shipping costs from one or more locations (basing points) to the price of the product, even if the product is not shipped from the basing point. Industry-wide basing point systems which involve phantom freight (billed shipping costs exceed actual shipping costs) are illegal in the United States.

<u>Learning Objective Five</u>: To be familiar with the major legal restrictions on pricing freedom.

The Robinson-Patman Act makes it illegal to give, induce, or receive discriminatory prices which result in a competitive advantage to one buyer over similar buyers unless there is <u>a priori</u> cost justification or the competitive situation demands it. Proportional services and discounts must be given to similar buyers. Brokerage allowances are illegal if the buyer controls the wholesaler or broker or if the buyer and wholesaler are the same entity.

Fair trade or resale price maintenance acts are state laws which prohibited middlemen from reducing a product's price below the price established by the manufacturer. In 1975, Congress passed an act that declared resale price maintenance laws which impacted on interstate commerce illegal. Unfair sales practices acts exist in many states. These acts specify that dealers must price certain products at a price no lower than minimum prescribed mark-ups above these products' costs. Other state and local laws exist which impact on pricing policies.

VOCABULARY BUILDING

Matching Exercise

Match the following by placing the letter of the concept or term on the blank preceding the phrase which best describes the concept or term. You should use a term or concept only once.

A.	Skimming price	J.	Delivered pricing
B.	Penetration price	K.	Basing point pricing
C.	Loss leader	L.	Uniform delivered pricing
D.	Bait pricing	M.	Cash discounts
E.	Bait and switch	N.	List prices
F.	Price lining	O.	Trade discounts
G.	F.O.B.	P.	Non-cumulative quantity discounts
H.	Odd prices	Q.	Cumulative quantity discounts
I.	Even prices	R.	Seasonal discounts

_____ 1. Designates the point at which the buyer is no longer responsible for shipping.

_____ 2. Discount to encourage large individual orders.

_____ 3. A price that is set at a low level to enter into a competitive market more effectively.

_____ 4. Charging customers shipping costs from a location other than where the product was shipped.

_____ 5. Discount to encourage prompt payment of bills.

_____ 6. Pricing strategy that involves determining "price points."

_____ 7. Price reductions for performance of wholesaling and retailing functions.

_____ 8. Basic price quote prior to any adjustments.

_____ 9. Pricing strategy used to attract customers by advertising low-priced models of a product with the expectation of trading the customer up to a higher margin model.

_____ 10. A price that is a few cents lower than the nearest round dollar price.

_____ 11. A relatively high price for new products which are estimated to have relatively inelastic demand.

_____ 12. A pricing strategy whereby an organization charges the same price for the product at all locations.

_____ 13. A price reduction to encourage purchase of products during an inappropriate time of the year.

_____ 14. A pricing ploy whereby the merchant has no intention of selling the low-priced model.

_____ 15. Price adjustment to encourage buyers to purchase products from the same seller over a period of time.

VOCABULARY BUILDING

Programmed Learning Exercise

1. The decision to go with a price determined by quantitative methods rests with the decision-maker's _____ .

   [judgment]

2. If an organization maintains a fixed price regardless of the buyer, the organization follows a _____ policy.

   [one-price]

3. A _____-price policy allows for haggling.

   [variable]

4. A product which is priced at a loss is referred to as a _____ _____ .

   [loss leader]

5. A _____ demand curve faces marketers of products sold at traditional prices.

   [kinked]

6. The kinked demand curve may also occur in _____ markets.

   [oligopolistic]

7. Odd prices are intended to have a _____ effect.

   [psychological]

8. "Second product at one-half price" is an example of a _____ price.

   [special/promotional]

324

9. An organization practices _____ pricing or _____ _____ pricing if the shipping charges are built into the price paid by the consumer.

[delivered, freight allowed]

10. _____ _____ are locations from which customers are charged transportation costs even though the merchandise may not be shipped from these locations.

[Basing points]

11. The most common form of price adjustment is _____.

[discounting]

12. A(n) _____ discount is an additional adjustment to encourage even faster payment.

[anticipation]

13. Unfair sales practices acts are state laws which specify that certain items must be sold at or above prescribed _____.

[mark-ups]

14. The _____ - _____ Act is a federal law intended to stop discriminatory prices by prohibiting wholesaler's discounts to businesses which do not meet specific criteria of wholesalers.

[Robinson-Patman]

15. The Robinson-Patman Act provides that discriminatory prices can be justified if the _____ situation demands it or on an a priori _____ justification basis.

[competitive, cost]

TRUE OR FALSE STATEMENTS

T F 1. Management's ultimate role in pricing is to chose from among the many types of prices and forms of discounts.

T F 2. Most U.S. retailers follow a one-price policy.

T F 3. A skimming policy is more effective for new products with a relatively strong elastic demand.

T F 4. Item profit pricing is appropriate for complementary products.

T F 5. Unfair sales practices laws impact adversely on leader pricing.

325

T F   6.   Both the loss leader and the cost leader are examples of bait pricing.

T F   7.   Traditional prices reduce pricing freedom.

T F   8.   Firms who use a price lining strategy may find price competition difficult to fend off.

T F   9.   Odd prices are traditional prices.

T F 10. The demand curve is very elastic below the odd price.

T F 11. "Even" prices work best for relatively expensive products.

T F 12. Gentleman's price or ethical price refers to pricing lower than the demand schedule would suggest because of humanitarian reasons.

T F 13. A buyer in Chicago would prefer F.O.B. St. Louis to F.O.B. Chicago.

T F 14. With zone pricing, all buyers in a given zone pay the same product price, but pay separately for delivery from the center of the zone.

T F 15. Rebates are price adjustments which ensure that the consumer gets the full benefit of the price reduction.

T F 16. An anticipation discount is a type of seasonal discount.

T F 17. Keystoning refers to a retailer's policy of doubling the wholesale price of an item and making this the regular price.

T F 18. Resale price maintenance or fair trade laws exist in most states today and permit manufacturers to set minimum prices below which their products cannot be sold.

T F 19. Unfair sales practices acts require that out-of-style merchandise cannot be sold below a minimum mark-up.

T F 20. Government influences pricing through its price support programs.

MULTIPLE CHOICE QUESTIONS

1. Which is not a pricing strategy that is available to marketing managers?
    a. Target market pricing.   c. Variable-price.
    b. Leader pricing.   d. Total profit pricing.

2. Which type of variable-price is illegal according to the Robinson-Patman Act?
   a. Similar organizational buyers receive different prices based on cost justification.
   b. Buyers are charged different prices based on time differences.
   c. Similar organizational buyers receive disproportionate non-cumulative quantity discounts on purchases.
   d. Similar organizational buyers receive different prices based on competitive situation.

3. A penetration price strategy is likely to be more effective than a skimming price strategy in pricing a new product under all conditions except
   a. elastic demand.   c. economies of scale.
   b. weak competitive threat.   d. mass market acceptance.

4. Which marketing strategy should a marketing manager select when introducing a new unique (difficult to imitate) product?
   a. Penetration pricing.   c. Total profit pricing.
   b. Prestige pricing.   d. Skimming pricing.

5. Which statement regarding traditional pricing is false?
   a. An increase in price decreases total revenue.
   b. Customary prices remain unchanged for long periods of time.
   c. Demand is elastic above the traditional price but inelastic below it.
   d. A decrease in price increases total revenue.

6. When Sears prices its paint at $9.95, $12.95, and $16.95 per gallon, Sears is following a(n) _____ strategy.
   a. total profit   c. even prices
   b. price lining   d. traditional

7. When McDonald's prices hamburgers at 39¢, McDonald's is following a(n) _____ pricing strategy.
   a. penetration   c. odd price
   b. item profit   d. variable

8. When a status price is charged for a product, this means that
   a. the high demand for the product is partly based on the high price.
   b. demand for that product increases as its price decreases.
   c. demand for the product is not based on price.
   d. the demand is not very responsive to price.

9. Phantom freight exists if
   a. actual shipping costs equal billed shipping costs.
   b. actual shipping costs exceed billed shipping costs.
   c. actual shipping costs are less than billed shipping costs.
   d. a company practices freight allowed pricing.

10. Adjustments to list price include all <u>except</u>
   a. price targets. c. rebates.
   b. quantity discounts. d. cash discounts.

11. An invoice for a $5,000 purchase quotes the terms 5/10 r.o.g., net 60. The cash discount, if taken, will be
   a. $100. c. $500.
   b. $250. d. indeterminant.

12. What is true of the functional discount given to the channel member as that middleman's role increases?
   a. The discount increases.
   b. The discount doesn't change at all.
   c. The discount is reduced.
   d. The discount doesn't change, but the marketing does.

13. If a retailer is quoted the terms 50/10/2 on merchandise priced at $842, the retailer's cost would be
   a. $842.00. c. $371.32.
   b. $522.04. d. $252.60.

14. Which statement is <u>incorrect</u>?
   a. Cash discounts are to encourage faster payment of bills.
   b. Cumulative quantity discounts are to encourage large orders.
   c. Trade discounts are payments to middlemen for marketing functions to be performed.
   d. Promotional allowances are to encourage middlemen to promote the product to their local customers.

15. In addition to influencing pricing decisions by law, the government also influences by
   a. court cases. c. norms.
   b. rules. d. threats.

QUICK QUIZ

1Q.
"Salespeople" at K-Mart do not have to be able to negotiate prices with customers because K-Mart follows a one-price policy. Salespeople dealing with certain products do have to be able to negotiate prices, and so they usually earn greater compensation than K-Mart employees. What are some of these products?

1A.
Some of these products are automobiles, real estate, furniture, home decorating and repair services, office equipment, jewelry, and furs.

2Q.
Why would adopting a policy of price lining make assigning prices to men's suits easier for a clothing store owner?

2A.
Once the individual price points are established, the retailer can simply "plug in" the price to be assigned to any particular item.

3Q.
Some people claim that "F.O.B. factory" is the fairest type of pricing. Why do they make that claim?

3A.
Because with a "F.O.B. factory" policy in effect, each buyer must pay the shipping charges to his or her own location, thus paying the actual costs that are incurred with no part of those costs borne by other buyers.

EXPERIENTIAL ACTIVITIES

17-A. Distribution-based Price Policies

Marketers can adjust the product's price through distribution-based price policies. The influence of transportation costs on price and/or the buyer's costs is examined in the situations described below.

Assignment

1. Kemco, Inc., a producer of industrial vacuum cleaners located in Kent, Ohio, prices its products F.O.B. factory as does a competitor located in Peoria, Illinois. Both producers quote a list price of $600 on comparable models. Should Industrial Robotics of Indianapolis purchase ten industrial vacuum cleaners from Kemco, Inc., or its competitor, if shipping costs are $55 from Kent and $50 from Peoria for each vacuum cleaner?

   a. Industrial Robotics should purchase the vacuum cleaners from

   _____

   b. Justification: _____

   _____

   _____

2. Holden's, Inc., is a producer of seed corn located in Williamsburg, Iowa. Holden's quotes the same price for a type of seed corn to all buyers. For example, Holden 810 costs $65 per bag. Assume that $5 delivery charges are built into the $65 price and that it costs 10 cents per mile to deliver each bag of seed corn. Farmers Kolosek and Hall live 20 and 60 miles respectively from Holden, Inc.. Kolosek and Hall each purchase 100 bags of Holden 810.

    a. Actual delivery charges to Kolosek are $_____.

        Calculations:

    b. Actual delivery charges to Hall are $_____.

        Calculations:

    c. Holden's had phantom freight of $_____ to Kolosek.

        Calculations:

    d. Holden's had freight absorption of $_____ to Hall.

        Calculations:

3. A producer of office furniture located in Chicago uses Indianapolis as a basing point city. The list price is $800 for an office desk. Transportation costs from Chicago and Indianapolis to customers located in Denver and Detroit are given below.

CHAPTER 18

AN OVERVIEW OF PROMOTION

OBJECTIVE

Effective marketing requires effective communication with an organization's customers. The promotion elements of personal selling, advertising, publicity, and sales promotion should be developed and coordinated to achieve effective communication with customers.

OUTLINE

I. The nature and purposes of promotion

   A. Promotion is an organization's communication with external publics, especially customers and potential customers.

   B. The basic purposes of promotion are to inform, persuade, and remind.

II. The elements of promotion

   A. Promotion consists of personal selling, advertising, publicity, and sales promotion.

      1. Personal selling is person-to-person communication between buyer and seller.

         a. Personal selling is expensive on a per contact basis.

         b. Flexibility is a major advantage of personal selling.

      2. Advertising includes any persuasive message carried by a paid mass medium for an identified sponsor.

      3. Publicity involves an unpaid and unsigned message delivered through a nonpersonal (mass medium) channel.

       a. Publicity differs from advertising in that the sponsor is not identified and there is no payment to the mass medium to deliver the message.

       b. Publicity can be positive or negative as it conveys newsworthy information about an organization.

       c. Brandstanding is a public relation's technique that links a product to an issue of public concern.

   4. Sales promotion consists of those promotional activities, other than personal selling, advertising, and publicity, that stimulate buyer purchases or dealer effectiveness in a specified time period.

       a. These are nonroutine, temporary promotional efforts designed to achieve short-term objectives.

       b. Sales promotion supports and is coordinated with other promotional activities.

   5. The characteristics of the four elements of promotion are summarized in Exhibit 18-1 in the Zikmund and d'Amico textbook.

  B. Packaging often reinforces other communication efforts.

III. The communication process

  A. Communication is the process of exchanging information and conveying meaning to others.

   1. The basic features of the communication process are message source, message, channel of communication or medium, receiver, encoding, decoding, feedback, and noise.

   2. For communication to take place, the receiver must understand the meaning of the message as intended by the sender (message source).

  B. Encoding is the process of translating the idea to be communicated into a symbolic message.

  C. The encoded message is sent through a channel of communication (salesperson, mass medium, or sales promotion activity).

  D. Decoding is the mental process by which the receiver interprets the meaning of the message.

E. Feedback is the communication of the receiver's reaction to the sender's message.

F. Noise interferes with perfect communication which would exist if the receiver decoded the message exactly as the encoder intended the message to be decoded.

    1. Commonality between the receiver's and the sender's psychological fields of experience enhances communication.

    2. Noise may disrupt any stage of the communication process.

IV. The hierarchy of communication effects

A. Repetition of promotional communications may be necessary to persuade a customer to change an attitude or to make a purchase.

B. The hierarchy of effects model acknowledges that promotion moves customers through a series of stages (unawareness, awareness, knowledge, liking, preference, conviction, and purchase) regarding a product or a brand.

    1. The hierarchy model suggests that promotion can be used to persuade buyers to change their attitudes and behavior toward a product, brand, or organization.

    2. This model also suggests that customers may be at different stages in the hierarchial effects continuum.

    3. The promotional message should be built around a target audience (target market) and its stage(s) in the hierarchial model.

    4. The hierarchy of communication effects model may not be appropriate for low involvement products.

C. Promotional messages often exist at several levels in the channel of distribution and emanate from several sources (different channel members).

V. The promotional mix

A. The integration of advertising, personal selling, sales promotion, and publicity to meet the information requirements of the target market(s) is referred to as a promotional mix or promotion mix.

337

B. The general relationship between advertising and personal selling varies by transactional stage and by type of industrial or consumer product classification.

    1. The relative importance of advertising, compared to personal selling, is typically greater during the pre-transaction and post-transaction stages and of lesser importance during the transaction stage.

    2. Personal selling is usually more significant than advertising in the promotional mix in marketing industrial products and in selling complex products; whereas, advertising has more significance in selling convenience products.

VI. Promotional strategies

A. A push strategy emphasizes promotional efforts aimed at channel members while a pull strategy emphasizes promotional efforts directed toward persuading ultimate consumers or buyers to demand the product.

B. Most manufacturers use a combination push-pull strategy.

C. The situation confronting a marketer determines whether to emphasize a push or a pull strategy.

    1. A push strategy is appropriate if a firm has limited funds or needs to obtain channel cooperation.

    2. A pull strategy can be emphasized for popular consumer products or if environmental conditions necessitate advertising to stimulate demand.

D. A promotional strategy can be hard sell (use aggressive promotion to convince buyers that they need the product) or soft sell (promotion that is less conspicuous in the direct asking for the order).

VII. Promotional campaigns

A. A promotional campaign involves a series of promotional activities that are designed to accomplish a specific objective.

B. Image building, product differentiation, and positioning are three major approaches to developing a promotional campaign for a mature product.

338

1. Image building stresses a product's, or a brand's, symbolic value rather than its product benefits.

2. A product differentiation promotional campaign emphasizes some dimension of a product or a product's solution to a customer problem, often in the form of a unique selling proposition (USP).

3. Positioning promotes a brand in relation to competing brands in a buyer's mind.

4. These three campaign approaches may overlap.

C. The total campaign must be coordinated so that each promotional element supplements and complements the other elements.

VIII. Determining the promotional budget

A. The task method or objective approach to determining the promotional budget necessitates first identifying the objectives or tasks to be accomplished and then determining the costs to achieve these tasks.

B. The percent of sales method may be based on planned, actual, or historical sales.

1. This method offers simplicity and relates promotion to sales.

2. A disadvantage with the percent of sales method is that promotion is a result of sales rather than sales being a result of promotion.

C. The comparative parity method determines the promotional budget based on what competitors do, usually matching their efforts.

D. The marginal approach to promotional budgeting is difficult to implement, though theoretically sound.

E. Some organizations with cash flow-related problems use an "all-you-can-afford" approach to determine the promotional budget, even if this amount is inappropriate for the task to be accomplished.

F. Most organizations use a combination approach to determine the promotional budget.

G. Marketers use vertical (channel members at different levels) and horizontal (channel members at the same level) cooperative programs to increase promotional budgets and efforts.

SUMMARY

Learning Objective One: To discuss the key role played by promotion in any successful marketing effort.

Promotion consists of those marketing mix activities (personal selling, advertising, publicity, and sales promotion) which involve an organization's external communication with various publics, especially customers. These promotional activities communicate information about other elements of the marketing mix. Types of communicated information include a product's benefits and its price, how a product is used, and where to obtain the product. In essence, the role of promotion is to make customers aware of the existence of the total product.

Learning Objective Two: To understand that, despite the comments of critics of advertising, promotion is necessary to the basic operation of our economy.

The critics of promotion, especially advertising, suggest that society could do without this element of the marketing mix. It is unlikely society could sustain, or even increase, its standard of living since the basic purposes of promotion are to inform, persuade, and remind potential buyers about an organization's total product. Promotion is communication—informing consumers about a product's benefits, persuading these customers to buy their brand in the competitive marketplace, and reminding loyal consumers that the organization or product has satisfied them over time. Without promotion, buyers would have less information available to make informed buying decisions and, possibly, even fewer product options as promotion enhances the competitive situation.

Learning Objective Three: To be able to define each of the four major elements of promotion and comment on their interrelationships within a promotional plan.

The four major elements of promotion are personal selling, advertising, publicity, and sales promotion. Personal selling involves direct (face-to-face) communication between a buyer and a seller where the seller's purpose is persuasion. Advertising includes any persuasive message carried by a mass medium and paid for by an identified sponsor. Publicity involves any unpaid and unsigned (no identified sponsor) message delivered through a nonpersonal (mass medium) channel. Sales promotion consists of those nonroutine, temporary promotional efforts, other than personal selling, advertising, and publicity, which are designed to stimulate buyer purchases or dealer effectiveness in a specified time period.

A promotional plan is designed to meet the different information requirements of potential buyers at different stages in the communication-effects hierarchy. Target market members who are unaware of a product require different promotional efforts than those potential buyers ready-to-purchase the product. In general, advertising and publicity tend to be more effective and efficient in creating awareness while personal selling and sales promotion stimulate purchases more effectively and efficiently. Thus, each promotional element supports, and must to be coordinated with, the other elements of promotion to achieve promotional objectives.

Learning Objective Four: To be familiar with the basic model that describes all communication processes, including promotion.

The basic communication model describes the process of conveying meaning from a message source to a receiver. For meaning to be conveyed, the receiver and message source must have some commonality in their psychological fields of experience. The message source encodes a message that is tailored to a receiver's psychological field of experience. This message is transmitted through some channel or medium to the receiver who must decode the message. Information is conveyed if the receiver interprets the meaning of the message as intended by the message source. The basic model includes a feedback mechanism from the receiver to the message source. Noise interferes with the communication process during encoding, transmitting, decoding, and feedback. The communication process must be built around the intended receiver.

Learning Objective Five: To know how promotional messages are varied to appeal to different target markets--customers ranging from those who are unaware of the product being offered to those who regularly purchase it.

The heirarchial communication effects model recognizes that buyers have different perceptions and attitudes toward a product and that promotion can influence change toward a product by moving customers through a series of psychological states (unawareness, awareness, knowledge, liking, preference, conviction, and purchase). The promotional message must be consistent with the target audience's psychological state. Promotional messages aimed toward consumers on the earlier psychological stages should inform the target audience of the product's existence (awareness) and the product's attributes and benefits (knowledge). For consumers on the liking and preference stages, promotional messages should be designed to stimulate favorable feelings and attitudes toward the product. If a customer is on the conviction step, the message should persuade the person that now is the time to buy. For those who have purchased the product, promotional messages should reinforce and remind the buyer of the product's value.

Learning Objective Six: To discuss the appropriateness of using specific promotional tools for particular products and marketing situations.

The effectiveness and efficiency of promotional tools vary by product, type of product, and marketing situation surrounding each product. Mass audiences can be informed efficiently and effectively by advertising. Personal selling is an effective tool at the conviction and purchase stages of the hierarchial effects model, especially for products which are expensive, innovative, or complex. Sales promotion activities can be used effectively to induce consumers to seek product information or, even, to purchase inexpensive consumer products. Each promotional element performs a role in moving buyers along the hierarchial effects continuum.

The general relationship between the mix of advertising and personal selling varies by the transactional stage of the buying process and by type of industrial or consumer product. Compared to personal selling, the relative importance of advertising is greater during the pre-transaction and post-transaction stages. These stages tend to stress information-related (awareness, knowledge, liking, and preference) and reminder-related (reassure and reinforce) objectives. At the transaction stage, personal selling is used to achieve persuasion-related (conviction and purchase) objectives. The role of advertising and personal selling varies from complex industrial products to frequently-purchased (convenience) consumer products. Personal selling increases in significance as the product moves from convenience products to complex industrial products while the role of advertising decreases along this same product classification continuum.

Learning Objective Seven: To be familiar with the various promotional strategies, such as push versus pull and the hard sell versus the soft sell.

A push strategy emphasizes promotional efforts directed toward members of a channel of distribution. Each channel member aims promotional activities toward the next channel member in order to move the product through the channel. Manufacturers who use a pull strategy direct their promotional efforts toward the buyer in order to stimulate demand for the product. This demand then pulls the product through the channel. Most marketing organizations use a combination push-pull promotional strategy.

A hard sell strategy emphasizes aggressive persuasion of individuals to convince these buyers that they need the product now. This strategy uses repetitive messages and refuses to accept "No" for an answer. Under the soft sell approach, promotional efforts are designed to create favorable feelings and attitudes toward the product using nonverbal as well as verbal symbols. The soft sell approach is more subtle in asking for the order.

Learning Objective Eight: To describe how the elements of promotion can be brought together to support one another in a promotional campaign.

A promotional campaign consists of a series of promotional activities that are designed to achieve a specific objective. For a mature product, a promotional campaign can be built around image building, product differentiation, or positioning. An image building approach stresses symbolic value associated

342

with the product (Marlboro man) rather than product features (Wendy's "Where's the beef?" campaign) as a product differentiation approach does. A positioning approach promotes a brand relative to competing brands as suggested by the classic example of 7-Up, the Uncola. Other promotional campaigns can be based on new product introduction, channel acceptance, or product deletion. In summary, the promotional approach provides a means to bring the promotion elements together into a unity of presentation.

Learning Objective Nine: To be able to name and describe the major approaches used by marketing managers to set promotional budgets.

The major methods used by marketing managers to set promotional budgets are percent of sales, comparative parity, all-you-can-afford, and the task method. Under the percent of sales method, the marketing manager takes a percentage of sales (planned, actual, or historical) and uses that amount as the promotional appropriation. The comparative parity method bases the appropriation on what competitors spend, usually matching their efforts. The marketer spends whatever dollars are available under the all-you-can-afford approach. The task method requires that marketing managers first identify the tasks or objectives to be accomplished with promotion, and then determine the costs needed to accomplish those tasks.

VOCABULARY BUILDING

Matching Exercise

Match the following by placing the letter of the concept or term on the blank preceding the phrase which best describes the concept or term. You should use a term or concept only once.

A. Promotion
B. Personal selling
C. Advertising
D. Pull strategy
E. Push strategy
F. Promotion mix
G. Feedback
H. Promotional campaign
I. Publicity
J. Positioning

K. Image building
L. Product differentiation
M. Noise
N. Decoding
O. Encoding
P. Communication
Q. Sales promotion
R. Vertical cooperative promotion
S. Horizontal cooperative promotion

____ 1. Promotional campaign approach based on symbolic value rather than product attributes.

____ 2. The integration of the totality of an organization's promotional efforts.

343

_A_ 3. Applied communication used by marketers to exchange persuasive messages and information between buyers and sellers.

_E_ 4. A promotional strategy aimed at channel members rather than to ultimate buyers of a product.

_R_ 5. A promotional approach where channel members at different levels jointly sponsor advertising.

_O_ 6. The stage in the communication process at which the sender translates the idea to be communicated into words, pictures, gestures, or other symbols.

_C_ 7. Any persuasive message carried by a mass medium which is paid for by a sponsor of the message.

_L_ 8. A promotional campaign approach that emphasizes product benefits.

_G_ 9. Communication of an individual's reaction back to the source of the message.

_I_ 10. An unpaid and unsigned promotional message transmitted through nonpersonal channels.

_M_ 11. Any interference or distraction that interrupts the communication process.

_P_ 12. The process of exchanging information and conveying meaning to others.

_Q_ 13. Short-term promotional activities that offer a material reward to customers, salespeople, sales prospects, or dealers.

_S_ 14. Promotional efforts sponsored by channel members at the same level.

_B_ 15. Person-to-person interaction between a buyer and a seller where persuasion is the purpose of the interaction.

VOCABULARY BUILDING

Programmed Learning Exercise

1. The essence of promotion is _____.

[communication]

2. The three basic purposes of promotion are to _____, _____, and _____.

[inform, persuade, remind]

3. The four subsets of promotion are _____, _____, _____, and _____.

[personal selling, advertising, publicity, sales promotion]

4. The promotion element which offers maximum feedback from the market is _____.

[personal selling]

5. Sales promotion activities are _____ offers of a material reward to customers, dealers, salespeople, or potential customers.

[temporary]

6. _____ is the mental process by which the receiver interprets a message's meaning.

[Decoding]

7. Communication is facilitated when the sender and the receiver have some commonality in their _____ _____ of experience.

[psychological fields]

8. Promotion becomes more effective with_____ .

[repetition]

9. Those people who have _____ the product are on the highest level on the promotional "staircase."

[purchased]

10. A satisfied or reinforced customer is the result when the purchase decision leads to a _____.

[reward]

11. Marketers selling complex industrial equipment would be more likely to use _____ than _____.

[personal selling, advertising]

12. The _____ promotional strategy attempts to stimulate ultimate consumers to demand the product at the retail level.

[pull]

13. A _____ _____ strategy is characterized by aggressive persuasion of individuals.

[hard sell]

14. A hard sell strategy emphasizes _____ of the promotional messages.

[repetition]

15. A promotional campaign is a series of promotional activities aimed at achieving a specific _____ .

[objective]

16. The term USP stands for _____ _____ _____ .

[unique selling proposition]

17. The _____ campaign approach promotes a brand relative to competing brands in a buyer's mind.

[positioning]

18. The _____ method of determining the promotional budget requires that the marketer first identify the objective to be accomplished and then determine the costs to accomplish that objective.

[task]

19. The _____ _____ method of determining promotional budgets is based on what competitors do.

[comparative parity]

20. Effective _____ requires effective communication.

[marketing]

TRUE OR FALSE STATEMENTS

T (F) 1. The old adage--"Build a better mousetrap and the world will beat a path to your door"--implies that no promotion is needed if your product is the best.

(T) F 2. A traditional definition of promotion is persuasive communication.

T (F) 3. Reminder promotion is more important for first-time buyers than for loyal customers.

T (F) 4. Advertising and publicity are similar in all aspects except that publicity involves a message carried by a mass medium which is not paid for by a sponsor.

T F 5. An example of a sales promotion activity is a supermarket offering free samples of fresh fruit and baked goods.

T (F) 6. Advertising has the lowest cost per contact among the four major elements of promotion.

346

(T) F 7. Packaging should convey the same unity of presentation as other promotional methods.

(T) F 8. An example of a promotional message is a sales presentation.

T (F) 9. The message source decodes a message in terms of the receiver's psychological field of experience.

T (F) 10. Sources of noise in the communication process are always external to the receiver.

T F 11. Identification of the target market is one of the first steps in developing promotional messages.

T (F) 12. Consumers who have low involvement in a product follow the steps in the model of hierarchy of communication effects.

T (F) 13. All firms within an industry use very similar promotional mixes since their promotional objectives are very similar.

(T) F 14. Personal selling is usually most effective in consummating the sale.

(T) F 15. A soft sell strategy is more subtle than a hard sell strategy in asking for the order.

T (F) 16. The unique selling proposition is the basis of an image building promotional approach.

(T) F 17. Simplicity is a major advantage of the percent of sales method of setting promotional budgets.

(T) F 18. The all-you-can-afford promotional budget approach is often used by organizations with cash flow problems.

(T) F 19. Cooperative promotional programs enable organizations to expand their promotional efforts.

(T) F 20. The Robinson-Patman Act influences marketers in developing cooperative promotional programs.

MULTIPLE CHOICE QUESTIONS

1. Which statement regarding promotion is false?
    a. A major goal of promotion is to inform potential buyers.
    b. Promotion is the most important marketing mix element.
    c. Persuasion is a primary goal of promotion.
    d. Promotion reminds loyal customers about products.

2. The most flexible element of promotion is
    a. personal selling.   c. publicity.
    b. advertising.   d. sales promotion.

3. Which is not a characteristic of sales promotion?
    a. It is designed to achieve short-term objectives.
    b. It offers nonroutine selling efforts.
    c. It is a personal mode of communication.
    d. It identifies the sponsor.

4. Which is not a characteristic of publicity?
    a. Publicity is not a regular and recurrent activity.
    b. Publicity involves an unpaid message transmitted through a mass
        medium.
    c. Publicity identifies the sponsor of the message.
    d. Publicity can be positive or negative.

5. The most expensive element of promotion on a per contact basis is
    a. personal selling.   c. publicity.
    b. advertising.   d. sales promotion.

6. The goal of communication is to have
    a. fast feedback.
    b. sales or communication effects.
    c. a behavior change.
    d. the receiver understand the meaning intended by the message source.

7. The encoding process is best illustrated by
    a. a salesperson who finishes a presentation and waits for the
        prospect's response.
    b. Marlboro developing an ad to suggest it is a masculine cigarette.
    c. a prospect who selectively perceives an ad for chocolate-covered
        broccoli.
    d. Levi Strauss tying a special promotion to the Olympic Games.

348

8. Which statement regarding the communication process is false?
   a. The message source must understand the receiver's psychological field of experience.
   b. Receivers interpret messages in different ways.
   c. All promotional messages are transmitted via mass media channels.
   d. Noise can affect encoding the message.

9. The lowest level on the promotion "staircase" consists of those people who
   a. have not tried the product.
   b. are aware of the product's existence.
   c. have not formed favorable attitudes and feelings toward the product.
   d. are unaware of the existence of the product.

10. A primary promotional objective for consumers on the knowledge step of the hierarchial effects model is to
    a. encourage favorable feelings toward the product.
    b. provide factual information.
    c. reinforce product benefits and value.
    d. encourage action by the consumer.

11. Which is not suggested to the marketer by the hierarchy of communication-effects model?
    a. Promotion can be useful to induce buyers to change.
    b. No matter where consumers are on the hierarchy, all marketers must do the same amount of educating consumers.
    c. It is necessary to identify first where the consumers are on the hierarchy.
    d. Different people may be at different stages on the hierarchy.

12. The promotional mix should
    a. meet the information requirement of all target customers.
    b. be aimed at those near the top of the hierarchy staircase.
    c. be directed at consumers rather than channel intermediaries.
    d. give equal treatment to all elements of promotion.

13. Personal selling is favored over advertising
    a. for frequently-purchased consumer products.
    b. during the pre-transactional stage.
    c. to remind buyers of the value of their purchase.
    d. to persuade customers to purchase a product.

14. Advertising is favored over personal selling in the marketing of
    a. telephone systems.   c. motor oil for automobiles.
    b. advertising specialties.   d. health programs.

15. An example of a push strategy is
    a. a consumer sweepstakes contest by Reader's Digest.
    b. a manufacturer offering retail salespeople a bonus for each can of Kiwi shoepolish sold.
    c. IBM advertising the PC jr. on national television.
    d. P & G using a 20¢ off coupon for Crest toothpaste.

16. If a company was just entering a market with a new consumer product and has limited funds, the company should probably
    a. try to promote the product heavily and directly to consumers.
    b. focus all their advertising dollars at the consumer level.
    c. make use of a hierarchical promotional technique.
    d. try to encourage the channels to help promote the product and use push promotion.

17. Which is not a major approach to the development of a promotional campaign for a mature product?
    a. Loyalty building.   c. Image building.
    b. Positioning.   d. Product differentiation.

18. An example of a product differentiation strategy is
    a. a flip-top box.
    b. from one beer lover to another.
    c. the mark of excellence.
    d. E.T.'s candy.

19. The most logical promotional budget-setting method is the
    a. percent of sales method.   c. task method.
    b. marginal approach.   d. comparative parity method.

20. Which best illustrates the use of a horizontal cooperative promotional program?
    a. A number of downtown merchants plan and promote jointly a downtown sidewalk sale.
    b. A manufacturer and its retailers split the cost of local ads.
    c. A manufacturer develops ads to be used by retailers.
    d. A manufacturer only advertises in the channels and does not use consumer-based promotion.

QUICK QUIZ

1Q.
There is considerable variation in the amount of money spent on the four major elements of promotion by American marketers. Money aside, which element is used most commonly by organizations? Which is actually employed by the most organizations?

1A.
The answer is personal selling. This is because many small and even some large organizations have been able to get along without advertising, publicity, and perhaps even sales promotion; but, it is almost impossible to imagine an organization which uses no forms of personal selling. Even a small machine shop, employing only one or two people, needs someone to meet the public, to deal with customers, and to find out what customers want. Thus, it seems unlikely that any organization can get along without some personal selling.

2Q.
What does "feedback" look like in terms of the model in Exhibit 18.2 in the Zikmund and d'Amico textbook?

2A.
Many diagrams show feedback as a dotted line intended to demonstrate a flow of information like this:

```
SENDER→ ENCODE→ TRANSMIT→ DECODE→ RECEIVER
   ↑                                  ↓
   L — — — — — ←FEEDBACK ← — — — — —J
```

Actually, what happens is that the sender and receiver "change places." That is, the individual who was the receiver now encodes and transmits ideas to the person who was the sender. That person must receive and decode the message. If there is a response, the positions and the tasks involved again change hands.

351

3Q.
Which is most important: advertising, personal selling, publicity, or sales promotion?

3A.
For most organizations the success of the promotional effort requires a smoothly coordinated effort composed of all elements of the promotional mix. Thus, if effective marketing is the criterion of "importance," the answer to the question is the same as the answer to the problem of identifying which chair leg is the most important.

4Q.
Throughout most of this chapter we have seen that marketers often concentrate on communicating their product's "image" rather than the product's real aspects and benefits. Why don't marketers concentrate more on the product itself?

4A.
"Image" is a part of the product regardless of what marketing's critics say. Customers want many things from the products they buy, not just the "real" product in the nuts and bolts sense. Many products, such as industrial goods, are promoted almost exclusively on their "real" benefits and characteristics.

EXPERIENTIAL ACTIVITIES

18-A. The Communication Process

The basic features of the communication process are the message source, message, channel (medium) of communication, receiver, and feedback. Any communication system involves the processes of encoding, decoding, and transmitting the message. Your task is to illustrate and to explain a communication system for an AIM toothpaste advertisement.

Assignment

  1. Identify each of the following for AIM toothpaste.

      a. Manufacturer (message source): _____

CHAPTER 19

PERSONAL SELLING AND SALES MANAGEMENT

OBJECTIVE

The marketing activities of personal selling and sales management are explored in this chapter. Professional selling reflects the marketing concept by identifying and fulfilling customer needs individually. Sales management involves planning, organizing, directing, and controlling the personal selling effort.

OUTLINE

I. The characteristics of personal selling

   A. Personal selling involves a person-to-person dialogue between a buyer (prospect) and a seller where the purpose of the interaction is personal persuasion.

   B. The closing of a sale by a salesperson can mark the beginning of a long mutually profitable relationship between a buyer and a seller.

   C. Personal selling is the most flexible promotional element because the salesperson can adapt the sales presentation to the potential buyer's problem.

   D. Personal selling is a selective medium as it allows the salesperson to concentrate on the best prospects.

   E. Limitations of personal selling include its high cost per call, its inefficiency in reaching mass audiences, and the problem of recruiting, selecting, training, and monitoring salespeople.

II. Importance of personal selling

   A. Virtually all organizations maintain some level of personal contact and sales effort with their customers.

B. Personal selling is the most significant promotional tool in terms of dollars spent and number of people employed (approximately 10% of the U.S. workforce which is about 8 million people).

III. The types of personal selling

A. Three basic categories of selling positions are order-taking, order-getting, and sales support.

B. Order-takers do little creative selling in performing their responsibilities of writing orders, checking invoices, and assuring timely order processing.

1. Order-takers "keep" sales rather than "make" sales.

2. There are "inside" and "outside" order-taking sales jobs.

C. Order-getters perform creative selling responsibilities as they apply a product's benefits to the needs of customers.

D. Most salespersons are assisted by a sales team comprised of various specialized sales support people.

1. Missionary sales personnel are salespersons who build goodwill by assisting customers rather than taking or getting orders.

2. Other types of sales support people include sales engineers, applications programmers, master salespersons, and sales correspondents.

IV. The creative selling process

A. Creative selling is an adaptive process which consists of a series of steps focusing on customer satisfaction.

B. The first step in the creative selling process is locating and qualifying prospects.

1. The activity of locating prospects or prospecting refers to those activities used to identify likely buyers.

2. Qualifying a prospect (preapproach) necessitates that a salesperson estimates the prospect's buying influence and sales potential and identifies the decision-maker and other influentials regarding the purchase.

358

C. The approach (step two in the creative selling process) involves contacting and establishing rapport with the prospect.

    1. The salesperson attracts the buyer's attention during the approach.

    2. The salesperson tailors each approach to a prospect's particular situation.

D. The sales presentation (step three) develops the prospect's interest and desire in the product usually by communicating persuasively the product's benefits as a solution to the prospect's problem or needs.

E. Handling objections is the next step in the creative process.

    1. Two-way dialogue in the sales presentation enables the customer to raise objections on concerned points.

    2. One tactic for handling objections is to agree with the prospect and then use a counter-argument.

F. Closing the sale (step five in the creative selling process) requires that the salesperson asks for the order.

    1. The salesperson can use a trial close to determine if the sale is imminent or if more persuasion is necessary.

    2. Types of closing techniques include the direct approach, the narrow-the-alternatives approach, the assumptive close, the "standing room only" approach, and the summative approach.

G. The follow-up (step six) involves providing post-sale services and ensuring that the order was handled as promised.

V. Sales management

A. Sales management deals with the planning, organizing, directing, and controlling of the sales force or personal selling effort.

B. Retail sales forces are easier to supervise than outside (field) sales forces, since retail salespeople operate in a rather controlled setting.

C. Sales managers need to establish sales objectives.

    1. Sales objectives must be precise, quantifiable, reasonable, and time specific.

2. Sales objectives can be expressed in total unit or total dollar sales, sales (unit or dollar) per call, sales calls (completed or new customers), sales increases, or market share.

D. A sales force can be organized on the basis of geographic territory, customer type, product line, or selling tasks.

   1. Geographically-based sales territories should take into consideration factors such as sales potential, physical size, transportation facilities, and existing and potential customers.

   2. Organization by customer type may result in more than one salesperson calling on a particular organization, but each salesperson calls on a different person within the organization.

   3. Organization by product line is appropriate when products require specialized knowledge by salespersons in order to serve buyers' needs better.

   4. Sales forces can be organized by selling tasks, such as sales development or sales maintenance.

E. Sales managers perform the important personnel function of recruiting and selecting sales personnel.

   1. Job specifications and salesperson qualifications, including a list of traits, need to be determined.

   2. Personality tests can be used as an aid in selecting a salesperson.

F. Sales training varies from company to company and by the background of the sales trainees.

   1. For new recruits, sales training can involve field experience or intensive training at regional offices and/or headquarters.

   2. A sales training program for recent graduates usually includes coverage of company policies and practices, industry and competitors' background, product knowledge, and selling techniques.

   3. Sales training should be an on-going process.

G. The compensation plan should incorporate the characteristics of simplicity, fairness, paycheck regularity, security, incentive, management control, and optimal purchase orders by customers.

360

1. Compensation plans range along a continuum from a straight salary method to a straight commission approach.

2. The straight salary method is appropriate when unequal selling opportunities exist and/or performance of nonselling activities is required.

3. A straight commission plan rewards sales performance and offers little security.

4. The commission with draw plan provides security and incentive to the salesperson and is appropriate for products with seasonal demand.

5. Under a quota-bonus plan, a salesperson's base salary is related to a quota total and a bonus is offered if quotas are exceeded.

6. The salary plus commission plan provides security and incentive to salespersons and enables management to have nonselling activities performed by salespersons.

H. Motivating the sales force involves periodic sales meetings, sales promotion activities (sales contests, bonus plans, trips, prizes, and sales conventions), and financial incentives.

I. The sales force needs to be evaluated and controlled in order to achieve an organization's overall marketing plan.

1. Performance should be measured against predetermined standards such as a sales quota.

2. Most sales representatives maintain a call report of their activities.

J. Management of a non-organizational sales force, including selling agents and manufacturers' agents, creates special management problems which, at times, are resolved through monetary incentives.

VI. Sales: the starting point for a marketing career

A. Selling is an effective training ground for a career path in management.

B. A sales position enables one to learn the company's products and the company's customers.

361

SUMMARY

<u>Learning Objective One</u>: To discuss the role of personal selling in the marketing mix.

The role of personal selling is to provide personal contact with customers. As an element of promotion, personal selling informs, reminds, and persuades customers about an organization's products. Salespersons are effective in closing the sale as they can adjust presentations to the best prospects, based on direct and immediate feedback from these prospects. In addition to imparting information to customers, sales personnel gather information as part of an organization's marketing information system.

<u>Learning Objective Two</u>: To identify marketing situations in which personal selling rather than advertising or other means of promotion would be most effective in reaching and influencing target buyers.

As previously noted, personal selling is effective in closing the sale. The salesperson is able to adjust the sales message, based on direct verbal and nonverbal feedback, and to ask for the order. By concentrating on the best prospects, personal selling is a selective medium which is more efficient and effective at the transaction stage of the buying process than advertising is. Personal selling works better than other forms of promotion for products which are technical, expensive, innovative, or complex. For frequently-purchased convenience products, personal selling is too inefficient in reaching consumers, but effective in calling on channel intermediaries. In general, personal selling is most effective at the conviction and purchase stages of the heirarchy of communication effects model.

<u>Learning Objective Three</u>: To describe the role of the professional salesperson in a modern marketing firm.

The role of the professional salesperson in a modern marketing firm is to apply the marketing concept to customer needs. The salesperson views selling as an adaptive and flexible process in identifying customer problems and solving those needs individually with the products, terms of sale, and distribution options that the organization has to offer. By viewing the creative selling process as adaptive, the professional salesperson adjusts the sales presentation to show how the product solves the customer's problem and can satisfy the needs of the customer. By effectively communicating benefits of the product, the final goal of customer satisfaction is achieved. Finally, the use of the sales team enhances professional selling.

Learning Objective Four: To discuss the several steps involved in a personal selling effort from prospecting for clients to closing the sale.

The personal selling effort should be structured around a series of steps that are referred to as the creative selling process.   The creative selling process consists of (1) locating and qualifying the prospect, (2) approaching the prospect, (3) making the sales presentation, (4) handling objections, (5) closing the sale, and (6) the follow-up.

The activity of locating prospects involves identifying likely customers from various sources such as previous customers and advertising inquiries. After identifying a likely prospect, the salesperson needs to qualify the prospect to determine if the prospect has (1) a need for the product, (2) the ability and willingness to pay for the product, (3) the authority to buy or the ability to indicate the person(s) that the salesperson should contact, and (4) the profit potential for an individual order or future orders.

After qualifying a prospect, the salesperson makes an initial contact (approach) and establishes rapport with the prospect in order to make a sales presentation.   The sales presentation is a persuasive sales message designed to arouse interest in the product and to develop desire for the product.   This presentation should be a two-way dialogue between the prospect and the salesperson in order to identify the prospect's objections and to enable the salesperson to present solutions to these objections.   An effective technique to handle objections is to accept the objection with reservation and then present a counter-argument.   The two-way dialogue provides the salesperson insight as to the proper timing of when to ask for the order (closing the sale).   The salesperson can use closing techniques such as the direct, straightforward approach, the assumptive close, the "standing room only" close, the summative approach, or narrow the alternatives to a choice.   The salesperson needs to follow-up the sale to ensure that customer satisfaction results from the sale.

Learning Objective Five: To be aware that the marketing process does not stop when the sale is made and be able to tell why this is the case.

The professional salesperson perceives obtaining an order as the beginning of an organization's relationship with a customer.   A satisfied customer results in repeat sales and positive word-of-mouth recommendations.   In order to ensure a long, enduring buyer-seller relationship, sales personnel should follow-up on orders to ensure that orders are delivered in proper condition on schedule, and, that post-sale services are performed.   Organizations that adhere to the marketing concept realize customer satisfaction results from effectively following-up on the sale.

<u>Learning Objective Six</u>: To be familiar with the major aspects of the sales manager's job.

The sales force, like other personnel in an organization, has to be managed in order to direct their efforts toward achieving organizational goals. A sales manager is responsible for (1) setting sales objectives, (2) organizing the sales force, (3) recruiting and selecting sales personnel, (4) training the sales force, (5) developing an effective compensation plan, (6) motivating the sales force, and (7) evaluating and controlling the sales force.

Sales objectives should be precise, quantifiable, reasonable, and time specific in order to provide direction to the sales force and to aid sales management in planning and controlling the sales activities. Sales representatives are assigned to sales territories organized on the basis of geographic areas, customer type, product line, or selling tasks. Recruiting and selecting sales personnel necessitate that job specifications and salesperson qualifications be specified, usually in a job description. Sources external and internal to the organization can be used to identify sales applicants. These applicants are screened, interviewed, and tested for the sales position. Sales training is an on-going activity that varies according to a sales representative's background--sales recruit or experienced salesperson. In addition to motivating sales personnel, the compensation plan should (1) be simple and fair, (2) provide security, incentive, and management control, and (3) encourage optimal customer orders. The compensation plan addresses the issues of salary, commissions, quotas, drawing accounts, and expense reimbursement. The sales manager can use sales meetings, sales promotion activities, and financial incentives, including compensation, to motivate the sales force. Evaluation and control of the sales force require that performance be measured against predetermined standards and that sales representatives maintain a call report of their activities.

<u>Learning Objective Seven</u>: To understand why personal selling positions are frequently the first steps on a successful career path.

In starting a career in personal selling, a sales trainee has the opportunity to learn the company's products and, more important, its customers. Every organization's success depends on selling its products to customers; thus, people who have had sales positions are very knowledgeable about the markets in which the firm operates. In addition, selling provides opportunities for sales trainees to (1) develop their interpersonal skills, (2) understand and appreciate the business decision process, and (3) accept individual responsibility for performance. Since successful careers are based on these attributes, a sales position is often the first step in one's career path in management.

VOCABULARY BUILDING

Matching Exercises

Match the following by placing the letter of the concept or term on the blank preceding the phrase which best describes the concept or term. You should use a term or concept only once.

A. Personal selling
B. Order-takers
C. Order-getters
D. Missionary sales personnel
E. Prospecting
F. Sales presentation
G. Closing
H. Qualifying the prospect
I. Approach
J. Handling objections

K. Trial close
L. Follow-up
M. Sales management
N. Straight salary method
O. Straight commission plan
P. Commission with draw
Q. Quota-bonus plan
R. Salary plus commission plan
S. Sales quota

_____ 1. Salespersons whose primary selling responsibility is to "keep" sales.

_____ 2. Specific goal or sales volume expectation for a given period of time.

_____ 3. The step in the sales process during which the salesperson attempts to obtain a commitment to buy.

_____ 4. A compensation plan that is not tied directly to sales performance due to unequal selling opportunities or performance of non-selling activities.

_____ 5. A personal selling tactic intended to elicit from a client a signal indicating if the client is ready to complete the sale.

_____ 6. A compensation plan that rewards sales performance only.

_____ 7. A salesperson's attempt to communicate persuasively the product's benefits and to explain appropriate courses of action to the buyer.

_____ 8. Support sales personnel who build goodwill.

_____ 9. The sales-process activity of identifying likely customers.

_____ 10. A step in the creative selling process where the prospect's potential for buying is evaluated.

_____ 11. Compensation plan that is commonly used when the product sold has a seasonal demand.

_____12. This step in the sales process attempts to ensure that customer satisfaction results from the sale.

_____13. A step in the selling process that is intended to gain the buyer's attention.

_____14. Salespersons whose primary selling responsibility is to make sales and to "seek" customers.

_____15. A step in the creative selling process where the salesperson responds to questions expressed by potential buyers.

VOCABULARY BUILDING

Programmed Learning Exercise

1. _____ _____ refers to person-to-person persuasive dialogue between a buyer and a seller.

[Personal selling]

2. The salesperson's job is to _____, _____, and _____.

[inform, remind, persuade]

3. _____ _____ is the most widely used method by which organizations communicate with their customers.

[Personal selling]

4. The average cost for a U.S. industrial sales call was about _____ in 1983.

[$200]

5. The three basic categories of selling positions are _____-_____, _____-_____, and _____ _____.

[order-getting, order-taking, sales support]

6. _____ _____ is the ability to interpret product and service features in terms of benefits to the buyer and to motivate the buyer to purchase the right quality and volume of the product.

[Creative selling]

7. Members of an organization who assist the salesperson in the selling process are referred to as the _____ _____.

[sales team]

8. The _____ _____ is a sales employee at an office who answers questions about delivery, installation, and service.

[sales correspondent]

9. Professional salespeople follow a series of steps known as the _____ _____ _____.

[creative selling process]

10. Qualifying a prospect is sometimes called the _____.

[preapproach]

11. The _____ _____ _____ closing technique indicates that the product's supply is limited.

["standing room only"]

12. A salesperson looks for signs or _____ _____ that are revealed by a prospect to suggest readiness to buy.

[closing signals]

13. _____ _____ is the marketing management activity dealing with planning, organizing, directing, and controlling the personal selling effort.

[Sales management]

14. _____ sales managers are directly concerned with outside salespersons who report to them.

[Field]

15. A _____ _____ is the sales volume or the sales tasks that are set as goals of the organization.

[sales objective]

16. A _____ _____ is the geographic area and/or specific accounts assigned to a salesperson.

[sales territory]

17. Sales forces can be organized according to the selling tasks of sales _____ and sales _____.

[development, maintenance]

18. Sales training is an _____ process.

[on-going or continuous]

19. The most commonly used sales compensation plan is _____.

[salary plus commission]

20. The _____ _____ is an activity record that sales representatives keep to inform managers of field activities and occurrences.

[call report]

TRUE OR FALSE STATEMENTS

T F 1. Closing of the sale should be viewed as the end of the selling process.

T F 2. Compared to other forms of promotion, personal selling allows the organization to concentrate on the best prospects.

T F 3. Personal selling is the most economical method of promotion to reach a mass audience.

T F 4. The job of the order-taker is to "get" orders.

T F 5. The "inside" salesperson has few opportunities to enlarge the order size.

T F 6. The least creative selling situation is the "canned presentation."

T F 7. Qualifying prospects involves identifying the person to be contacted by the salesperson.

T F 8. A professional salesperson is justified in posing as a government official to get past the secretary.

T F 9. Non-verbal messages are important aspects of a sales presentation.

T F 10. The trial close is used only when the salesperson perceives the customer wants to buy.

T F 11. The performance of the follow-up activities represents a major difference between marketing and simply selling.

T F 12. Selling is not a primary responsibility of sales managers.

T F 13. Retail sales forces require less direct supervision than field sales forces.

T F 14. Good sales objectives should be qualitative and reasonable given company resources and the competitive situation.

T F 15. The best way to organize a sales force is based on convenience to the sales force, and this explains the popularity of geographically-based sales territories.

T F 16. The personnel function is one of the most important functions that sales managers perform.

T F 17. Personality tests can prove that an individual will or will not be a good salesperson.

T F 18. Successful salespeople are more like the people to whom they are trying to sell than those who are not successful salespeople.

T F 19. An ideal compensation plan should offer security and incentive.

T F 20. Performance of sales personnel should be measured against pre-determined standards.

MULTIPLE CHOICE QUESTIONS

1. Which is not a responsibility of the professional salesperson?
   a. To keep existing customers informed about company products.
   b. To keep management aware of developments in the market.
   c. To persuade potential customers through nonpersonal channels.
   d. To show potential customers how their problems can be solved by the product.

2. The main advantage of personal selling over other forms of promotion is
   a. cost.   c. reach.
   b. flexibility.   d. efficiency.

3. Which is not a disadvantage of personal selling?
   a. Managing salespeople.   c. Cost per call.
   b. Reaching mass audiences d. Effectiveness in closing.

4. Which statement regarding personal selling is correct?
   a. Fewer dollars are spent annually on personal selling than on advertising.
   b. Most small companies rely on promotional tools other than personal selling because of its high cost per call.
   c. Personal selling employs about 20 percent of the U.S. workforce.
   d. The importance of personal selling varies across organizations.

5. Order-takers' primary responsibilities do <u>not</u> include
   a. identifying how much a customer wants.
   b. checking invoices for accuracy.
   c. seeking new customers.
   d. writing up orders.

6. Rich Esposito works for a cosmetics firm. His major job responsibilities are to distribute product information to retailers and to assess the service level provided to these retailers. Rich would be
   a. a missionary salesperson.   c. an order-taker.
   b. a creative salesperson.   d. an order-getter.

7. Which is <u>not</u> true regarding the "canned sales presentation"?
   a. It requires the least well-trained salespersons.
   b. It is given with little or no variation to all prospects.
   c. It doesn't work well, so relatively few companies use it.
   d. It is often found in telephone selling.

8. The first step in the creative selling process is
   a. locating and qualifying prospects.
   b. approaching the prospect.
   c. understanding the customer's needs.
   d. preparing the sales presentation.

9. Which activity is <u>not</u> involved in qualifying sales prospects?
   a. Determining the sales potential of that account.
   b. Determining whether or not the prospect has a real need for the product.
   c. Identifying the people who may be involved in the decision process.
   d. Approaching the sales prospect.

10. In analyzing effective sales presentations, it should be noted that
    a. good salespeople always bring the product to show the prospect.
    b. interest must be followed by development of desire.
    c. it is sufficient to just get the prospect interested in the product.
    d. the ultimate goal is to get the prospect interested in the product.

11. Which tactic is <u>not</u> recommended as a way to handle objections during the sales presentation?
    a. Argue with the prospect over the objection.
    b. Agree with the prospect's objections.
    c. Accept the objection with reservation.
    d. Use objections to clarify the sales presentation.

12. Which is not a closing technique?
    a. Counter-argument approach.
    b. Direct, straightforward request for the order.
    c. Assumptive close.
    d. Narrow-the-alternatives approach.

13. Which is not a closing signal?
    a. Prospect raises the same objection again.
    b. Prospect reexamines the product carefully.
    c. Prospect comments "I like dealing with your company."
    d. Prospect asks "What colors are available?"

14. Which step in the creative selling process is likely to ensure future sales?
    a. Qualifying prospects.   c. Closing the sale.
    b. Sales presentation.   d. Follow-up.

15. Management of the personal selling effort encompasses all of these activities except
    a. setting sales objectives.
    b. monitoring the sales effort.
    c. calling on customers to get orders.
    d. developing compensation plans.

16. When a company's products have different applications in different industries, the form of sales organization it should use is by
    a. geography.   c. sales task.
    b. product.   d. customer type.

17. In developing geographically-based sales territories, the sales manager considers all of these factors except
    a. potential customers within the territory.
    b. provision for close supervision of salespersons within the territory.
    c. sales potential within the territory.
    d. transportation within the territory.

18. Which statement is not true regarding the various methods of compensating the sales force?
    a. The straight salary method maximizes management control over the salesperson's time.
    b. A straight commission motivates salespersons to develop new accounts.
    c. A commission with draw allows for protection of the salesperson during off-periods.
    d. A straight commission offers incentive to sell.

19. Jan Swanson's selling-related responsibilities include obtaining orders from past customers, developing new accounts, and setting up store displays. Her compensation plan is most likely to be one of
   a. straight salary.   c. quota-bonus.
   b. straight commission.   d. salary plus commission.

20. The use of sales promotion techniques with regard to the motivation of salespeople is such that
   a. they are used only with a quota-bonus compensation system.
   b. they do not motivate salespeople as much as a straight salary does.
   c. contests and prizes can be useful motivators for salespeople.
   d. most salespeople do not need such management motivation.

QUICK QUIZ

1Q.
How does the effective salesperson know when and how customer's objections may be adapted to the product or service offered?

1A.
Personal selling is communication and, as such, involves the same communications model presented in the last chapter . . . ENCODE, TRANSMIT, etc. This model included FEEDBACK. Personal selling, among all promotional tools, is uniquely able to make use of feedback. For example, a customer who mentions that her firm cannot afford to purchase the salesperson's product for at least two months may prompt the sales representative to explain the various credit terms available to the prospect. By adapting to feedback, the salesperson "makes the sale."

2Q.
How does the professional salesperson operate in the international market place?

2A.
As we have seen, the steps involved in creating a sale are sensible and follow an orderly progression. Of course, salespeople must modify their words and actions to fit other cultures,

cultures which may not value quick decisions or overly friendly attitudes. A Japanese business person once complained that an optical testing machine ordered from a large U.S. company arrived in Japan seriously damaged because it was not packed in a crate suitable for international shipping and was without proper import papers. The conclusion of the Japanese business person was that American companies and their sales personnel do not care about doing things right and don't really want Japanese business.

3Q.
Of the various types of sales organization . . . by geographic territory, customer type, and product line . . . which is the most consistent with the marketing concept?

3A.
On the surface, the answer would seem to be "by customer type" since the marketing concept so strongly stresses focusing on the customer. A bit of thought, however, shows that organization by product line is closely related to organization by customer type since the users of one product line are likely to be one type of customer while users of other products are of another type. Organizing by geographic territory would seem to be more for the convenience of the seller than the buyer. Geographically-based sales territories can reduce costs which is also consistent with the profit aspect of the marketing concept. However, users of this organizational structure must feel that their customers are homogeneous enough that such a method is satisfactory.

EXPERIENTIAL ACTIVITIES

19-A. The Creative Selling Process

You are a sales representative for Specialty Promotional Products, Inc. The company has recently added golf towels to their product mix of specialty products. This line of golf towels includes standard and deluxe models. The standard model is a one-color 11" by 18" towel. The available colors include green, red, royal blue, tan, brown, white, orange, and black. The deluxe model is a two-color 11" by 18" towel which includes a brass rivet and hook. Each towel can be imprinted with the name, address, telephone number, and logo of a customer. Price and commission rates for these two golf towels are presented in Table 19-1. Each additional letter or number over 35 costs $20 per 250 towels, of which you receive $10. Each additional color costs $100, of which you receive $50.

Table 19-1
Specialty Promotional Products, Inc. Commission Rates for Golf Towels

Quantity	Standard Model		Deluxe Model	
	Per Unit Cost	Commission Rate	Per Unit Cost	Commission Rate
50 – 99	$3.35	8%	$2.95	10%
100 – 149	2.80	9%	2.45	11%
150 – 249	2.55	10%	2.25	12%
250 – 449	2.30	11%	2.10	14%
500 – 999	2.12	13%	1.87	15%
1,000 – 1,499	1.84	14%	1.59	17%
1,500 or more	1.62	15%	1.42	18%

You are preparing for a sales presentation to the advertising and sales promotion director of Glass Specialties Companies, Mary Lynn. Glass Specialties is in the glass replacement business for automobiles, light trucks, and trucks in seventeen states. Their industrial customers include insurance companies and agencies, commercial accounts, such as Ryder Trucks and United Van Lines, and automobile body repair shops. Secretaries are influentials for insurance agencies. In addition, the company has a large retail business where individuals bring their automobiles to company branches for glass-related problems. Finally, you have not met Mary Lynn.

Assignment

1. Outline a sales presentation with the intended goal of the presentation to obtain an order. Your outline should consider the six steps in the personal selling process (locating and qualifying prospects, the approach, the sales presentation, handling objections, closing the sale, and the follow-up). Questions that will concern Mary Lynn during the presentation are noted below.

    a. Why would Glass Specialties want golf towels as sales promotional devices?

    b. Why not some other type of sales promotion, or even some other type of golf towel from a competitor?

    c. Is the price reasonable?

    d. What about color and slogan?

    e. Should the decision be made now?

2. If your professor requests, you should be prepared to make a presentation in class.

CHAPTER 20

ADVERTISING

OBJECTIVE

Effective advertising campaigns must be developed as part of an organization's overall marketing strategy. Planning and developing an advertising campaign requires the development of specific advertising objectives, advertising strategy, advertising budget, creative strategy, advertising messages, media strategy, media schedule, and measures of effectiveness.

OUTLINE

I. Product and institutional advertising

   A. Messages can be consummatory (immediate-action) or instrumental (longer-term action).

   B. Product advertising emphasizes a specific product and may be either direct-action or indirect-action.

   C. Institutional advertising promotes corporate image, goodwill, or generic demand.

I. Planning and developing advertising campaigns

   A. Planning and developing an advertising campaign requires decisions regarding advertising objectives, advertising budget, media selection, and creative strategy.

   B. Advertising objectives need to be developed as part of an organization's marketing strategy.

   C. Advertising objectives relate to communication goals.

1. Advertising's broad communication goals are to generate attention, to be understood, to be believed, and to be remembered.

2. Advertising campaigns require specific advertising objectives.

D. Specific advertising objectives are the basis for the creative strategy.

1. Specific advertising objectives are influenced by opportunities in the marketplace, competitive advertising campaigns, target markets, and other marketing strategy decisions.

2. Advertisements must contribute to the accomplishments of advertising goals.

E. Advertising objectives vary over the product's life.

1. Changes in advertising strategy and advertising objectives over the product's life cycle are summarized in Exhibit 20-2, in the Zikmund and d'Amico textbook.

2. At the introductory stage, the advertising strategy is to develop primary or generic demand for the product.

F. Mature products require selective demand (brand) advertising.

1. Advertisements for mature products emphasize psychological benefits and competitive advantages.

2. Advertising objectives for mature products are intended to increase the number of buyers or to increase the rate of usage among current users.

III. Creative strategy

A. The creative process in advertising refers to the generation of ideas and development of the advertising message.

B. The advertising appeal (what to say) is the central idea or theme of an advertising message.

1. The appeal's purpose is to convey to potential buyers what a product offers and why the product should appeal to them.

2. An advertising theme provides continuity to an advertising campaign using different advertisements.

3. Creativity is a competitive tool.

C. The execution of an appeal involves how to say it.

  1. "How to say it" is as important as, if not more important than, "what to say."

  2. Major execution formats, or styles of presentation, are storyline, product uses and problem solutions, slice-of-life, demonstration, testimonial, use of a spokesperson, life-style, association, montage, and jingle.

     a. The storyline advertising format tells a story or gives the history of a product.

     b. The product uses and problem solutions format incorporates a unique selling proposition that stresses a product's uses, attributes, benefits, or availability.

     c. The slice-of-life format dramatizes a problem and then introduces the product as the problem-solver.

     d. The demonstration format shows how the product can benefit the consumer by illustrating the product's features or by proving some advertised claim, utilizing comparative advertising when appropriate.

     e. Product endorsement by an individual, spokesperson or other, is the basis of the testimonial format.

     f. Life-style advertisements associate product usage to the target market's life style.

     g. The association format draws an analogy concerning another situation or product which is communicated to the target market.

     h. The montage format blends a number of situations, demonstrations, and other visual effects into one advertisement so that the total effect conveys the product appeal.

     i. Jingles serve as memory aids to enhance product recall by potential consumers.

D. Advertising departments and advertising agencies handle most creative and media aspects of advertising.

1. Advertising departments usually function as staff, rather than line, within a company's organizational structure.

2. The typical advertising agency structure consists of creative services (creative people, production, traffic), client services (account supervisors and executives), marketing services, and administration and finance.

IV. Producing the advertisement

A. Copy refers to any words that may be printed or verbalized in an advertisement.

B. Art refers to all non-copy aspects (layout, whitespace, pictures) of an advertisement used to attract attention or to illustrate a fact or idea.

C. Copy and art complement each other to achieve communication objectives by using the AIDA formula (attention, interest, desire, action) as a guideline for developing an advertisement.

V. Measuring the effectiveness of advertising

A. Advertising effectiveness research encompasses pretesting and post-testing.

B. Pretesting is conducted to develop better advertisements by testing the basic appeal, copy and art ideas, advertisement "roughs," and finished advertisements through the use of such research methods as focus group interviews, in-mall intercepts, and experiments.

C. Post-testing research is used to determine if the specific advertising objectives, such as brand recognition and recall, attitude change regarding the product or brand, inquiries generated, or sales, were accomplished.

1. Brand recognition and recall can be measured using unaided, aided, or related recall techniques.

2. A before and after study is necessary to measure changing attitudes about a product.

3. Counting the number of inquiries can measure an advertisement's pulling power.

4. Though sales is the bottom line for all advertisements, sales is not an accurate measurement of advertising effectiveness, unless the advertisement is a direct-action commercial designed to accomplish a specific sales-related advertising objective.

VI. Media selection

A. A media selection strategy considers the message, the audience, the desired effect, and the budget in order to determine which media to use and when to schedule these media.

B. Which media to select will depend on how the message can best be conveyed to the desired target audience.

1. Lengthy messages are appropriate for print (newspaper and magazine) media; outdoor media are effective for reminder messages; television is especially effective for visual comparisons and demonstrations; and radio is effective for image building.

2. Media planners should match the profile of the medium or media to the profile of the target market.

C. The advantages and disadvantages of advertising media are summarized in Exhibit 20-4, in the Zikmund and d'Amico textbook.

D. Reach, frequency, timing of advertisements, availability of media, and costs are important media scheduling considerations.

SUMMARY

Learning Objective One: To know how to define and use such terms as product advertising, institutional advertising, and direct-action advertising.

Product advertising is intended to encourage the purchase of an organization's products by promoting attributes, uses, benefits, and images of these products. Direct-action advertising is intended to stimulate an immediate action by the receiver, such as clip and/or use a coupon worth 10¢ off on the purchase of one quart of milk. Institutional advertising promotes an organization's image, its goodwill, or other nonproduct specific goals rather than focusing on a product.

Learning Objective Two: To know the differences between primary demand and selective demand advertising.

Selective demand advertising promotes a specific brand within a product category; whereas, primary advertising promotes the product category.

Primary or generic demand advertising is used during the introductory stage of the product life cycle or by trade associations (drink milk, use railroads, eat pork). Brand advertising utilizes psychological dimensions as well as differentiating product attribute characteristics.

Learning Objective Three: To discuss the process followed in the development of an advertisement.

Advertising combines with other marketing mix activities to sell a product. As an element in the marketing mix, advertising strategy must be developed as part of the organization's marketing strategy. Advertising strategy requires that specific advertising objectives be established. These objectives are usually communication-oriented, but must contribute toward the achievement of sales objectives. These objectives influence the advertising budget, creative strategy and tactics, media strategy, and advertising evaluation.

Creativity is an important aspect of developing an advertisement. Information, insight, and a decision framework ignite the creative spark which triggers the creative process. The creative process should result in a creative strategy which identifies the advertising appeal (what to say) and the execution format (how to say the appeal). Creative people use this strategy in the development of an advertisement. To combine copy and art effectively in most advertisements, creative people follow the AIDA formula. That is, each advertisement must attract attention, arouse interest, create desire, and initiate action. Pretesting of advertisements, including the basic appeal, major components, and roughs, should be done prior to transmitting the message. Of course, in producing the actual advertisement, verbal, visual and/or audio elements are used. Most advertisements use copy and art to accomplish the communication objectives.

After a message has been pretested and selected, the media strategy (media selection and media scheduling) is implemented. In addition to budgetary considerations, reach and frequency are important inputs in developing the media strategy. The effectiveness of the advertisements is assessed through post-testing research.

In summary, the development of an advertisement involves: (1) establishing specific advertising goals consistent with marketing strategy; (2) determining creative strategy; (3) developing advertising messages; (4) determining media strategy; (5) measuring advertising effectiveness; and (6) establishing an advertising budget.

Learning Objective Four: To be familiar with the role communication objectives play in the advertising process.

Advertising's function is to communicate with target markets. As such, advertising objectives should be communication-oriented. An advertisement's broad communication goals are to generate attention, to be understood, to be believed, and to be remembered. If these broad goals are not achieved, more specific advertising objectives cannot be accomplished. Thus, creativity is essential in determining advertising strategy and in the development of an advertising message.

Learning objective Five: To show how advertisements are likely to change over the course of a product life cycle.

During the introductory stage of the product life cycle, advertisements are designed to develop generic or primary demand for the product. The purpose of primary demand advertising is to develop product awareness and distribution while explaining what the product is and how it works. As the product matures, advertisements are designed to be reflective of this maturing process. Brand (selective demand) advertising is initiated to foster product acceptance and brand preference during the growth stage of the product life cycle. Advertisements for mature products (maturity stage) become more symbolic as they stress psychological benefits, as well as product features, in their attempt to maintain market position and to enhance brand loyalty. Such advertisements, hopefully, will increase the number of buyers and/or rate of usage (among current users). During the decline stage of the product life cycle, advertisements, though fewer in number, are designed to phase out the product.

Learning Objective Six: To explain the nature of an advertising appeal and to name and describe several commonly used formats to execute these appeals.

An advertising appeal is the central idea of an advertising message. This appeal conveys to a target audience (market) what benefits the product offers. The execution format indicates the way an advertising appeal can be presented. Major formats include storyline, product uses and problem solutions, slice-of-life, demonstration, testimonial, life-style, association, montage, and jingle. The storyline format tells a story or gives the product's history. A unique selling proposition based on a product's uses, benefits, or attributes is the focus of the product uses and problem solutions format. The slice-of-life format is a dramatization of the problem solution format. The demonstration format illustrates how the product can be beneficial to the consumer either by proving some advertising claim or by dramatizing a product feature. Comparative advertising is one demonstration method. The testimonial format uses product endorsements that are made by individual users or by spokespersons. The life style format relates product usage to a target market's life style; whereas, the association format draws an analogy concerning another product or situation (Marlboro man) which is communicated to the target audience. The montage format combines a number of situations, demonstrations, and visual effects into one advertising message to convey the appeal's total effect. The jingle format uses a jingle as a memory aid to enhance brand recall.

Learning Objective Seven: To be familiar with the various measures of advertising effectiveness and advertising research techniques.

Advertising effectiveness research encompasses pretesting and post-testing techniques. Pretesting techniques assist in the development and refinement of advertising copy. Pretesting is conducted to test basic appeals, copy, art, rough advertisements, and finished advertisements. Appropriate pretesting research techniques include concept testing, consumer juries (advertisements shown to a sample audience), focus groups, in-mall intercepts, laboratory experiments (trailer tests, in-home projector tests), or inquiries. Post-testing effectiveness research is designed to determine if the specific advertising objective (awareness, brand recognition or recall, attitude change, inquiries, sales) has been accomplished. Recall tests (aided, unaided, related) can be used to measure brand awareness, brand recognition, and recall. Such techniques as day-after recall, coincidental (telephone survey while program and commercial are being aired) survey, or the Starch Advertisement Readership Service illustrate various types of recall tests. In order to measure attitude change, a before and after study (survey or experiment) is necessary. Inquiries can be counted to measure the pulling power of an advertisement.

Learning Objective Eight: To be able to identify the advantages and disadvantages of different advertising media.

Selected advantages and disadvantages of advertising media are presented in Exhibit 20-4, in the Zikmund and d'Amico textbook. In general, print media (newspapers and magazines) are appropriate for lengthy messages; outdoor media are appropriate for reminder (short) messages; television provides visual demonstration; radio offers selectivity and flexibility; and direct mail is an extremely selective medium. Demographic market selectivity is offered by magazines, radio, and direct mail. Newspapers provide flexibility and a short lead time compared to magazines, but poorer quality print production and short-life advertisement capability. Broadcast media (radio and television) have perishable messages and clutter. Outdoor advertising is appropriate for short messages only and has limited locations. Direct mail can be expensive on a cost per person basis, especially when reader interest is limited.

VOCABULARY BUILDING

Matching Exercise

Match the following by placing the letter of the concept or term on the blank preceding the phrase which best describes the concept or term. You should use a term or concept only once.

A. Product advertising
B. Direct-action advertisement
C. Indirect-action advertisement
D. Institutional advertising
E. Advertising appeal
F. Advertising theme
G. Execution format
H. Storyline format
I. Slice-of-life format
J. Demonstration format
K. Comparative advertising
L. Testimonials

M. Life-style advertisement
N. Association advertising format
O. Montage format
P. Copy
Q. Art
R. AIDA
S. Pretesting research
T. Post-testing research
U. Recall tests
V. Related recall tests
W. Reach

_____ 1. The style or format by which an advertising message will be presented.

_____ 2. Words contained within an advertisement.

_____ 3. Central theme of an advertisement.

_____ 4. Number of people exposed to an advertisement in a given medium.

_____ 5. Advertising that features a specific product.

_____ 6. Product advertising intended to stimulate sales over the longer run.

_____ 7. Advertising where one brand of a product is contrasted directly with another brand.

_____ 8. A type of advertising that concentrates on drawing an analogy or other relationship to convey its message.

_____ 9. All aspects of an advertisement other than its verbal portions.

_____ 10. Post-testing research done to determine the extent to which people can remember having seen particular advertisements.

_____ 11. A type of advertising in which an individual makes a statement that (s)he owns, uses, or supports the product.

_____12. A type of advertising that blends a number of situations, demonstrations, and other visual effects into one commercial.

_____13. Post-testing research that measures the ability of a person to repeat specific messages contained in an advertisement.

_____14. Hierarchy of effects model, based on consumer behavior theory about mental activities of consumers, that is used in the development of an advertisement.

_____15. A type of advertising that shows a clear-cut example of how the product can be used to benefit the consumer by proving some advertising claim or by dramatically illustrating product features.

VOCABULARY BUILDING

Programmed Learning Exercise

1. _____ messages are delivered with the intent that something be done soon while _____ messages are intended to have some longer-term effects.

   [Consummatory, instrumental]

2. Most retail advertising emphasizes _____ action.

   [direct]

3. The type of advertising that focuses on the corporate image or generic demand is _____ advertising.

   [institutional]

4. _____ demand advertising promotes specific brands of products while _____ demand advertising promotes demand for a product class.

   [Selective, primary or generic]

5. Advertising for mature products are more likely to focus on _____ dimensions than advertising for new products.

   [emotional or psychological]

6. The generation of ideas and the development of the advertising message is called the _____ process

   [creative]

7. _____ _____ involves answering the questions of "what to say" and "how to say it."

   [Creative strategy]

8. The advertising _____ provides continuity among advertisements of a campaign.

    [theme]

9. _____ is the lifeblood of advertising.

    [Creativity]

10. A variation on the testimonial appeal is where a _____ represents the company and directly addresses the audience and urges the purchase of the product.

    [spokesperson]

11. _____ is a special association advertising format.

    [Fantasy]

12. The commercial jingle serves as a _____ _____.

    [memory aid]

13. _____ refers to the arrangement of the visual elements of an advertisement.

    [Layout]

14. Places where neither pictures nor words appear in print media are called _____.

    [whitespace]

15. The acronym AIDA stands for _____, _____, _____, and _____.

    [attention, interest, desire, action]

16. Advertising research can be divided into the _____ and _____ phases.

    [pretesting, post-testing]

17. _____ _____ strategy refers to determining which media are most appropriate for a particular advertisement.

    [Media selection]

18. _____ offer demographic market selectivity, long-life advertisement capability, and editorial support.

    [Magazines]

19. _____ advertising promotes impulse buying as well as "sells" in a nonpersonal environment.

    [Point-of-purchase]

20. Media scheduling is influenced by decisions regarding reach and
_____.

[frequency]

TRUE OR FALSE STATEMENTS

T F   1. The difference between direct-action and indirect-action adver-
            tisements is that direct-action advertisements sell products and
            indirect-action advertisements are institutional advertisements.

T F   2. The effect of product and institutional advertisements does not
            overlap.

T F   3. A general communication objective for advertising is "to be
            understood."

T F   4. Advertising should be based more on creativity than on advertising
            objectives.

T F   5. Advertising developed for an innovative product should emphasize
            and develop primary demand rather than selective demand.

T F   6. Advertising objectives are relatively constant as environmental
            conditions change.

T F   7. Creativity is necessary for all aspects of the marketing mix.

T F   8. The terms "advertising appeal" and "advertising theme" mean the
            same.

T F   9. Account supervisors coordinate the relationship between the adver-
            tiser and its agency.

T F   10. What to say refers to the execution format.

T F   11. The storyline advertisement focuses on the unique selling propo-
            sition.

T F   12. The slice-of-life format dramatizes the problem solutions format.

T F   13. Comparative advertising is used more often by non-leading firms in
            an industry.

T F   14. A spokesperson gives a testimonial about the product.

T F 15. Advertisements consist of visual elements, verbal elements, and/or audio elements.

T F 16. The function of pictures in an advertisement is to attract attention or to illustrate an idea or fact.

T F 17. Each advertisement should move a receiver through the AIDA stages with one exposure.

T F 18. Sales are the most accurate measure of advertising effectiveness.

T F 19. Media selection is influenced substantially by knowledge about the target market.

T F 20. A disadvantage of a directory is its limited customer usage.

MULTIPLE CHOICE QUESTIONS

1. Which type of advertisement makes use of a soft sell approach calculated to stimulate product sales over the longer run?
   a. Consummatory.
   c. Indirect-action.
   b. Direct-action.
   d. Comparative.

2. Sears recently advertised on television that all of its stores will sell radial tires at a 50% discount off list price during the next week. Which best describes Sears' advertising message?
   a. Consummatory.
   c. Instrumental.
   b. Institutional.
   d. Comparative.

3. The purpose of institutional advertising is to
   a. increase the sale of specific products offered by an organization.
   b. supplement the efforts of an organization's sales force.
   c. cause consumers to take a direct and immediate action.
   d. promote corporate image and to build goodwill.

4. Which is not one of the four broad goals of advertising?
   a. To be believed.
   c. To be remembered.
   b. To sell.
   d. To generate attention.

5. Advertising for mature products should
   a. avoid emphasizing psychological benefits.
   b. build awareness among various channel intermediaries.
   c. promote the product's competitive benefits.
   d. not use communication-oriented objectives.

6. Which is not true regarding advertising's role during the introductory stage of the product life cycle?
   a. Advertising should develop demand for the product category.
   b. Trade advertising may be needed to attract and interest channel members in carrying the product.
   c. Brand awareness may have to be stressed.
   d. Advertising developed at this point must not be changed throughout the life cycle.

7. Which is not a type of advertising objective for mature products?
   a. To appeal to new market segments.
   b. To inform the market about benefits of this product type.
   c. To reduce brand switching among current users.
   d. To inform customers of new uses.

8. Which is least likely to influence creative ideas for advertisements?
   a. Marketing information.   c. Insight.
   b. Marketing objectives.   d. Media execution.

9. The typical advertising agency structure includes the two unique functions of
   a. client services and creative services.
   b. marketing services and client services.
   c. creative services and marketing services.
   d. production and marketing services.

10. A comparison of the relative importance of the creative idea (what is said) versus the execution of that appeal (how it is said) shows that
   a. what is said is always more important than how it is said.
   b. how the message is said is always more important than what is said.
   c. the style of the message is always more important than the message itself.
   d. there is no rule regarding which is always more important.

11. Which is not a major execution format?
   a. Montage.   c. Copy positioning.
   b. Slice-of-life.   d. Association.

12. A wine advertisement that tells about the history of the wine is known as a _____ advertisement.
   a. storyline   c. copy positioning
   b. product use   d. association

13. An advertisement showing two students commenting on how a micro-computer helps them on their take-home assignments is an example of a _____ advertisement.
   a. problem solutions
   b. slice-of-life
   c. testimonial
   d. demonstration

14. One major difficulty of comparative advertising is that these advertisements
   a. are usually illegal.
   b. provide publicity for competitors' products.
   c. are relatively ineffective.
   d. are not supported by governmental agencies such as the FTC.

15. The rule about developing advertisements and selecting media is that
   a. advertisements should be developed before the media decisions are made.
   b. creative strategy must be decided before the media strategy.
   c. media strategy must precede any creative decisions.
   d. there is no rule regarding which comes first.

16. Which statement regarding the measurement of advertising effectiveness would be least acceptable to marketing and advertising managers?
   a. Certain tools can provide an exact measure of an advertisement's effectiveness.
   b. Managers are reluctant to spend their budgets on advertisements which have not been pretested.
   c. Post-testing is more important than pretesting.
   d. Measuring advertising effectiveness in terms of sales is difficult.

17. Which technique would be most appropriate to measure a change in brand awareness?
   a. Recall test.
   b. Awareness test.
   c. Before and after survey.
   d. Recognition test.

18. Which is not a major consideration in developing a media selection strategy?
   a. Which media to use?
   b. What audience you want to reach?
   c. What effectiveness measuring technique will be used?
   d. What media schedule to use?

19. Which is not an advantage of newspapers?
   a. Editorial support.
   b. Flexibility.
   c. Geographic market selectivity.
   d. Demographic market selectivity.

20. The advertising medium which offers the opportunity for the best audience selectivity is
   a. magazines.
   b. direct mail.
   c. television.
   d. radio.

QUICK QUIZ

1Q.
Communication theory recognizes two forms of message, the consummatory and the instrumental. Of the advertisements discussed so far, which is the consummatory type and which is the instrumental type?

1A.
Direct-action product advertisements are the consummatory messages communicated by advertisers because they seek immediate action. Advertisements which seek to influence people over time are the instrumental messages. Thus, institutional advertisements and indirect-action product advertisements are of this type.

2Q.
Much is made of the cost of TV advertising. How much does it cost?

2A.
Television advertising can cost as much as the marketer is willing to spend. This is partially because the costs of production can be very low if an ad is a locally produced videotape of a businessperson speaking directly into a camera, or very high if, for example, the advertiser hired the Disney Studios to assemble a special-effects-laden minute of thrills. Rates also vary. Some stations charge only $30-$50 per 30-second commercial, while stations in New York, Los Angeles, and other big markets charge many times as much.

c. Television budget: $_____

3. This media schedule costs AAMCO Transmission $_____
    less using local rates than using national rates.

4. Determine the budget for the above media schedule for a local
    newspaper, a local radio station, and a local television station. The
    national rates can be found in the Standard Rate and Data Service
    (SRDS) books available in your library. If not available, disregard
    this part.

    a. Newspaper budget: $_____

    b. Radio budget: $_____
        (Station _____)

    c. Television budget: $_____
        (Station _____)

    d. Total media budget: $_____

ANSWERS TO OBJECTIVE QUESTIONS

MATCHING

1.	G	4.	W	7.	K	10.	U	13.	V
2.	P	5.	A	8.	N	11.	L	14.	R
3.	E	6.	C	9.	Q	12.	O	15.	J

TRUE OR FALSE

1.	F	5.	T	9.	T	13.	T	17.	F
2.	F	6.	F	10.	F	14.	F	18.	F
3.	T	7.	T	11.	F	15.	T	19.	T
4.	F	8.	F	12.	T	16.	T	20.	T

MULTIPLE CHOICE

1.	c	5.	c	9.	a	13.	b	17.	c
2.	a	6.	d	10.	d	14.	b	18.	c
3.	d	7.	b	11.	c	15.	d	19.	d
4.	b	8.	d	12.	a	16.	a	20.	b

CHAPTER 21

INDUSTRIAL/ORGANIZATIONAL MARKETING

OBJECTIVE

Industrial marketing involves the marketing of a broad array of products ranging from raw materials to intangible services to organizations. An understanding of the special characteristics of industrial markets and the buying behavior of organizational buyers is essential to designing marketing strategies for industrial goods and services.

OUTLINE

I.   The nature of industrial demand

   A.   The demand for industrial products is derived from consumer demand.

      1.   Derived demand occurs because of, or is based on, demand for another product, i.e., demand for steel occurs because of automobiles demanded by consumers.

      2.   The effects of derived demand are described by the acceleration principle which explains that a small increase in demand at one level in the distribution system greatly increases the demand at a subsequent level in the channel system.

      3.   Industrial marketers can stimulate the demand for consumer products under certain circumstances.

   B.   Industrial demand is relatively inelastic in the short run.

      1.   Industrial buyers can pass along the price increase.

      2.   In general, the price of any one industrial product is an insignificant part of the total price of the final product.

C. Industrial demand fluctuates in response to business conditions and expectations of industrial buyers about the future.

II. Characteristics of the organizational market

    A. Industrial markets are concentrated, both geographically and numerically, in limited areas, and a few customers may account for a large proportion of sales.

    B. Industrial buyers often prefer to buy directly from producers and manufacturers.

    C. Industrial buyers evaluate products and vendors carefully, taking into consideration product specifications, terms of sale, service, and guarantees.

    D. Industrial markets are dynamic.

III. Organizational buying behavior

    A. Organizational buying may involve a number of people in an organization depending on the cost, risk, technical complexity, and purchase frequency of the anticipated purchase.

    B. Organizational buying is a multi-stage decision-making process consisting of a series of buy phases (see Exhibit 21-3, in the Zikmund and d'Amico textbook).

    C. The amount of time and effort spent on buying depends on the type of buying decision.

        1. In the straight rebuy situation, buying is virtually automatic as the organization is satisfied with suppliers and the products supplied.

        2. In the modified rebuy situation, an organization re-evaluates vendors as it is known what products are needed.

        3. The new task situation requires the organization to evaluate products and vendors.

    D. Suppliers should vary marketing effort to buyers according to the type of buying situation: straight rebuy, modified rebuy, or new task.

IV. Organizational buying motives

A. Industrial buyers compare product characteristics to the product specifications established for the purchase.

B. Vendors and products are evaluated against the product-related services desired by an industrial buyer.

C. Price can be the single most important factor in the buying decision, especially when competitive bids are solicited.

D. The need to operate an organization is the overriding factor in industrial buying.

V. The buying center

A. The buying center is comprised of people and groups that participate in the purchasing process.

B. Five roles can be identified within buying centers although any single person within an organization may play more than one role and a group of people may play a single role.

  1. Users are those who actually use the products.

  2. Gatekeepers are persons who control the flow of information to other buying center members.

  3. Influencers affect the purchase decision by supplying information to other members of the buying center.

  4. Deciders are those people who make the actual purchase decision.

  5. Buyers are persons who have the formal authority to purchase the product.

C. Membership and influence in the buying center changes as the purchasing process progresses through its stages.

D. Individuals in the buying center who are found throughout the organization have an official place in the organization and an unofficial one in the buying center.

VI. Classification of industrial markets

A. The Standard Industrial Classification (SIC) system is used by the U.S. Government to classify different segments of industry.

B. The major SIC divisions are: agriculture, forestry, fishing, hunting, and trapping; mining; construction; manufacturing; transportation, communication, electric, gas, and sanitary services; wholesale trade; retail trade; finance, insurance, and real estate; services; and public administration.

C. SIC codes are used to designate industries, products, product items, and individual industry members.

D. Information published by the government uses SIC codes as a guide to data grouping and aggregation; and, such information is often used by industrial marketers to estimate market potential and geographic sales quotas by industry.

VII. Classifications of industrial goods

A. Raw materials are unprocessed or semi-processed products which are used to make other products and which become part of the finished product.

B. Installations are long-term investments in capital goods.

C. Fabricating materials and component parts are manufactured (processed) materials and parts which become part of the finished product.

D. Process materials are used to make other products but do not become part of the finished good.

E. Accessory equipment are capital goods which typically involve a straight rebuy situation and have a shorter life than installations.

F. Operating supplies are "convenience" products used by an organization in the course of operating the business.

G. Services are intangible products, often contracted, to operate the organization.

SUMMARY

Learning Objective One: To understand why demand for industrial products is derived demand.

Demand for industrial products is dependent on demand for consumer products. Most industrial products either become part of consumer goods or are used to make consumer products. Demand for industrial products such as construction materials for highways and dams fluctuates in response to business cycles which are driven by consumption. The concept of derived demand has impact in the areas of price and promotion of industrial goods. Because demand for industrial products depends on demand for consumer products rather than changes in price, demand for industrial products tends to be price inelastic. Stimulating demand for consumer products rather than for pertinent industrial goods may have greater impact on sales and profitability of industrial firms.

Learning Objective Two: To discuss the buying criteria and motives at work in the industrial market.

Industrial buyers evaluate a potential purchase primarily on the bases of product specifications, price, and services. Product characteristics are frequently an important buying criterion since many industrial products are made to buyer specifications to perform a given task. Service-related factors (delivery, repair, technical support, and after-sale services) are important motives in acquiring the industrial customer as well as building a long-term relationship with this customer. Price is an important consideration for parity products and when competitive bids are requested from suppliers. Price considerations include the list price, discounts, terms of sale, and credit opportunities. Other buying motives relate to safety, security, and protection.

Learning Objective Three: To know some of the major characteristics of the industrial marketplace in general.

The industrial marketplace is highly concentrated both geographically and with respect to buyers. Industrial buyers tend to be sophisticated buyers who prefer to buy direct from suppliers and to follow specified buying procedures.

Learning Objective Four: To be familiar with the three basic buying situations that occur in industrial marketing: the straight rebuy, the modified rebuy, and the new task purchase.

The straight rebuy requires no review of product specifications or vendors--the order is placed automatically when the need to buy occurs. The modified rebuy requires no review of product specifications but vendors are re-evaluated. The new task situation requires both product specifications and identification and review of possible vendors.

Learning Objective Five: To understand what a buyer of organizational products seeks in the products to be purchased, and be able to explain how marketers can react to these needs.

Different members of an organization (members of the buying center) evaluate products according to different attributes (initial cost, operating cost, reliability, complexity, energy savings, pollution, and other uses). Depending upon the type of buying situation (straight rebuy, modified rebuy, or new task) and the member's role (user, gatekeeper, influencer, decider, or buyer), the industrial marketer will need to adjust the marketing mix. Strategies that "in" suppliers and "out" suppliers can use in the three types of buying situations are summarized in Exhibit 21-5, in the Zikmund and d'Amico textbook.

Learning Objective Six: To be familiar with the basics of the SIC system and its usefulness to marketers.

The SIC coding system is used to classify different segments of industry in terms of economic activity. This system can be used to specify industry, function, product category, product, and individual manufacturers and products. It is common, however, to use only the four-digit codes which designate industry, function, and product category. These codes are widely used to classify information published by federal and state governments, trade associations, and industry sources. Such information is used to develop geographic market potentials and to gain insights relative to the economic structure of geographic areas.

Learning Objective Seven: To know the basic categories of industrial goods and be able to relate them to the marketing approaches associated with each.

Industrial products are classified as raw materials, installations, fabricating materials and component parts, process materials, accessory equipment, operating supplies, and services. Marketing activities for raw materials focus on the distribution component as raw materials are bulky and relatively inexpensive. Processing plants are located near sources of raw materials to minimize transportation; and, vertical integration (vertical marketing systems) is common. The marketing approach for installations stresses personal selling, including team selling. The ability to meet buyer specifications is a key consideration in selecting a supplier for fabricating materials and component parts. Thus, the marketing mix typically stresses dealing directly with buyers which, at times, may utilize some consumer advertising as an ingredient in a pull strategy. Process materials tend to be parity products which are marketed on the basis of buyer's specifications, price, and delivery and often involves contract buying. These variables are stressed in the marketing approach which evolves around a direct sale. Advertising, price and non-price competition, and use of intermediaries are aspects of the marketing approach for accessory equipment. Suppliers of operating supplies use a sales force to service major accounts and to approach potential future customers. Smaller accounts typically visit the supplier's outlet or telephone the order. Negotiation and direct channels of distribution are key marketing activities for suppliers of services.

Learning Objective Eight: To understand the importance of the buying center concept to industrial marketing.

The buying center is an informal, cross-departmental decision unit comprised of all the people and groups that have a role in the decision-making process associated with purchasing. Roles of the members in the buying center change as the decision-making progresses. These roles have been identified as users, gatekeepers, influencers, deciders, and buyers. The importance of the buying center concept to industrial marketers is that marketing activities should not be overly focused on one individual or group to the exclusion of other individuals or groups. Marketing activities should be directed to influentials in an organization wherever possible. Identification of likely buying center members for important purchases and direction of information to these members can improve the selling effort.

VOCABULARY BUILDING

Matching Exercise

Match the following by placing the letter of the concept or term on the blank preceding the phrase which best describes the concept or term. You should use a term or concept only once.

A.	Industrial marketing transaction	L.	Buyers
B.	Derived demand	M.	Standard Industrial Classification system (SIC)
C.	Acceleration principle	N.	Raw materials
D.	Straight rebuy	O.	Installations
E.	Modified rebuy	P.	Fabricating materials
F.	New task buy	Q.	Component parts
G.	Buying center	R.	Process materials
H.	Users	S.	Accessory equipment
I.	Gatekeepers	T.	Operating supplies
J.	Influencers	U.	Services
K.	Deciders		

_____ 1. People who have the formal authority to purchase the product.

409

_____ 2. Sheet metal, cloth, or like product that becomes part of the final product.

_____ 3. Small increases in demand at one level greatly increase the demand at another level in the channel.

_____ 4. Buying situation where there is no change in product requirements but vendors are re-examined.

_____ 5. An informal, cross-departmental unit in which the primary objective is the acquisition, impartation, and processing of relevant purchasing-related information.

_____ 6. Persons who control the flow of information to other buying center members.

_____ 7. Materials used to make other products but which do not become part of finished goods.

_____ 8. Buying situation where product requirements must be determined and possible suppliers are not known.

_____ 9. Persons who make the actual purchase decision.

_____10. Industrial products in an essentially unprocessed state that are used to produce other products and become part of the finished product.

_____11. A type of "convenience" industrial product.

_____12. A person who supplies information for purchasing decisions.

_____13. Activities performed on a contract basis by individuals not employed by the purchasing organization.

_____14. Automatic and regular purchase of familiar products from familiar suppliers.

_____15. An industrial product that is standardized and has a short life, but does not become part of the finished product.

VOCABULARY BUILDING

Programmed Learning Exercise

1. An _____ marketing transaction takes place whenever a good or service is sold for any use other than personal consumption.

[industrial]

2. The _____ market is far larger than the _____ market.
[industrial, consumer]

3. The _____ _____ is the largest single buyer of industrial products.
[federal government]

4. Industrial demand is _____, _____, and fluctuating.
[derived, inelastic]

5. Industrial demand is derived from _____ demand.
[consumer]

6. Industrial buyers tend to buy _____ from manufacturers or producers.
[direct]

7. The _____ _____ situation describes a buying situation for an organization faced with a new problem or need.
[new task]

8. In the _____ _____ situation, the buyer buys the same products from the same suppliers virtually automatically.
[straight rebuy]

9. In the _____ _____ situation, buyers know what products are needed and who the likely suppliers are, but wish to "shop around" before purchasing.
[modified rebuy]

10. Important buying criteria in the industrial marketplace are _____ _____, _____ _____, and _____.
[product characteristics, related services, prices]

11. _____ products are products which are more or less the same.
[Parity]

12. _____ will actually use the product under consideration.
[Users]

13. The _____ _____ usually performs the role of "buyer."
[purchasing agent]

14. The flow of information to other members of the buying committee is controlled by _____.
[gatekeepers]

15. _____ affect the purchase decision by supplying information to _____ who make the actual purchase decision.

[Influencers, deciders]

16. The _____ _____ _____ system is a numerical coding system developed by the federal government to classify industrial segments.

[Standard Industrial Classification]

17. _____ materials and _____ _____ or component parts are industrial products used to make other products and which become part of the finished product.

[Raw, fabricating materials]

18. _____ are major industrial products which are expensive and expected to have a long life, but do not become part of the finished product.

[Installations]

19. Operating supplies have been called the _____ goods of industrial marketers.

[convenience]

20. Opportunities for _____ advantage in industrial marketing should be sought in the areas of price and distribution.

[differential]

TRUE OR FALSE STATEMENTS

T F 1. The industrial market includes producers, processors, and manufacturers but not wholesalers and retailers.

T F 2. The purchase of a case of canned apple juice by a local hospital in a supermarket would be classified as an industrial transaction.

T F 3. Short-term price reductions for industrial goods are unlikely to affect the quantity demanded of these goods.

T F 4. Industrial demand tends to be stable over long periods of time.

T F 5. Demand for aluminum cans is dependent on the price of processed aluminum material.

T F 6. Compared to consumer markets, industrial markets are geographically concentrated.

T F 7. The purchase of paper supplies such as stationery will always be a straight rebuy situation.

T F   8. Rapid changes in the competitive environment for suppliers will likely trigger a modified rebuy situation.

T F   9. Reputation and prestige of the supplier are important motives in the industrial market.

T F   10. Because the demand for industrial products is relatively price elastic, any single industrial buyer will not pay attention to the price of an industrial product being evaluated for possible purchase.

T F   11. Buying centers are the formalized organizational units formerly known as purchasing departments.

T F   12. A firm's purchase of word processing equipment is likely to be influenced by many different types of people in an organization.

T F   13. Members of a buying center are appointed for specific periods of time and return to their regular official positions after this period of time.

T F   14. Gatekeepers initiate the purchase process and may develop product specifications.

T F   15. SIC codes do not classify retailers.

T F   16. Frequent users of the SIC system use the term "industry" to refer to a four-digit grouping within the SIC.

T F   17. Price is not a key concern to buyers of component parts.

T F   18. Advertising is not an important marketing activity for marketers of process materials.

T F   19. The purchasing agent is likely to play the most important role in the purchase of operating supplies.

T F   20. Price and promotion are the most important variables in the industrial marketing mix.

MULTIPLE CHOICE QUESTIONS

1. The industrial market would not include
    a. retailers.   c. manufacturers.
    b. farmers.   d. consumers.

2. Between 1971 to 1973, demand for crude oil increased by 6.5% per year due to increased motor gasoline consumption (from pollution control devices, more convenience equipment, increased car weight from safety regulations, and the surge in new car sales) and distillant, and heavy fuel consumption needed to substitute for natural gas, coal, and nuclear power supplies which were in short supply. This is an illustration of
   a. cross-elasticity.
   b. derived demand.
   c. fluctuating demand.
   d. price inelasticity.

3. The price of "Arab light" crude oil increased from about $2.00 per barrel late in 1972 to about $10.50 late in 1974 even though the demand for oil increased substantially during this same period. This is an illustration of
   a. cross-elasticity.
   b. derived demand.
   c. fluctuating demand.
   d. price inelasticity.

4. When coffee crops fail in Columbia, coffee brokers and food manufacturers are likely to "stock-up" on coffee beans even in the face of rapid price increases. This is an illustration of
   a. cross-elasticity.
   b. derived demand.
   c. fluctuating demand.
   d. price inelasticity.

5. Which is not a characteristic of the industrial market?
   a. Preference to purchase through intermediaries.
   b. Few customers.
   c. Geographically concentrated.
   d. Formalized buying processes.

6. When increases in the price for a processed material drive marginal suppliers of component parts out of business, a buyer of component parts is likely to engage in
   a. straight rebuy.
   b. modified rebuy.
   c. new task buy.
   d. demarketing.

7. When a soft-drink manufacturer anticipates a serious sugar shortage, but cannot incur additional costs for the manufactured product, what type of buying situation is likely to occur?
   a. Straight rebuy.
   b. Modified rebuy.
   c. New task buy.
   d. Demarketing.

8. Which is not a characteristic of the straight rebuy situation?
   a. A recurring requirement exists.
   b. Purchasing agent has primary responsibility for buying.
   c. Product specifications change.
   d. Buyers may make a request for accelerated delivery time.

9. Which is not a characteristic of a new task purchase situation?
    a. This situation may arise because of outside events.
    b. Extensive information is collected.
    c. This situation occurs infrequently.
    d. No relevant past buying experience exists.

10. Which is not a buy phase?
    a. Recognition of likely solutions.
    b. Development of product specifications.
    c. Acquisition and analysis of proposals.
    d. Establishment of a buying center.

11. Which is not a common buying criterion for industrial products?
    a. Price.   c. Product characteristics.
    b. Special promotions.   d. Technical support.

12. Which does not describe a buying center?
    a. Formal.   c. Cross-departmental.
    b. Unstable membership.   d. Multiple roles.

13. When a purchasing agent sends a sample of a micro-processor supplied by a vendor to an electronics engineer, this purchasing agent is performing the role of a(n)
    a. gatekeeper.   c. decider.
    b. influencer.   d. buyer.

14. The electronics engineer sends a memo to the purchasing agent which evaluates the micro-processor favorably in terms of product specifications. What role is the engineer playing?
    a. Gatekeeper.   c. Decider.
    b. Influencer.   d. Buyer.

15. What role is played by the purchasing agent when placing the order for the micro-processor?
    a. Gatekeeper.   c. Decider.
    b. Influencer.   d. Buyer.

16. The reason a knowledge of the workings of the SIC system is important to marketers is that
    a. any marketing research information needed by marketers is obtainable through the SIC system.
    b. the SIC contains so much data that it eliminates the need to do original research.
    c. vast amounts of published information utilize the SIC system as a means to organize that information.
    d. as SIC information becomes computerized, it will virtually eliminate the need for marketing managers to make decisions.

415

17. The purchase of a micro-processor for the manufacturer of a personal computer would be classified as a(n)
    a. installation.
    c. process material.
    b. component part.
    d. fabricating material.

18. The purchase of dry cleaning materials by a dry cleaning establishment would be classified as a(n)
    a. raw material.
    c. operating supplies.
    b. process material.
    d. fabricating materials.

19. Petroleum as it comes from the well, totally untreated and ready to be refined into various petroleum-based products, is a
    a. fabricating material.
    c. component part.
    b. process material.
    d. raw material.

20. The purchase of scanner type POS (point of sale) terminals and an information storage and retrieval computer-based system by a super-market chain would be classified as a(n)
    a. process materials.
    c. installation.
    b. accessory equipment.
    d. service.

QUICK QUIZ

1Q.
What are the basic differences be-tween industrial marketing mixes and consumer marketing mixes?

1A.
Industrial marketing, compared to consumer marketing, tends to use shorter channels of distribution and relies more on personal sell-ing in order to perform services before and after the sale that en-courage repeat purchases and to establish a long-term relationship.

2Q.
Are emotional buying motives as important in industrial buying situations as in consumer market-ing?

2A.
No. Even though emotional buy-ing motives are used in industrial marketing, such motives are of secondary importance in motivat-ing an industrial buyer to pur-chase from a given supplier.

9 ___ ___ ___ ___ ___
10 ___ ___ ___ ___ ___
11 ___ ___ ___ ___ ___
12 ___ ___ ___ ___ ___
13 ___ ___ ___ ___ ___
CBD ___ ___ ___ ___ ___

2. Have the distribution targets been achieved for Birmingham, Alabama? _____ Explain. _____

_____
_____
_____
_____
_____
_____

3. What recommendations do you have?

_____
_____
_____
_____
_____
_____
_____
_____
_____
_____

Table 21-A.
Number of Establishments by Kind of Business for Major Retail Centers
and Central Business Districts in Birmingham, Alabama: 1977.

SIC Code	Kind of Business	Major Retail Centers[1]							
		No. 1	No. 2	No. 3	No. 4	No. 5	No. 6	No. 7	No. 8
53	General Merchandise Group Stores	7(4)	4(1)	4(1)	6(3)	3(1)	4(1)	4(0)	4(1)
531	Department Stores	3(1)	3(1)	3(0)	-(-)	2(0)	4(1)	3(0)	4(1)
533	Variety Stores	1(1)	1(1)	1(1)	4(2)	1(1)	-(-)	-(-)	-(-)
539	Misc. General Merchandise Stores	3(2)	-(-)	-(-)	2(1)	-(-)	-(-)	1(0)	-(-)
591	Drug and Proprietary Stores	3(1)	3(1)	2(0)	7(2)	1(1)	-(-)	4(2)	3(1)

SIC Code	Kind of Business	Major Retail Centers (Continued)							
		No. 9	No. 10	No. 11	No. 12	No. 13	SMSA[2]	City	CBD[3]
53	General Merchandise Group Stores	5(2)	5(1)	3(0)	3(1)	1(0)	203	59	15(2)
531	Department Stores	4(1)	1(0)	1(0)	2(0)	-(-)	36	17	3(0)
533	Variety Stores	1(1)	2(0)	1(0)	1(1)	-(-)	84	24	5(1)
539	Misc. General Merchandise Stores	-(-)	2(1)	1(0)	-(-)	1(0)	83	18	7(1)
591	Drug and Proprietary Stores	5(2)	4(2)	3(1)	2(0)	4(1)	230	86	11(4)

Source: U.S. Department of Commerce, Bureau of the Census, 1977 Census of Retail Trade (RC77-C-1) for Birmingham, Alabama, pages V, VI, VII, 1-14, 1-15.

[1] Concentrations of retail stores (located inside the SMSA but outside the CBD) having at least $5 million in retail sales and at least 10 retail establishments, one of which was classified as a department store (SIC 531).

[2] Standard Metropolitan Statistical Area. This designation was changed to MSA for the 1980 Census of Population.

[3] Central Business District is the defined downtown retail area of an SMSA central city.

422

ANSWERS TO OBJECTIVE QUESTIONS

MATCHING

1. L	4. E	7. R	10. N	13. U
2. P	5. G	8. F	11. T	14. D
3. C	6. I	9. K	12. J	15. S

TRUE OR FALSE

1. F	5. F	9. F	13. F	17. T
2. T	6. T	10. F	14. F	18. T
3. T	7. F	11. F	15. F	19. T
4. F	8. T	12. T	16. T	20. F

MULTIPLE CHOICE

1. d	5. a	9. a	13. a	17. b
2. b	6. b	10. d	14. b	18. b
3. d	7. c	11. b	15. d	19. d
4. c	8. c	12. a	16. c	20. c

CHAPTER 22

MARKETING IN THE MULTINATIONAL ENVIRONMENT

OBJECTIVE

Multinational marketing requires that marketers follow the principles of effective marketing to be successful and to avoid the negative effects of ethnocentrism. Marketing mixes of multinational organizations should be made with regard to a global strategic approach and local adjustments in tactics to reflect environmental differences among international markets.

OUTLINE

I. A world perspective

   A. Multinational marketing involves the marketing of products across national boundaries.

   B. International marketing involves the development and implementation of marketing strategies that distinguish between foreign and domestic strategies.

   C. The same basic marketing concepts (market segmentation, marketing mix strategy, and environmental analysis) apply to both domestic and international marketing; however, there are some strategic and tactical differences based on environmental (cultural, economic, political, and legal) factors.

II. The importance of world marketing

   A. Multinational marketing impacts the domestic economy by (1) increasing the standard of living, (2) stimulating domestic competition, and (3) triggering economic growth.

   B. The costs of world trade can include "culture shock" and trade deficits.

C. American exports are about seven percent of the United States GNP.

III. Getting involved in multinational marketing

    A. Decision 1: Do we get involved in international marketing?

        1. The economic concept of comparative advantage states that trade between two countries will benefit both because of benefits associated with specialization.

        2. Factors that encourage international marketing include (1) saturated domestic market, (2) obsolete domestic product, (3) domestic government or environment becomes anti-business, (4) foreign market opportunities, (5) foreign production opportunities, (6) formation of economic communities (EEC and LAFTA), and (7) General Agreements on Tariffs and Trade (GATT) accords.

        3. Tariffs, import quotas, embargoes, and other restrictive foreign government controls discourage international marketing.

    B. Decision 2: Which international markets?

        1. This segmentation decision involves criteria related to market size, market growth, costs of entry, competitive activity, level of economic development, degree of political stability, existence of compatible marketing systems, political regulations on businesses, and cultural compatibility.

        2. Differences between cultures must be identified and understood while the attitude of ethnocentrism needs to be avoided.

        3. The political environment (government policies toward international trade and degree of political stability) of the target host country must be examined and evaluated.

        4. A country's level of economic development (undeveloped country, less-developed country, developing country, or developed country) will impact on appropriate marketing strategies.

        5. Demographic-related factors impact on the profitability of marketing efforts.

    C. Decision 3: How much commitment in each market?

        1. An organization's commitment may involve exporting, joint-venturing, and/or direct investment.

426

2. Exporting is the least risky commitment to international marketing while direct investment involves the most risk.

3. Exporting may be indirect through an intermediary, such as a buyer for export, or direct whereby the domestic firm may use salespeople, a domestic-based department, or establish overseas sales offices, branches, or distributors to market their products.

4. Various forms of joint venturing (domestic and host countries jointly establish production and marketing facilities) are licensing, international franchising, contract manufacturing, and joint ownership.

5. Direct foreign investment in production and marketing facilities in a host country is a long term commitment of resources and effort.

D. Decision 4: How should we organize for international marketing?

1. The organizational structure should be consistent with the level of commitment to international marketing (decision 3).

2. The organization could establish an export department (for direct and indirect exporting) or an international department (for investment in or contract with the host country).

3. An international company has a perspective of a domestic-based company while a multinational company's perspective goes beyond a home or domestic orientation to a global orientation.

E. Decision 5: How much should we change our domestic-based marketing?

1. The international marketer should have a corporate-wide strategy which is adjusted to reflect local conditions.

2. International marketing research is essential in identifying market potentials and characteristics even though secondary data are less accurate and not as available as in the United States.

3. Product planning options are to market (1) the same product, unadjusted, (2) the same product, adapted to the market, and (3) a totally new product invented for the market.

4. Promotion planning involves decisions similar to those for product planning and must consider media availability, literacy, type of media, language, and media habits.

5. Price planning tends to be cost-plus but needs to reflect inflation, devaluation, and dumping.

6. Distribution planning can be quite complex due to less developed distribution systems and the requirement that less efficient traditional methods of distribution be used to obtain distribution.

7. Marketing mix planning involves investigating local conditions and then altering the marketing mix to fit those decisions.

SUMMARY

<u>Learning Objective One</u>: To describe the impact of international marketing on our domestic economy and on the economies of our trading partners.

Today, many of the products that we consume are made available because of international marketing. Foreign products are imported into the United States because they are less expensive or because local manufacturers or producers are unable to meet domestic demand. Similarly, the United States exports its products abroad. Multinational marketing helps nations to develop their economies in addition to satisfying consumer needs. International marketing enables each country to specialize in the production and marketing of those products in which it is most efficient and to exchange those products for other nations' products. Thus, multinational marketing promotes global efficiency through the development of specialization. For example, imports stimulate domestic competition and industrial growth, both of which helps to increase the standard of living. Costs associated with international marketing are trade deficits and "culture shock" for some countries.

<u>Learning Objective Two</u>: To be able to discuss the many cultural, linguistic, and political pitfalls that the successful international marketer must overcome.

For an organization to market its product successfully to an international market, the marketer must take a non-ethnocentric attitude toward cultural and political environments. Customs, habits, lifestyles, and languages differ from market to market. For instance, the Western culture perceives being late for a business meeting as an inappropriate behavior, but this would be an acceptable behavior in an Eastern culture. An understanding of a nation's, or a market's, cultural values is essential to avoid misinterpretations of language subtleties, appropriateness of colors, women and men roles, and other traditions. Cultural differences are not the only barrier as obstacles can be rooted in the political environment in terms of a government's attitude toward international trade and its stability. A government can impose restrictions (tariffs, embargoes, import quotas, and other nontariff barriers) on trade with another country. An international marketer must overcome these obstructions. Most

428

likely, all or some of these differences will impact the marketing strategy and will require that the strategy suit local conditions.

Learning Objective Three: To understand the powerful negative effects ethnocentrism can have on a multinational firm's marketing plan.

Ethnocentrism is the tendency for an international marketer to use his or her culture as the acceptable way of doing things.   This attitude disregards that people differ worldwide and that nations vary in terms of culture, economic development, resources, purchasing power, and national priorities.   It would be disastrous to impose one's customs, lifestyle, or management philosophy on people of a different culture.   In general, the organization which used this self-reference criterion to market a highly successful domestic product in a foreign country will not be an effective marketer.

Learning Objective Four: To show the progression of steps a domestic marketer must complete in analyzing and developing overseas markets.

The decision sequence that any domestic company must complete when getting involved in international marketing necessitates answers to several questions.

1.   Do we get involved in international marketing?
2.   If yes, which international markets?
3.   How much commitment to each market?
4.   How should we organize for international marketing?
5.   How much should we change our domestic-based marketing?

An organization's managers must balance factors encouraging and discouraging international trade.   Only if the analysis indicates that international marketing will be a profitable expansion strategy, should target markets be evaluated and selected.   Selection of target markets involves consideration of the cultural, political, economic, and demographic environments to assess current and future potential, expected sales, costs, profits, and return on investment. Next, the company has to decide whether it wants its level of involvement to be exporting (direct or indirect), joint venture (licensing, international franchising, contract manufacturing, or joint ownership venture), or direct foreign investment.   The level of commitment to each market will impact the organizational structure (export or international department) and organizational perspective (multinational or international company).   Market characteristics and marketing research will help to determine what changes need to be made in each specific marketing mix element.   The objective of such detailed investigation and planning is to adapt to local conditions and needs.

429

<u>Learning Objective Five</u>:   To understand how otherwise clever American
marketing organizations have failed to penetrate other nations' markets.

This chapter provides numerous examples of American-based organizations which have not been successful in ventures in foreign host countries.
Many of these failures can be traced to an attitude of ethnocentrism, inadequate environmental analyses, inadequate marketing research, and inappropriate application of marketing concepts to foreign countries' needs and
problems.

<u>Learning Objective Six</u>:   To have seen how the basic marketing mixes devel-
oped for domestic markets must be modified for use overseas, but that despite
modification, the principles of effective marketing still apply.

Target marketing necessitates that meaningful target markets be identified and that the marketing mix be matched to these target markets.   Since
foreign markets differ from domestic markets, the basic marketing mix will
need to be adapted to local conditions of the foreign market.   Otherwise,
ethnocentrism can have negative effects on a multinational organization's
marketing plans.   Effective multinational marketers make marketing mix decisions based on a global strategic approach and local adjustments in tactics.
Their planning of the marketing mix involves first investigating local conditions
and then determining the extent to which the strategic approach needs to be
modified for a local market.   Each of the four basic marketing mix components
can be adjusted to reflect local conditions.

VOCABULARY BUILDING

Matching Exercise

Match the following by placing the letter of the concept or term on the
blank preceding the phrase which best describes the concept or term.   You
should use a term or concept only once.

A. International marketing
B. Comparative advantage
C. European Economic Community
    (Common Market)
D. General Agreement on
    Tariffs and Trade (GATT)
E. Tariff
F. Import quotas
G. Embargo
H. Ethnocentrism
I. Boycott

J. Undeveloped countries
K. Less-developed countries
L. Developing countries
M. Developed countries
N. Indirect exporting
O. Direct exporting
P. Joint venturing
Q. Licensing
R. International franchising
S. Contract manufacturing
T. Joint ownership venture

_____ 1. A government restriction that prohibits the importing of particular goods from particular countries.

_____ 2. An agreement in which a U.S.-based company agrees to permit an overseas manufacturer to produce and market a product in that overseas country.

_____ 3. Tendency to consider one's culture and way of life as the natural and normal way of doing things.

_____ 4. Nations where small-scale industry and market activities exist.

_____ 5. Selling goods to an intermediary that specializes in selling products in international markets.

_____ 6. Limits set on the amounts of certain types of goods that may be legally imported into a country.

_____ 7. Nations that are characterized by social change, increasing marketing activity, and growth of selective industries.

_____ 8. Arrangement between domestic and host companies to establish some production and marketing facilities in overseas markets.

_____ 9. Tax imposed on goods brought into a nation.

_____ 10. A series of agreements and understandings intended to encourage international trade by reducing international trade restrictions and by achieving reductions in trade tariffs.

_____ 11. The development and implementation of marketing strategies that emphasize geographic market segmentation and the distinction between foreign and domestic markets.

_____ 12. Nations that are the most economically advanced.

_____ 13. An arrangement in which the domestic and foreign partners both invest capital and share ownership in a business operation.

_____ 14. Direct sale of products to customers located outside of the domestic market.

_____ 15. A form of licensing in which the domestic-based company establishes an overseas business.

VOCABULARY BUILDING

Programmed Learning Exercise

1. _____ are the foreign products you purchase domestically while _____ are domestically produced products sold in foreign markets.

    [Imports, exports]

2. American exports are approximately _____ percent of the U.S. GNP.

    [seven]

3. The same fundamental, procedural marketing concepts that apply in domestic marketing apply in _____ marketing.

    [international]

4. The economic theory of _____ _____ states that trade between two countries will benefit each other.

    [comparative advantage]

5. Two important cooperative economic communities are the _____ and _____.

    [ECC, LAFTA]

6. The most extreme form of a quota is a(n) _____.

    [embargo]

7. The economy of _____ countries is primarily agricultural-based.

    [undeveloped]

8. Exporting activities may begin to emerge in _____ countries.

    [developing]

9. The types of commitment a domestic-based company can make to international marketing are _____, _____ _____, and _____ _____.

    [exporting, joint venturing, direct investment]

10. _____ is the lowest level commitment that a company can make to international marketing.

    [Exporting]

11. A widely used measure of the national income available in a country is _____.

    [GNP]

12. A _____ is a type of merchant intermediary that purchases goods from domestic firms to sell in international markets.

    [buyer for export]

432

13. The simplest method of joint venturing is _____ .

[licensing]

14. Contract manufacturing, compared to licensing, offers a U.S.-based company more _____ _____ .

[market control]

15. The highest level of foreign investment in a nation is _____ foreign investment.

[direct]

16. An _____ department manages the firm's international marketing operations while an _____ department deals directly or indirectly with overseas customers.

[international, export]

17. A(n) _____ company has a more global perspective than a(n) _____ company.

[multinational, international]

18. The three product-oriented adjustments that can be made in international marketing are _____ , _____ , and _____ .
[same product unadjusted, same product adjusted, new product invention]

19. _____ is the practice of a government to decrease the value of its currency relative to other currencies.

[Devaluation]

20. The practice of pricing products for a foreign market below their comparable fair market value in a domestic market is referred to as _____ .

[dumping]

TRUE OR FALSE STATEMENTS

T F 1. The same fundamental marketing concepts that apply in domestic marketing apply in multinational marketing.

T F 2. On a conceptual marketing level, the most obvious barrier in international marketing is language.

T F 3. A "self-reference" shock may occur as trade develops between developed and less-developed countries.

T F 4. The formation of economic communities simplifies trade among nations.

433

T F   5.   Culture consists of the values, beliefs, patterns of living, and social institutions shared by members of a society.

T F   6.   Foreign cultures need little analysis in order to understand cultural differences.

T F   7.   An element of concern in the political environment is the attitude of government toward international trade.

T F   8.   Literacy, technology, and distribution structure are among factors related to the level of political development.

T F   9.   The U.S. has the largest GNP and GNP per capita.

T F 10.   Japan has the highest population density.

T F 11.   Direct exporting may take the form of traveling salespeople, a domestic-based export department, or overseas sales offices, branches, or distributors.

T F 12.   Exporters may modify products and instructional materials slightly to suit each foreign market.

T F 13.   Contract manufacturing offers the opportunity to utilize less expensive labor to reduce the price of products.

T F 14.   International marketing research frequently involves the usage of much readily-available secondary data.

T F 15.   The simplest product strategy for international marketing is to adjust the existing product.

T F 16.   Product invention can take the form of backward invention and forward invention.

T F 17.   Most companies can effectively wage a single worldwide promotion when they expend effort in this direction.

T F 18.   Cost-based pricing is the common base of pricing overseas.

T F 19.   In terms of distribution planning, the marketer must be concerned with adapting to the existing distribution structure of each nation.

T F 20.   Logistics systems are similar for both domestic and international markets.

MULTIPLE CHOICE QUESTIONS

1. Multinational marketing involves the adaptation of a marketing strategy based on market segmentation by
   a. socio-economic factors.
   c. geographic factors.
   b. product use.
   d. life style.

2. Which is not a basic marketing decision to be made in foreign markets?
   a. Analysis of environmental factors.
   b. Analysis of domestic expenditures.
   c. Determination of target markets.
   d. Development of marketing mix strategy.

3. Which is not true regarding the influence of world trade involvement by a nation?
   a. World trade can raise the nation's standard of living.
   b. World trade may be necessary to fill some basic needs of that nation.
   c. World trade may result in cultural change in that nation.
   d. World trade usually serves to discourage domestic competition and production.

4. Which consideration about the domestic market does not encourage a domestic company to move into international marketing?
   a. Market saturation.
   c. Technological obsolescence.
   b. Lack of new markets.
   d. Tariffs on products.

5. Which is not a discouraging factor when an organization is contemplating getting involved in international marketing?
   a. Domestic government anti-business perspective.
   b. Tariffs.
   c. Import quotas.
   d. Restrictive foreign government controls.

6. The decision sequence to get involved in international marketing includes all except
   a. which international market(s).
   b. what management's philosophy is towards world trade.
   c. how much commitment to each international market.
   d. how to organize for each international market.

7. The selection of an international market does not include estimating and/or forecasting
   a. market potential.
   c. past market activities.
   b. return on investment.
   d. sales potential.

435

8. Which factor is <u>least</u> likely to affect a marketer's decision to select an international market?
   a. Market growth.   c. Costs of entry.
   b. Competitive activity.   d. Compatible marketing systems.

9. Which criterion becomes more important in international marketing decisions than in domestic marketing decisions?
   a. Degree of cultural compatibility.
   b. Size of the market.
   c. Estimated return on investment.
   d. Potential of the market.

10. An ethnocentric philosophy towards international markets is likely to result in
   a. an unstable political environment in a host nation.
   b. correctly interpreting cultural differences among people.
   c. a marketing strategy based on mistaken beliefs about the foreign market behavior.
   d. highlighting the differences between the foreign and domestic market conditions.

11. Which is <u>not</u> true regarding the marketer's concerns about the political environment in international marketing?
   a. Many nations need imports and encourage world trade.
   b. Trade laws are often written out of political, not economic, motives.
   c. Many nations will not permit full ownership of business by foreign companies.
   d. This environment is more predictable internationally than in the U.S.

12. In evaluating a foreign market's potential, one of the best available measures of market size is
   a. disposable income.   c. real income.
   b. GNP.   d. balance of trade.

13. Which stage of economic development is best described as having a local market orientation and functions such as limited marketing activities, specialization, and separation of production and marketing?
   a. Undeveloped country.   c. Developing country.
   b. Less-developed country.   d. Developed country.

14. When a foreign government imposes high tariffs, restricts foreign ownership, and has a high tax on royalty payments, an organization should
   a. only import from the country.
   b. enter into a joint venture with a local national firm.
   c. make a direct foreign investment.
   d. select another country or market.

436

15. Which is not a characteristic of indirect exporting?
    a. Companies export on a continuous and planned basis.
    b. Companies elect to sell periodically a portion of its inventory to some U.S.-based exporter.
    c. Companies may view the international market as a place to dispose of products.
    d. Companies make no systematic effort to be in the international market.

16. A comparison of joint venturing and exporting shows that
    a. joint venturing involves some agreement for overseas production.
    b. exporting always results in higher profits.
    c. exporting will be used more often in low-risk markets.
    d. neither joint venturing nor exporting involves overseas production.

17. The difference between the multinational and the international company is that
    a. there is no difference; the two are synonymous.
    b. multinationals do business in more than one foreign country; internationals do not.
    c. international companies are controlled by several countries; multinationals are not.
    d. multinationals have a larger, more global perspective.

18. Which is the first step an organization should take to investigate a potential foreign market?
    a. Conduct primary research.
    b. Review available secondary data to analyze the existence of an opportunity.
    c. Decide on a marketing strategy.
    d. Ask permission of host country.

19. An essential step involved in international marketing mix decisions is to
    a. investigate language barriers.
    b. determine overall social patterns.
    c. determine the extent to which decisions are transferable among markets.
    d. investigate national conditions.

20. A major reason for differences between international and domestic marketing is that
    a. different countries have different GNP's.
    b. all countries impose restrictions and tariffs on business.
    c. the political environment is radically different from country to country.
    d. beliefs and values of people and business institutions differ from country to country.

QUICK QUIZ

1Q.
Even though nations differ linguistically, do most nations have a common language?

1A.
No. In general, English-speaking, French-speaking and Spanish-speaking nations tend to be more linguistically homogeneous than other nations. For example, the official language of India is Hindi and is spoken regularly by only 30 percent of the population. The various language families include Indo-European (which includes Hindi), Dravidian, Tibeto-Chinese, and Austric. The percentages of persons speaking each language family are 73%, 25%, 1%, and 1% respectively. Source: Edward A. O'Neal (1978), "India: Unreal Expectations," The Wilson Quarterly, Autumn, p. 120; Vern Terpstra (1978), The Cultural Environment of International Business (Cincinnati, Ohio: South-Western Publishing Company, p. 11).

2Q.
Do U.S.-based companies use barter in their international marketing?

2A.
U.S.-based companies have barter transactions with less developed nations in order to expand sales, reduce balance of payments problems, and alleviate payment problems. One form of bartering is countertrading in which a U.S.--based company would agree to buy or market abroad products of equivalent value to pay for products the U.S. company sold. Countertrading is increasing in importance as a means to sell to countries which don't have cash

to pay for products such as the U.S. and Soviet Pepsi arrangement.

3Q.
What are projected to be the world's most populous areas?

3A.
In the year 2000, according to a United Nations forecast, the 10 largest urban areas and their projected populations in millions will be Mexico City (31.0), Sao Paulo (25.8), Tokyo-Yokahama (24.2), New York-N.E. New Jersey (22.8), Shanghai (22.7), Peking (19.9), Rio de Janeiro (19.0), Greater Bombay (17.1), Calcutta (16.7), and Djakarta (16.6).

EXPERIENTIAL ACTIVITIES

22-A. Which International Market?[1]

An international cereal manufacturer, headquartered in the United States, is investigating the establishment of a manufacturing and marketing facility in India. You are retained as a consultant by the manufacturer to prepare a preliminary report regarding this decision. In preparing your report, you obtained these facts regarding India.

1.   India's population exceeds 650 million people.

2.   India is the tenth largest industrial nation.

3.   India's distribution and marketing system is adequate.

4.   The two other cereal manufacturers in India are local firms.

5.   The Indian government is not very receptive to foreign investment, especially if the investment does not enhance economic development through modern technology.

---

[1]The material in this case was presented by Sunil Patel, graduate student, Illinois State University. Used with permission.

Assignment

1. Should the cereal manufacturer consider the Indian market for expansion? _____

2. Justification: _____ _____

_____

_____

_____

_____

_____

_____

_____

_____

_____

_____

_____

_____

22-B. Basic Multinational Strategies[2]

A United States television manufacturer has decided to market a product in the European Economic Community (ECC). The manufacturer is not sure how much ownership and managerial commitment to make to the ECC. The options are exporting (indirect or direct), joint ventures (licensing, international franchising, contract manufacturing, or joint ownership venture), and direct foreign investment.

Previous research has indicated that:

1. average labor costs are lower in ECC countries than in the United States;

2. the ECC imposes high tariff rates on television sets and components;

---

[2]The material in this case was presented by Sunil Patel, graduate student, Illinois State University. Used with permission.

3. the quality of television sets currently sold within the ECC is lower than the quality of the sets produced by the U.S. manufacturer; and

4. there are few television manufacturers whose products are sold in all of the member countries.

Assignment

1. What multinational strategy would you recommend? _____

2. Justification: _____

_____

_____

_____

_____

_____

_____

_____

_____

_____

_____

_____

ANSWERS TO OBJECTIVE QUESTIONS

MATCHING

1. G	4. K	7. L	10. D	13. T
2. S	5. N	8. P	11. A	14. O
3. H	6. F	9. E	12. M	15. R

TRUE OR FALSE

1. T	5. T	9. F	13. T	17. F
2. T	6. F	10. F	14. F	18. T
3. F	7. T	11. T	15. F	19. T
4. T	8. F	12. T	16. T	20. F

MULTIPLE CHOICE

1. c	5. a	9. a	13. c	17. d
2. b	6. b	10. c	14. b	18. b
3. d	7. c	11. d	15. a	19. c
4. d	8. d	12. b	16. a	20. d

CHAPTER 23

MARKETING AND SOCIETY

OBJECTIVE

Marketing has a social and ethical responsibility toward competitors, consumers, and the general public. Effective marketers can fulfill these responsibilities best by properly applying the marketing concept.

OUTLINE

I   Social responsibility

    A. Social responsibility concerns the ethical consequences of an individual's or an organization's marketing activities on the interest of others.

    B. Social responsibility is more encompassing than legal responsibilities.

    C. A major question concerns the compatibility between corporate social responsibility and the corporate profit motive.

    D. Social institutions must operate within a society's rules of conduct.

II. The question of ethics

    A. Ethics refer to moral principles that guide one's conduct.

    B. Social norms define ethical issues which influence the choice of marketing actions.

        1. Norms indicate what ought to be done.

        2. Difficult choices emerge when conflict exists between two norms since an ethical problem arises.

C. No permanent, objective ethical standards exist to guide market actions, even though codes of ethics do exist.

III. Ethical dimensions of the marketing mix

    A. Marketing is accountable to three publics--consumers, competitors, and the general public.

        1. Marketing's social responsibility to these publics relate to consumerism issues, fair competitive practices, and quality of life issues.

        2. The social institution of government oversees marketing's interaction with its three publics, intervening when necessary.

    B. Marketing has a macro-responsibility to society (macromarketing) as well as an individual organizational micro-responsibility (micromarketing) to customers and competitors.

    C. The responsible actions of marketing managers toward competitors concerns fair competition.

        1. Procompetitive laws guide marketers' actions toward fair competitive practices.

        2. Some marketing practices, such as price collusion and horizontal price fixing, are prohibited specifically by law; while other practices, such as fraud and misleading advertising, fall under a law which deals with a general issue rather than mentioning the specific offending marketing practice.

        3. A small minority of marketers are criminals.

    D. Consumerism is a broad social movement to protect individuals rights as consumers and it reflects some marketers neglect of their social responsibilities.

    E. Marketing's responsibility to consumers evolves around the four basic consumer rights: (1) the right to safety; (2) the right to be informed; (3) the right to choose; and (4) the right to be heard.

        1. Consumers have the right to be protected from unnecessary risks and danger in the consumption of a product (right to safety).

            a. The right to safety has moved from a caveat emptor philosophy to a philosophy that makes the seller responsible.

444

b. Failure to protect customers is not consistent with the marketing concept.

2. The right to be informed entitles customers to be protected from fraudulent, deceitful, or grossly misleading information.

  a. Misleading or deceptive advertising and bait and switch are two areas of primary concern to marketers.

  b. The FTC can mandate corrective advertising for misleading or deceptive advertising.

  c. Puffery or a slight advertising exaggeration is permissible.

3. Consumers have the right to choose from among a wide variety of satisfactory quality products that are fairly priced.

  a. Product obsolescence is an issue confronting marketers.

  b. Fashion obsolescence and planned obsolescence are more controversial than technological obsolescence and physical obsolescence.

4. The right to be heard provides consumers the opportunity to express their feelings through complaints and letters to sellers and legislators, and through establishing consumer organizations and consumer advocate groups.

5. Other consumers rights, such as a right to a clean environment, exist.

F. Effective marketers respect consumer rights.

1. The marketing concept stresses consumer satisfaction.

2. Organizations that are not consumer-oriented do not survive.

3. Societal measures to ensure consumer protection include prevention, restitution, and punishment.

IV. Quality of life

A. Quality of life reflects a sense of well being by members of a society.

B. Businesses are expected to be economically efficient, preserve the environment, and conserve national resources as they serve the public.

C. It is unclear who (consumers, businesses, or both) should bear the cost of a clean environment.

D. Recycling is a means to ensure a cleaner environment and to conserve resources.

E. Privacy issues are of increasing importance to marketers.

F. Public standards or perceived public standards determine law and ethics.

G. The quality of children's lives is affected by advertising.

H. Society expects marketing to deliver a standard of living efficiently and effectively.

   1. A complex distribution system has emerged to deliver the wide variety of goods demanded by society.

   2. Marketing has been criticized for creating false needs and proliferating the market with unnecessary brands.

V. The ethics of persuasion

A. Advertising is attacked by critics frequently.

B. Critics want informative advertising rather than persuasive advertising.

VI. Marketing and higher prices

A. Critics of marketing charge that marketing activities such as advertising and packaging waste resources.

B. Marketers point out that such activities, especially advertising, conserve resources and make mass production possible.

C. Distribution does not cost too much as marketing intermediaries must perform channel functions more efficiently and more effectively than manufacturers in order to survive.

446

SUMMARY

Learning Objective One: To understand the place of ethical behavior in marketing.

Marketing organizations have to exercise social responsibility in their interaction with various publics of society. Ethical actions are subjective and judgmental, depending on the current norms of society. These norms define ethical issues which, in turn, influence actions of marketers. Thus, ethics should guide the actions of marketers.

Learning Objective Two: To understand the difficulties encountered in fulfilling marketing's responsibilities.

Difficulties related to fulfilling marketing's responsibilities arise when society's and an organization's interests conflict or when different segments of society have conflicting social values and norms. Incompatibility between corporate social responsibility and the corporate profit motive can place an organization at a competitive disadvantage through increased costs associated with fulfilling a corporate social responsibility. Conflicts of this nature are usually resolved by legislation that requires these costly socially desirable features be added. Conflicts between different norms are difficult to resolve as permanent ethical standards are not available. Marketing managers can use codes of ethics as well as the marketing concept to guide their actions in these instances. Long-term considerations, rather than short-term considerations, can enhance resolving these ethical issues related to marketing's role.

Learning Objective Three: To describe the several publics toward which marketers must act ethically.

Marketing is responsible to three publics: (1) competitors; (2) consumers; and (3) the general public. The interests of these groups are interrelated and, consequently, must be considered when making marketing-related decisions. Government influences the interrelationships among these members, including marketing, by overseeing their actions and intervening when one or more of these members behaves irresponsibly.

Learning Objective Four: To have a sense of the importance of the consumerism movement.

The consumerism movement is a social response to marketers who have not been socially responsible. If all marketers followed the marketing concept, consumerism would not be necessary. The consumerism movement centers around four basic consumer rights. These rights are: (1) the right to safety; (2) the right to be informed; (3) the right to choose; and (4) the right to be

heard. The movement has made marketers more responsible toward the consumer in their actions and indicates the importance of organizations to adhere
to the marketing concept in their marketing efforts.

Learning Objective Five: To identify areas in which marketing's social responsibilities are particularly great.

Marketing has social responsibility in the areas of fair competitive practices, consumerism, and quality of life. Responsible action toward competitors
is enhanced by procompetitive laws which delineate marketing actions which are
prohibited. Responsible action to consumers evolves around assuring that the
four basic rights of consumers are protected. At the macro level, marketing
as an aggregate social institution must provide for an improved quality of life.
Thus, marketing must (1) ensure a clean environment, (2) protect natural
resources, (3) provide an efficient system to deliver products, and (4) adhere
to public standards in matters such as privacy, pricing, advertising, product
planning, personal selling, sales promotion, and distribution.

Learning Objective Six: To explain how the free market system serves to
guide and evaluate the decisions of marketing managers.

If marketing managers make socially irresponsible decisions, market
mechanisms operate such that good products drive out bad products. Consumers will not continue to buy: (1) inferior quality products; (2) products
perceived to be too expensive; (3) products about which they are improperly
informed; or (4) products available at inferior locations. Consumers vote for
the products which survive--through their repeat purchases. Furthermore,
consumers, competitors, and other concerned groups can guide and evaluate
marketing decisions through legislation and other social actions (e.g., boycotts). In summary, ethics, social norms, and public standards need to be
considered prior to making a marketing decision.

VOCABULARY BUILDING

Matching Exercise

Match the following by placing the letter of the concept or term on the blank preceding the phrase which best describes the concept or term. You should use a term or concept only once.

A.	Social responsibility	K.	The right to choose
B.	Ethics	L.	Product obsolescence
C.	Norms	M.	Fashion obsolescence
D.	Value system	N.	Technological obsolescence
E.	Consumerism	O.	Planned obsolescence
F.	The right to safety	P.	Physical obsolescence
G.	The right to be informed	Q.	The right to be heard
H.	Deceptive advertising	R.	Quality of life
I.	Bait and switch	S.	Privacy issues
J.	Puffery		

_____ 1. Sense of well-being perceived by a society's citizens.

_____ 2. Practice of conscientiously introducing new products at planned intervals of time to make existing products out of date.

_____ 3. Concerns ethical consequences of an individual's or an organization's marketing activity on the interests of others.

_____ 4. Promotional messages that mislead consumers.

_____ 5. Practice of making existing products out of date by introducing new products that are more technologically advanced.

_____ 6. System of preferences within a society that guides ethical norms.

_____ 7. Pattern of products becoming out of date because of changes in the preferences for particular styles.

_____ 8. Grew out of the desire to protect individuals from practices that infringe on their rights as consumers.

_____ 9. Moral principles that guide conduct.

_____10. Practice of making slight advertising exaggerations that society, in general, considers harmless.

_____11. The potential annoyances caused by marketers who make contacts with consumers.

_____12. Breakdown of a product due to wear and tear.

_____13. Rules of conduct to be followed in particular social circumstances.

_____14. Variety of products available to enable consumers to select products that best meet their particular needs.

_____15. A condition that occurs when existing products become out of date due to the introduction of new products.

VOCABULARY BUILDING

Programmed Learning Exercise

1. Social responsibility designates the _____ consequences of how one's marketing activity might affect the interest of others.

   [ethical]

2. _____ suggest what ought to be done under given circumstances.

   [Norms]

3. Problems arise when two _____ are in conflict.

   [norms]

4. The three major publics to which marketing is held accountable are _____, _____, and the general public or citizens.

   [competitors, consumers]

5. _____ oversees the interrelations between marketing and its three major publics.

   [Government]

6. _____ is the study of marketing which focuses on contributions and faults of the marketing systems, a societal view of marketing.

   [Macromarketing]

7. Laws such as the Sherman Anti-Trust Act that favor and foster competition are called _____ laws.

   [procompetitive]

8. _____ price fixing exists when competitors get together to determine prices.

   [Horizontal]

9. The four basic consumer rights are the right to _____, the right to be _____, the right to _____, and the right to be _____.
[safety, informed, choose, heard]

10. The right to safety means that consumers have the right to expect the products they purchase to be free from _____ risks.
[unnecessary, hazardous, or dangerous]

11. The right to safety is a move away from _____ _____ or the philosophy to let the buyer beware.
[caveat emptor]

12. Consumers have the right to obtain _____ that is required to make an intelligent choice from among available products.
[information]

13. _____ involves advertising a low-priced product, which is not available, with the intent of selling a more expensive product item.
[Bait and switch]

14. The right to be _____ assures consumers that their interests and concerns will receive full and sympathetic consideration.
[heard]

15. The three major types of measures that are used to ensure consumer protection are _____, _____, and _____.
[prevention, restitution, punishment]

16. Recycling involves the use of a _____ channel.
[backward]

17. Matters of law and ethics are frequently decided on the basis of _____ _____ or beliefs as to what is right and proper.
[public standards]

18. The task of marketing from a macromarketing perspective is the delivery of a _____ _____ _____.
[standard of living]

19. _____ is frequently a substitute for the more expensive promotional element of personal selling.
[Advertising]

20. _____ makes mass production of a large volume of standardized items possible.
[Advertising]

TRUE OR FALSE STATEMENTS

T   F   1.   All of society's rules of conduct have been formalized into laws.

T   F   2.   Social responsibility is broader than legal responsibility.

T   F   3.   Consensus exists on what is ethical behavior.

T   F   4.   Social responsibility of marketing organizations extends beyond its traditional economic role.

T   F   5.   Rights and obligations of social institutions are dictated by society's norms.

T   F   6.   An ethical decision today will be an ethical decision in the future.

T   F   7.   Ethical decisions impact on the development and implementation of the marketing mix.

T   F   8.   Ethical decisions are consistent in all nations.

T   F   9.   Organizations should respect the rights of citizens only if the citizen is a customer or a competitor.

T   F   10. Issues that affect a specific educational institution such as Texas Tech University are a micromarketing issue.

T   F   11. Most individuals feel price collusion is unethical, thus laws have been enacted to settle this ethical issue.

T   F   12. Procompetitive laws are designed to protect consumers.

T   F   13. The right to safety is a step toward caveat emptor.

T   F   14. Retailers have been held accountable for harmful products they have sold.

T   F   15. The Federal Trade Commission Act makes it illegal to have dishonest advertisements.

T   F   16. Critics of product obsolescence, especially fashion obsolescence, advocate that consumer's functional needs are more important than their social and emotional needs.

T   F   17. Physical obsolescence is more controversial than planned obsolescence.

452

T F 18. Corrective advertising is a type of punishment.

T F 19. Marketers must consider privacy issues in developing and implementing their marketing activities.

T F 20. In general, distribution does not cost too much in the United States.

MULTIPLE CHOICE QUESTIONS

1. Which statement is <u>incorrect</u> regarding social responsibility?
    a. Social institutions must operate within society's rules of conduct.
    b. Social institutions cannot be isolated from the context of a larger society.
    c. Social responsibility is narrower than legal responsibility.
    d. Social responsibility may be good for a business.

2. Questions of marketing's social responsibility focus on how marketing activities affect
    a. profits.   c. sales.
    b. customer satisfaction.   d. the interests of others.

3. If manufacturers seem to be unwilling to add expensive safety feature to their products, a feature which might raise the prices of their products and result in sales lost to competitors, the usual result is
    a. that manufacturers add the safety features just so they can avoid yet another government interference.
    b. that legislation is necessary to require all manufacturers to add the expensive safety feature.
    c. one competitor adds the safety feature just to "prove" that it is a socially responsible company.
    d. safety features never are added to products.

4. Moral principles that guide our conduct can be referred to as
    a. norms.   c. values.
    b. ethics.   d. standards.

5. A manager is faced with an ethical problem when
    a. two or more norms are in conflict.
    b. two or more people disagree on the strategy to pursue.
    c. an organization has exceptional growth in profits.
    d. an organization has sustained a loss for several quarters.

453

6. Which statement regarding ethics is <u>incorrect</u>?
   a. The responsible marketing manager will be faced with an ethical problem when any goal or preference conflicts with another.
   b. There is no fixed standard by which to judge actions.
   c. Objective standards as evidenced by codes of ethics exist.
   d. Available standards may not endure the test of time.

7. Issues constituting marketing's area of social responsibility do <u>not</u> include
   a. governmental regulations.
   b. fair competitive practices.
   c. quality of life issues.
   d. consumerism issues.

8. Which question does <u>not</u> address a macromarketing concern?
   a. Is the United States distribution system efficient?
   b. Do we have too many electronic games available in the United States?
   c. Should General Motors offer fewer automobiles to remain competitive?
   d. Should advertising to children be permitted?

9. An example of a procompetitive law is the
   a. Pure Food and Drug Act.
   b. Consumer Product Safety Act.
   c. Fair Packaging and Labeling Act.
   d. Sherman Anti-Trust Act.

10. The consumerism movement began because many
    a. businesses charged high prices.
    b. businesses offered inferior products.
    c. business practices infringed on consumer rights.
    d. marketing practices are unethical or illegal.

11. Which is <u>not</u> one of the four <u>basic</u> consumer rights?
    a. The right to be heard.
    b. The right to a clean environment.
    c. The right to be informed.
    d. The right to choose.

12. If all organizations could adopt the marketing concept and make it work perfectly, there would be no need for
    a. consumerism.
    b. marketing.
    c. business failures.
    d. social responsibilities.

13. An advertisement that is clearly misleading would appear to violate the consumer's
    a. right to be heard.
    b. right to choose.
    c. right to a clean environment.
    d. right to be informed.

14. Which of these advertising claims is an example of puffery?
   a. Double coupons on all purchases on Tuesday.
   b. Best automobile produced in America.
   c. All tires 10% off regular price this week.
   d. Buy the first shirt at regular price, second shirt is ½ of regular price.

15. The right to choose
   a. guarantees consumers many available products.
   b. states that consumers can buy what they want.
   c. implies that products offered will be priced fairly and be of satisfactory quality.
   d. indicates that product obsolescence is an acceptable business practice to consumers.

16. Organizations that survive over the long-run are, by definition,
   a. consumer-oriented.   c. growth-oriented.
   b. sales-oriented.   d. ethical.

17. Quality of life issues include all except
   a. ecology.   c. privacy.
   b. consumer protection.   d. the system's efficiency.

18. Which statement is true?
   a. Marketing creates demand.
   b. Marketing makes people need products.
   c. Marketing creates false needs.
   d. Marketing tries to offer products that can satisfy demand.

19. Consumer groups who criticize advertising would agree that
   a. all advertising is unnecessary.
   b. informative advertising is least expensive.
   c. advertising contributes to raising the standard of living.
   d. persuasive advertising is wasteful and manipulative.

20. The matters of ethics and efficiency in marketing are difficult to discuss with assurance and certainty. A good "bottom line" statement is that
   a. American marketing is inefficient and it is difficult to "fix" it.
   b. if the marketing concept is followed, a free market in effect "tells" marketers what is right and wrong with their efforts to satisfy customers.
   c. marketing alone, among all fields of study, holds the correct solutions to the world's problems.
   d. marketing is a business-related activity and questions of right and wrong have no place in marketing.

QUICK QUIZ

1Q.
Did the organization which adopted the name "Federal Express" choose that name to suggest some sort of tie-in to the U.S. Government or to give the impression that Federal Express is some sort of "official" agency?

1A.
As with most questions raised in this chapter, the answer must be, "What do you think?" It's worth noting that in other countries certain names cannot be used to suggest non-existent government approval. In Great Britain, an organization cannot claim to be the "royal" anything without specific government permission.

2Q.
If a manufacturer sets up a "sting" operation to trap retailers seeking to cash-in coupons for products which could not have been sold because they never existed, is that manufacturer acting ethically? Remember, the retailers could be fined or jailed for fraud.

2A.
Fraud is a crime and it is arguable that the dishonest retailers deserve what they get. However, in 1981, the "ABSCAM" case had the FBI filming Congressmen accepting bribes from phony "Arab sheiks" looking for "favors". Many people felt that intentionally tempting these Congressmen was as wrong as, or even worse than, the acceptance of the bribes.

3Q.
Should consumers be informed about everything that's in the products they buy?

3A.
Before saying "yes", consider "high fiber" products like certain breads, and that old favorite, the hot dog. Many high fiber products contain sawdust. The sawdust is fibrous and apparently safe, even beneficial, to consume. Hot dog labels used to say "Contains beef, pork, and spices." Now they say, "Contains lips, feet, ears, and udders." Do we really want to know everything?

4Q.

Time sells its mailing list to other magazine publishers. Penthouse sells its list to purveyors of a certain class of merchandise. The buyers of these lists then write to, phone, or even visit people on the lists. Is this ethical?

4A.

Maybe not, but your favorite charities sell their lists to other charities, and even to non-charities. Churches sell lists of members to organizations selling religious books and magazines. Even the government sells lists (e.g., of new car buyers to interested sellers of auto-related products). Since the money made on the lists goes to "more or less" good causes, is selling your name and address the right thing to do?

EXPERIENTIAL ACTIVITIES

23-A. Social Responsibility

Marketing actions need to be socially responsible. Unfortunately for many issues, a socially-responsible decision involves a trade-off among conflicting interests of various social groups. Responsible marketers may perform a cost/benefit analysis prior to making a marketing decision. For each situation described below, please indicate which marketing decision should be made and explain your decision.

1. An independent grocer is considering the use of unit pricing. She knows that sales volume must increase by one percent to offset the cost of unit pricing. A majority of food shoppers (65%) prefer unit pricing according to a recent study of area grocery shoppers. However, these shoppers ranked low prices and better value as the two most important decision factors when purchasing food items. Currently, only one of the five major area competitors uses unit pricing. Should the independent grocery use unit pricing?

   Decision: _____

   Justification: _____

   _____

   _____

   _____

457

2. A video arcade owner is discussing a media schedule with a salesperson from WBNQ-TV. The owner notices that the schedule includes 30-second spot advertisements on programs directed toward children under age 12. There is an extremely active ACT (Action for Children's Television) group in this city. Should the arcade owner advertise to children under age 12?

Decision: _____

Justification: _____

_____

_____

23-B. Code of Ethics

As an Assistant to the Corporate Vice President of Marketing for a large multinational firm, you have been reviewing field reports from company sales representatives. You note that these sales representatives have asked numerous ethical questions which are not covered in current corporate policies. Currently, the multinational organization has no code of ethics.

Assignment

1. The purpose of a corporate code of ethics is _____

_____

_____

2. Identify five issues that a corporate code of ethics should address.

Issue one: _____

Justification: _____

_____

_____

Issue two: _____

Justification: _____

_____

_____

Issue three: _____

Justification: _____

_____

_____

Issue four: _____

Justification: _____

_____

_____

Issue five: _____

Justification: _____

_____

_____

ANSWERS TO OBJECTIVE QUESTIONS

MATCHING

1.	R	4.	H	7.	M	10.	J	13.	C
2.	O	5.	N	8.	E	11.	S	14.	K
3.	A	6.	D	9.	B	12.	P	15.	L

TRUE OR FALSE

1.	F	5.	T	9.	F	13.	F	17.	F
2.	T	6.	F	10.	T	14.	T	18.	F
3.	F	7.	T	11.	T	15.	T	19.	T
4.	T	8.	F	12.	F	16.	T	20.	T

MULTIPLE CHOICE

1.	c	5.	a	9.	d	13.	d	17.	b
2.	d	6.	c	10.	c	14.	b	18.	d
3.	b	7.	a	11.	b	15.	c	19.	d
4.	b	8.	c	12.	a	16.	a	20.	b

STUDENT FEEDBACK FORM

This feedback form has two sections. The first section concerns your overall evaluation of each pedagogical section of the learning guide. The second section solicits your comments and suggestions regarding each chapter in the textbook, Marketing, and the Student Learning Guide. Your feedback will enable us to improve the next edition of the textbook and learning guide.

SECTION I. Overall Feedback of Each Pedagogical Section

Part A

For each pedagogical section, please indicate how helpful the section was in assisting you in understanding and learning the concepts and strategies of marketing.

	Very Helpful						Not Helpful
Chapter Objective	___ :	___ :	___ :	___ :	___ :	___ :	___ :
Chapter Outline	___ :	___ :	___ :	___ :	___ :	___ :	___ :
Chapter Summary	___ :	___ :	___ :	___ :	___ :	___ :	___ :
Matching Exercise	___ :	___ :	___ :	___ :	___ :	___ :	___ :
Programmed Learning Exercise	___ :	___ :	___ :	___ :	___ :	___ :	___ :
True or False Statements	___ :	___ :	___ :	___ :	___ :	___ :	___ :
Multiple Choice Questions	___ :	___ :	___ :	___ :	___ :	___ :	___ :
Quick Quiz	___ :	___ :	___ :	___ :	___ :	___ :	___ :
Experiential Activities	___ :	___ :	___ :	___ :	___ :	___ :	___ :

Part B

For this section you are asked to rank the nine pedagogical sections from most useful (1) to least useful (9) as an aid in the learning guide.

Pedagogical Section	Rank
Chapter Objective	____
Chapter Outline	____
Chapter Summary	____
Matching Exercise	____
Programmed Learning Exercise	____
True or False Statements	____
Multiple Choice Questions	____
Quick Quiz	____
Experiential Activities	____

SECTION II. Chapter Feedback

For each chapter in the textbook and the learning guide, please make any comments or suggestions which you feel will strengthen either of them as learning aids. Your constructive criticism will enable us to incorporate student feedback in subsequent revisions.

Chapter 1. The Nature of Marketing

Overall evaluation (circle one):   excellent   good   average   poor

Comments:

Chapter 2. Environmental Opportunities and Constraints

Overall evaluation (circle one):   excellent   good   average   poor

Comments:

Chapter 3. Developing Marketing Strategy

Overall evaluation (circle one):   excellent   good   average   poor

Comments:

Chapter 4. Market Segmentation

Overall evaluation (circle one):   excellent   good   average   poor

Comments:

Chapter 5. Overview of the Marketing Research Process

Overall evaluation (circle one):   excellent   good   average   poor

Comments:

Chapter 6. The Marketing Information System and Sales Forecasting Methods

Overall evaluation (circle one):   excellent   good   average   poor

Comments:

Chapter 7. Sociological Factors in Consumer Behavior

Overall evaluation (circle one):   excellent   good   average   poor

Comments:

Chapter 8. Psychological Influences in Consumer Behavior

Overall evaluation (circle one):   excellent   good   average   poor

Comments:

Chapter 9. The Elements of Products and Services

Overall evaluation (circle one):   excellent   good   average   poor

Comments:

Chapter 10. The Product Life Cycle and Related Strategies

Overall evaluation (circle one):   excellent   good   average   poor

Comments:

Chapter 11.   Marketing New Products

Overall evaluation (circle one):   excellent   good   average   poor

Comments:

Chapter 12.   The Nature of Distribution

Overall evaluation (circle one):   excellent   good   average   poor

Comments:

Chapter 13.   Distribution Institutions

Overall evaluation (circle one):   excellent   good   average   poor

Comments:

Chapter 14. Physical Distribution Management

Overall evaluation (circle one):   excellent   good   average   poor

Comments:

Chapter 15. Introduction to Pricing Concepts

Overall evaluation (circle one):   excellent   good   average   poor

Comments:

Chapter 16. Costs and Demand: How They Influence Pricing Decisions

Overall evaluation (circle one):   excellent   good   average   poor

Comments:

467

Chapter 17.   Pricing Strategies and Tactics

Overall evaluation (circle one):   excellent   good   average   poor

Comments:

Chapter 18.   An Overview of Promotion

Overall evaluation (circle one):   excellent   good   average   poor

Comments:

Chapter 19.   Personal Selling and Sales Management

Overall evaluation (circle one):   excellent   good   average   poor

Comments:

Chapter 20. Advertising

Overall evaluation (circle one): excellent good average poor

Comments:

Chapter 21. Industrial/Organizational Marketing

Overall evaluation (circle one): excellent good average poor

Comments:

Chapter 22. Marketing in the Multinational Environment

Overall evaluation (circle one): excellent good average poor

Comments:

469

Chapter 23. Marketing and Society

Overall evaluation (circle one):   excellent   good   average   poor

Comments: